POWER AND CONFLICT

VIOLENCE, COOPERATION, PEACE

AN INTERNATIONAL SERIES

Editors: Francis A. Beer, *University of Colorado, Boulder* and Ted Robert Gurr, *University of Maryland, College Park*

Violence, Cooperation, Peace: An International Series focuses on violent conflict and the dynamics of peaceful change within and among political communities. Studies in the series may include the perspectives and evidence of any of the social sciences or humanities, as well as applied fields such as conflict management. This international book series emphasizes systematic scholarship, in which theory and evidence are used to advance our general understanding of the processes of political violence and peace.

Volumes in the Series

POWER AND CONFLICT
Toward a General Theory

Hubert M. Blalock, Jr.

VIOLENCE, COOPERATION, PEACE

AN INTERNATIONAL SERIES

SAGE PUBLICATIONS
The International Professional Publishers
Newbury Park   London   New Delhi

To our grandchildren,
Jennifer and Trevor,
with hopes for all their generation

For information address:

SAGE Publications, Inc.
2455 Teller Road
Newbury Park, California 91320

SAGE Publications Ltd.
6 Bonhill Street
London EC2A 4PU
United Kingdom

SAGE Publications India Pvt. Ltd.
M-32 Market
Greater Kailash I
New Delhi 110 048 India

Printed in the United States of America

Library of Congress Cataloging-in-Publication Data

    Blalock, Hubert M.
      Power and conflict : toward a general theory / Hubert M.
    Blalock, Jr.
        p. cm.—(Violence, cooperation, peace ; 4)
      Bibliography: p.
      ISBN 0-8039-3594-3. — ISBN 0-8039-3595-1 (pbk.)
      1. Social conflict. 2. Power (Social sciences) I. Title.
    II. Series.
    HM136.B54   1989
    303.6—dc20
                                      89-10215
                                          CIP

SECOND PRINTING 1990

Contents

Preface

The orientation of this book is very general. As a student of race and ethnic relations, I have long been convinced that power and conflict processes are so closely intertwined that they cannot be separated without doing injustice to the one topic or the other. Furthermore, power and conflict processes, as applied to the field of race and ethnic relations, have much in common with similar processes in the realm of international relations or with much more micro processes, as for example those that occur within the family. Yet there are important differences, according to the type of party being considered and the social environments within which it is placed. It therefore becomes critical to attempt to pinpoint just what these similarities and differences are, and this in turn requires a more general theory. Therefore the birth of this book, as one more effort—among many others—to provide a reasonably systematic but yet comprehensive synthesis of a very large body of literature.

We all have values and biases that also help determine which projects we undertake and which we leave to others. Like many of these others, my own orientation toward conflicts is one of ambivalence. Conflicts very often turn out to be "bad," in the sense that they involve far more injury and misery than was originally anticipated. Actors rarely correctly predict either the duration or intensity of conflicts, generally erring in the direction of underestimating both. Conflicts generally turn out to be much more difficult to terminate than to begin, given the dynamics of escalation coupled with changes in individuals' motivation to gain revenge for what they perceive as "wrongs" inflicted by their opponents. Often, neither party can afford to appear willing to concede ground or to be the first to suggest a compromise resolution. So conflicts often grind on, long after either party has anything to gain from them. And, of course, many innocent victims suffer unnecessarily. This is why many of us tend to abhor conflicts and hope for a world in which no such conflicts ever occur, or at least one in which they can be brought to a much more speedy and far less costly resolution.

Yet the world is also filled with powerful groups and individuals who tend to dominate and exploit others. In such instances, conflict may be the only mechanism through which subordinated parties can hope to turn the tables or gain a measure of freedom from exploitative relationships. Many conflicts are initiated by such weaker parties, often with the hope that the mere threat of conflict will be sufficient to achieve their objectives. Sometimes such threats are effective in inducing the stronger party to "back off" and treat the subordinate party more favorably. This all depends on the circumstances and on expectations of costs and benefits, however. Miscalculations on both sides often prevail, so that actual costs are grossly underestimated and benefits exaggerated. In many instances, weaker parties are placed in even more unfavorable positions after the conflict has subsided. In others, however, the stronger party may either be sufficiently weakened that it can no longer exploit the other party, or it may recognize that it has more to lose than to gain by doing so. It is obviously critical to learn more about the circumstances under which such "successful" outcomes will occur, as compared with those under which the conflict will merely result in terrible losses for both sides and no effective change in the status quo.

No theoretical work provides definitive general answers to important questions of this sort. As we shall note over and over again, both power and conflict processes are exceedingly complex. Numerous variables are needed to help explain such processes, with the number of combinations of possible causal interrelationships among these variables being so large that our verbal theories used to account for them must be supplemented by rather complex, but also more compact, causal diagrams. Furthermore, there will be a variety of different kinds of special cases that require elaborations of some portions of our models, though permitting simplifications in others.

Perhaps the most that any reasonable general theory can accomplish is basically that of a sensitizing function: calling attention to factors that are likely to be neglected in overly simplistic accounts, suggesting how the actions of one party bring about reactions in the other that are often not anticipated, and indicating how the pieces of the general puzzle fit together. If these things can be accomplished, then the analysis of particular conflicts, as special cases, can be improved. As particular conflicts are described and analyzed within a reasonably common framework, knowledge can then cumulate far more systematically than is possible if one begins with the stance that each and every conflict situation contains so many idiosyncratic features that we can learn very little about future conflicts from studies of prior ones, or that our understanding of conflicts of a certain type cannot shed light on those that involve very different kinds of parties or environmental settings.

My aim in this book is to present a reasonably complete and somewhat abstract theory. In doing so, I have made no effort to "summarize the literature" or to focus in detail on a few specific instances of conflicts as case studies. Instead, attention is given to those theoretical works—representing several disciplines and spanning a number of decades—that have the most direct bearing on the arguments being presented, and to illustrate the ideas concerned primarily with a view to their clarification. In no way, then, will there be an attempt to present an encyclopedic coverage of what has become a vast and highly diverse body of literature. Readers who expect such an encyclopedic coverage will therefore be doomed to disappointment. In my own view, it is far preferable to locate the forest amidst the trees, prior to attempting a much more detailed and closer look at a more microscopic portion of the entire scene. This is basically what theory is all about.

Over the many years that I have thought about power and conflict processes, I have lost track of the many persons and individual ideas that have influenced my own thinking. A few of these will be cited in the pages that follow, but there are many others whose contributions have been more indirect, though no less important. Among the American sociologists whom I can definitely single out as having had such an impact are: James S. Coleman, Lewis Coser, E. Franklin Frazier, George C. Homans, Floyd Hunter, Paul Lazarsfeld, Robert K. Merton, Herbert A. Simon, and Robin M. Williams, Jr. Among my colleagues, former colleagues, and students who have had comparable, though more personal, impacts are Karen S. Cook, M. Richard Cramer, Richard M. Emerson, William A. Gamson, Amos H. Hawley, Michael Hechter, Guy B. Johnson, Gerhard E. Lenski, Paul H. Wilken, and Everett K. Wilson. Finally, I am also grateful, for their careful reading of the original manuscript, to the editors of the Sage series in which this volume appears, Francis Beer and Ted R.

Gurr, and to the three anonymous readers they selected to review it. I would also like to thank April Ryan for her conscientious work in producing the diagrams.

Chapter 1

Introduction

Social conflicts are ubiquitous, come in many forms, and involve vastly different kinds of parties, ranging from individual persons to large macro units such as nation-states. Some are dramatic and well-publicized, whereas others are much more subtle and hidden from public view. Social scientists have in general focused their attention more on the former than the latter, but this does not imply that the basic processes involved are all that different. Conflicts are perhaps most obvious when the contestants are either individual persons, as for example in marital conflicts, or major corporate actors, such as two nations at war. Conflicts also involve much more loosely knit quasi-groups such as social classes or ethnic groups, the boundaries of which are often fuzzy and difficult to define. Conflicts may involve overt physical violence, at the one extreme, or much more subtle punitive processes, at the other.

Do these various and sundry conflicts have much in common? How do our explanatory models have to differ if we try to generalize from interpersonal conflicts to international ones, or from those involving extreme violence to much more benign behaviors? Is any really general theory of conflict possible, with each of the diverse forms of conflict being subsumed as a special case? Is it necessary to treat international and interpersonal conflicts as totally distinct? How can a general theory of conflict be constructed, given the very distinctive bodies of literature that have developed around each of these very different kinds of conflict? Can the important differences among such forms of conflict be incorporated into a general theory, and can we make use of a single body of concepts or variables that pertain to such a variety of different forms? And what if such a general theory cannot be constructed? Does this mean that we will require a different theory for each and every type of conflict that we wish to study? Can we learn nothing about some new form of conflict by studying past ones?

The purpose of the present work is to construct such a general theory, and so our tentative answers to the above questions are already implied. At the very outset, however, it is necessary to anticipate that any such general theory must be highly complex but must also allow for simplifications that may differ according to the nature of the specific conflict process being studied. If, for example, we wish to include variables that seem necessary when we are dealing with organizational problems faced by a loose-knit quasi-group such as a racial or ethnic minority, we must anticipate that many of these variables will become irrelevant in studying conflicts within marital dyads. In our view, a general theory will ordinarily be more complex than are specialized versions, in which certain variables may be totally ignored by, say, setting their coefficients equal to zero or bypassing them in a causal diagram.

Why bother with the more complex general theory, then? As we shall argue below, one practically always discovers in a reasonably thorough literature review that different authors stress different sets of variables in their theories, so much so that there may be little or no overlap among several theoretical points of view. Even where social scientists may be dealing with basically the same *dependent* variables, their lists of independent variables may be entirely different. Often, a particular theorist will begin an argument by attempting to discredit alternative theories, usually by considerably oversimplifying the basic theses involved. It may rightly be claimed that these alternatives do not explain 100 percent of the variance or they cannot account for some phenomenon that the theorist deems critical. The new and presumably more adequate theory is then presented as an *alternative* to the previous formulations, rather than as a supplement to them. As a result, theorists often pass each other in the night, so to speak, without adequately addressing questions concerning the incompleteness of their own theories or the desirability of synthesizing them or augmenting each "alternative" theory so as to include important features of the others. The greater the diversity of the situations being treated and the more intellectual disciplines and theoretical orientations that are involved, it seems, the more difficult it becomes to develop genuine syntheses of such varying perspectives.

The view taken in the present work is that a general theory of conflict processes must in principle incorporate the major features of a large number of relatively more simple theories that have been developed from a diversity of perspectives. This is not to say that all arguments must count equally or that in each specific application one or another perspective cannot be safely neglected, at least as a first approximation. But we do assume that the general puzzle is highly complex and that, in putting it together, we stand a much better chance if we begin with a highly inclusive perspective and only *then* attempt to decide, on the basis of the empirical evidence, which kinds of variables can safely be ignored under a given set of circumstances.

Several decades ago there were claims—particularly by sociologists with a Marxian orientation—that American sociologists had neglected the study of conflict processes and that structural-functionalist arguments were heavily biased in the direction of assuming a consensus model of social systems. I do not believe that such a thesis was valid for all subfields, such as the vast sociological literature on race and ethnic relations that existed prior to that time. Regardless of the merits of the argument, however, it is certainly true today that we are blessed with a massive social science literature dealing in one way or another with conflict processes. Our problem is not so much with a paucity of *theoretical* positions on conflict as it is with the shortage of careful, quantitative empirical studies that involve comparable measures of critical variables.

Thus, if anything, it is the empirical side that is relatively weak and not well-melded with the theoretical literature. Unfortunately, it is beyond the scope of the present work to attempt a systematic review of this rather spotty empirical literature or even to assess the degree to which our own theoretical arguments are or are not supported by the empirical evidence that does exist. Since our formulations are intended to be highly general in nature, such literature reviews would be far more fruitful if applied to a series of specific cases, such as international conflicts, revolutions and internal warfare, interethnic conflicts, intrafamilial ones, and so forth.

Whereas the number and diversity of theoretical discussions are considerable, this does not necessarily imply that they are easy to "add up" or even evaluate constructively. One problem we encounter is a lack of consensus on the basic concepts or variables, or even for that matter on the kind of definition of social conflict that is being used. Syntheses of divergent theoretical arguments become very difficult under such circumstances. We shall make the effort only in an indirect and roundabout manner by attempting to build the most important arguments of different authors into our own distinctive formulation. Where possible, we shall use their vocabulary, provided that it does not lead to undue confusion.

Not only does the literature of immediate concern involve a wide range of social science disciplines and theoretical orientations, but it is also diverse in another important respect. A part of the literature is highly systematic, involving mathematical models or other relatively formalistic approaches. Another portion, perhaps the bulk of the literature, is largely descriptive in nature, being concerned with the details of single case studies or at most a comparison of three to six historical instances involving social conflicts. This latter literature exists primarily at the macro level, where interest rather naturally tends to be focused on "important" instances of conflict: wars between nations, major social revolutions, and so forth.

Finally, there is an extensive literature having a heavily ideological flavor, usually being focused primarily on special kinds of conflict, as for example that between social classes or between races or ethnic groups. Notions such as exploitation, class warfare or colonialism are prevalent in this type of literature, which is often written in polemic style and oriented to convincing the reader that one or the other side in the particular conflict of concern should be favored. This last type of literature, though one-sided, often contains useful insights as to variables that have been neglected in more mundane descriptive accounts or the more analytic literature. As expected, it also tends to emphasize the importance of ideological factors and hidden biases on the part of many of those analysts who purport to be presenting a more balanced view. In this sense it is a corrective to the other two kinds of orientations we have described.

Taken together, these rather distinctive bodies of literature are far too vast to receive our detailed consideration in the present work. Furthermore, systematic literature reviews are also undoubtedly best accomplished in connection with discussions of more restricted kinds of social conflicts, especially since very different vocabularies and concepts are used in each of these several domains. Our own review of this literature is therefore far more eclectic than encyclopedic in nature. The aim is to select from this huge body of literature those works that seem most amenable to incorporation into our own power-conflict framework. The models developed in later chapters are sufficiently complex that it seemed wise to keep the arguments as succinct as possible, without unnecessary excursions into lengthy critiques of lines of thought that are only tangentially related to those we shall develop. At the same time, it is necessary to discuss in some detail those theoretical arguments that form the building blocks of our own subsequent models. Our literature coverage is therefore consciously uneven in this sense.

Power considerations nearly always enter into discussions of conflict, but to varying degrees and with different emphases. Our own models will be explicitly built on a power-dependence framework that will be outlined in the next chapter. It is our view that power and conflict processes, though possibly analytically distinct and only partially overlapping, need to be joined to provide a reasonably complete orientation. Certain intellectual traditions, such as game theory approaches, introduce power notions only implicitly, as for example in rules of the game and the payoff matrices that are usually taken as givens, rather than treated as problematic or modifiable by the players themselves.

Other approaches, such as Richardson's (1960) arms-races equations and similar reactive process models, also do not deal with power factors except implicitly through the use of certain parameters which are taken as constants in the models. Bargaining approaches deal with power issues more directly but also sometimes treat power resources and mobilization factors as givens or as variables that the bargainers may use to influence the other party but that are not themselves subject to modification. A more complete theoretical formulation, we argue, must incorporate power factors in such a way that they are subject to control, manipulation, and change over the course of the conflict process itself. In other words, they are endogenous as well as exogenous variables that cannot easily be separated from other variables in our conflict process models.

Much of our subsequent argument will presume a kind of modified rational-actor model, based on subjective expected utilities. We shall allow, however, for a multiplicity of goals that include not only "economic" motives but also those that may be largely shaped by ideological factors or by interests that are basically irrelevant to the conflict at hand. Subjective probabilities, as well, may be influenced by misperceptions, ideological biases, deception, and a host of other factors that have little to do with so-called "objective" experiences, as for example frequencies of other actors' prior behaviors. Our basic argument will be that the kinds of rational-actor models that have characterized economic modeling and game-theory approaches are far too simplistic to be applied to realistic forms of social conflict. Yet the strategy of theorizing used in such modeling efforts is basically sound, as far as it goes. Our central thesis will be that modified rational-actor theories must be combined with considerations of power and dependency in order to account for the interactions that actually occur in most real-world conflict settings.

General theories of the type we shall be concerned with cannot, almost by their very definition, deal with highly specific causes of particular conflicts. Indeed, if one were to attempt to catalogue such immediate causes the gamut would range from competing territorial claims, overpopulation, needs for natural resources or for access to seaports, all the way to fanatical religious beliefs, personal rivalries, domestic quarrels, marital infidelity, paranoid or justified perceptions of impending treachery, hostile remarks made in the barroom, and many other sorts of idiosyncratic factors. Therefore the reader of this work should not look for discussions of specific kinds of exogenous variables or initial causes expected to be appropriate at a highly general level. Efforts to extend our general models to important special cases, however, need to be concerned with just such lists of exogenous variables that are thought to be relevant for the specific kind of conflict under discussion, whether this be international warfare, racial conflict, labor-management struggles, or interpersonal encounters.

Instead, our models will focus much more heavily on conflict *processes*, whatever the immediate causes of the conflicts may have been. As we shall see, many of these processes can be considered as having causal importance in their own right. Bargaining processes and miscalculations of the opponent's responses can lead to overt hostilities and may, themselves, be affected by the outcomes of prior conflicts. One important type of cause may be the accumulation or deployment of resources by one party and the interpretation the other party gives to *changes* in the other party's resources or patterns of behavior. Modifications in belief systems and changes in leadership or the internal makeup of one or both parties may also be important factors, not only in instigating a conflict but also in keeping it going or in facilitating its termination. Therefore, although we shall not be concerned with exogenous causes of conflicts, which will often be peculiar to each specific conflict situation, our models will contain a number of variables that may have important impacts on the conflict process as it later unfolds and eventually terminates.

We shall also not focus on the consequences or functions of conflict for the actors concerned or for other kinds of processes, as for example future exchange behaviors. Lewis Coser's (1956) excellent analysis of the functions of conflict is therefore only tangentially relevant to our own discussion, which should be regarded as complementary to his. Like Coser's, our formulation is in the spirit of the theoretical work of Georg Simmel (1955), who emphasized the forms, rather than the content of specific conflicts. Our own discussion will therefore be abstract and will use specific instances merely as illustrations of general points. Although it has a very different flavor from that of Simmel's pioneering work, its objective is much the same.

Definition of Social Conflict

By social conflict we shall mean the intentional mutual exchange of negative sanctions, or punitive behaviors, by two or more parties, which may be individuals, corporate actors, or more loosely knit quasi-groups. This definition seems to come reasonably close to general usage, without incorporating causes or consequences into the definition itself. Even so, it contains four features that in some instances may be problematic: the notions of negative sanctions, intent, mutuality, and parties.

By negative sanctions we shall mean the same thing as punitive behaviors, which we shall define as those courses of action by party X that decrease the probabilities of party Y's obtaining those goals to which it attaches positive values or utilities, or that increase the probabilities of Y's attaining negatively valued goals (Blalock and Wilken, 1979, pp. 346–47). In lay usage, the notion of "punitive behaviors" generally connotes a set of responses, say by X, to prior "bad" behaviors by Y. Although our own definition will usually coincide in most applications with this lay usage, there may be some instances where X may apply negative sanctions to Y without Y having "deserved" them. Of course a third party may interpret such prior actions of Y in a manner completely differently from X. Whereas X may believe that Y deserves punishment, both Y and such a third party may interpret Y's actions as totally innocent. We prefer to sidestep this question of Y's responsibility for X's actions and therefore choose to define "negative sanctions" or "punitive behaviors" in the above manner.

There is, however, an implied causal connection in our definition, namely that X's punitive actions actually affect Y's outcomes. The notion of intent has also been built into the definition so as to exclude those behaviors by X that only inadvertently impact negatively on Y. Suppose, for instance, that X and Y are two competitors for the same job. If X works hard to obtain impeccable credentials, this may result in Y's not getting the job, but we do not wish to suggest that X's actions have been punitive. If, however, X attempts to threaten Y or induce a third party to injure Y, and if Y responds similarly, we would consider their mutual behaviors to involve social conflict as well as impersonal competition.

There is a certain slipperiness here, and we shall attempt to handle it by introducing needed complications into the models we ultimately construct, which will include party X's (and Y's) beliefs and interpretations, values, goals, and other subjective variables, along with structural and behavioral factors. We shall also allow for the possibility that although X may attempt to sanction Y, it may fail to do so or may be only partly successful, perhaps because of a highly inefficient strategy or a lack of the necessary power resources. What we wish to rule out from our models, however, are the numerous kinds of situations in which two parties may negatively affect each other's outcomes without intending to do so, and perhaps not even being aware of each other's existence. Thus we rule out impersonal kinds of competition, including games in which there is a zero-sum, or near zero-sum, feature. If parties X and Y are playing such a game, however, and if X threatens Y by putting a gun on the table or kidnapping its children, and if Y responds in kind, then we have a conflict as well as a competitive situation on our hands.

Some authors consider conflict and competition to be basically interchangeable or treat conflict as representing an extreme form of competition. For instance, Kenneth Boulding (1962, p. 5) defines conflict as "a situation of competition in which the parties are *aware* of the incompatibility of potential future positions and in which each party *wishes* to occupy a position that is incompatible with the wishes of the other" (italics in original).

Other authors seem to imply in their definitions that competition is a basic feature of conflict. Coser (1956, p. 8) defines social conflict as "a struggle over values and claims to scarce status, power and resources in which the aims of the opponents are to neutralize, injure or eliminate their rivals." Ralf Dahrendorf (1959, p. 135) says, "I am using the term 'conflict' in this study for contests, competitions, disputes, and tensions as well as for manifest clashes between social forces." Dahrendorf later (p. 208) elects to include conflicts "of emotion and emotion within one individual" and (on p. 238) supplies still a third kind of definition: "any antagonistic relationship between organized collectivities that can be explained in terms of patterns of social structure." The thrust of his work, however, focuses on competition and "conflicts" of interest between classes in hierarchically arranged structures. In a much later formulation, Joseph Himes (1980, p. 14) defines social conflict as "purposeful struggles between collective actors who use social power to defeat or remove opponents and to gain status, power, resources, and other scarce values." Himes also stresses that social conflict involves purposeful behavior.

All of these definitions, including our own, have much in common and in many specific instances will be essentially interchangeable. For our purposes, however, it is inadvisable to build the notion of competition into the definition itself. Although many if not most instances of conflict will involve competition for scarce resources, we wish to allow for other possibilities so as to broaden the concept. Party X may attack Y for idiosyncratic reasons, perhaps a sadistic desire to destroy Y or a paranoid belief that Y intends to attack X. Perhaps party X wishes to dominate Y in order to spread a religious ideology or to prevent Y's political doctrines from influencing its own. Parties X and Y may be involved in a barroom brawl initiated by a disagreement over the relative merits of two breeds of hunting dogs. Or party X may be exploited by Y, rather than being in competition with Y for the same scarce resources. Perhaps there is a sense in which a master and a slave may be in competition for the slave's labor, but this seems to be stretching the meaning of the term "competition" to the breaking point. The slave may rebel because he values his freedom, whereas the owner may whip the slave becauses he desires his cheap labor. Thus conflicts may arise because of competition for valued resources, but they may also be due to other factors as well. Therefore it seems wise to keep the two ideas distinct.

Apart from our having built intent into the definition in order to rule out inadvertent impacts of the one party on the other's outcomes, we also wish to exclude various emotional states from our definition, though they may be incorporated in our conflict models as separate variables, where appropriate. Thus conflict is often accompanied and sometimes even caused by mental states such as anger, hatred, distrust, an unwillingness to forgive the other party for prior actions, negative stereotypes or other beliefs which justify retaliation, and an unwillingness to "let go" of the conflict even when the objective costs outweigh the benefits. Many of these subjective factors will be difficult to measure and may be disguised or otherwise manipulated so as to influence the opponent. This does not mean that they do not belong in our theoretical models, however, even though it seems unwise to build them into the *definition* of conflict itself.

The notion of conflict is also sometimes ambiguously used to refer to various kinds of inconsistencies or incompatibilities. For instance, writers—as in the case of Dahrendorf (1959)—may refer to internalized conflicts within a single individual, value conflicts, or conflicts of interest that may or may not have behavioral outcomes. If two sets of beliefs within a single ideological system are inconsistent, for example, we would prefer to use some term other than "conflict" to refer such an incompatibility. If two parties have "conflicting interests," we would prefer to treat this as a possible cause of "conflict" in the behavioral sense of the term, as we are using it, rather than including it within the definition itself. Instead, we shall refer to inconsistencies or incompatibilities in goals, values or interests, reserving the term "conflict" for actual or threatened exchanges of negative sanctions.

Our definition refers to the *mutual* exchange of negative sanctions, and therefore we must allow for asymmetry in the sense that party X may apply more negative sanctions than does Y, and probably the sanctions that each applies will differ both in nature and effectiveness. In order for conflict to exist, however, there must be at least some negative sanctions applied by each party. Given that all social interactions will involve some combination of both positive and negative sanctions, there is a sense in which our definition can become trivialized. Although conflict may technically exist, whenever negative sanctions are few or minor in comparison with positive sanctions there will usually be little interest in studying it as a *conflict* process, except possibly to note that some degree of conflict inevitably exists in all social interactions. Our own concern will be with social conflicts that are much more intense and important, but with the proviso that cooperative interactions can at any point turn into conflicts and that threatened negative sanctions may be implicit in nearly all forms of social interaction.

The problem of defining the notion of "negative sanction" also arises. Given an existing exchange arrangement, for example, does the reduction of a positive sanction, or the withholding of a reward, constitute a punishment or negative sanction? If party X comes to expect an annual pay raise of 10 percent but receives one of only 5 percent, does this imply a negative sanction? If X then provides Y with less work in return for such a disappointing pay raise, does this mean that X and Y are engaged in a "conflict" process, with each "punishing" the other for its prior behaviors?

There is a certain arbitrariness here which may be resolved by letting the parties, themselves, define what they perceive to be "negative" sanctions. This may mean, however, that X perceives Y's behavior as involving punitive acts whereas Y regards them in a more positive light. Indeed, many kinds of important social conflicts involve disagreements such as these. The kinds of conflict situations in which we are generally most interested may begin in this way but will rather quickly evolve to a point where the sanctions being applied by both parties are obviously negative, both to the opposing party and to outside observers. Therefore we need not be concerned with the subtleties involved, except to note that it is the *perceptions* of the actors concerned that impact directly on their own behaviors and thus indirectly on those of the opposing party.

Types of Parties

The term "parties" may also be ambiguous. In brief, party boundaries may in some instances be diffuse and therefore difficult to define. This will rarely be the case when one is dealing with corporate actors but will become problematic whenever one or both parties are quasi-groups, such as social classes, racial or ethnic groups, or overlapping generations. In such instances there may be highly active members of both parties but also many others whose behaviors and loyalties are difficult to classify as being clearly on the one side or the other.

Under some circumstances it may be sensible to consider such marginal "members" as constituting third parties, whose potential behaviors are taken into consideration by the central actors. Perhaps at one stage of a conflict they may be genuine third parties, but at another they may be drawn into the conflict and considered as members of a more inclusive party directly engaged in the conflict. If so, however, coordination and mobilization problems may increase. In any particular situation, then, the delineation of the parties that are actually engaged in the conflict may be somewhat arbitrary, and party boundaries may indeed shift as the conflict progresses.

How can such a diversity of parties be handled in a single model, and does it even make sense to attempt to do so? Any general theory can be simplified by removing particular causal links, by assuming certain variables to be constants in special cases, or by setting specific coefficients equal to zero. For example, our later models will refer to the heterogeneity of a party's membership and to consensus on means. Where the party consists of a single person, heterogeneity could either be ignored or assumed to take on a constant zero value. This implies that such variables may be "blocked out" or ignored when they are irrelevant. Thus there will inevitably be special cases that permit simplifications of the general model, depending on the nature of the parties of concern and perhaps other factors as well.

Corporate actors may also in many instances be treated as simpler parties than quasi-groups in that it may become possible to focus almost entirely on a centralized decision-making elite, or even a single ruler, whose goals and policies are sufficiently dominant that those of other members may be ignored for purposes of simplification (Bueno de Mesquita, 1981). Usually, however, there will be internal constraints operative within even the most centralized bureaucracy or totalitarian government, so that the possibly incompatible interests of other members will have to be taken into consideration in assessing degree and efficiency of mobilization, as well as many other factors that will subsequently be introduced into our discussions. Even so, our models may permit greater simplifications in the case of corporate actors than in instances where boundaries between opposing parties are not clear-cut, where loose coalitions may easily form and break up, and where coordination, consistency of behaviors, and internal cleavages become major factors that need to be considered. In particular, as a conflict wears on, as fatigue begins to predominate, and as rival factions vie for power, it may make a considerable difference whether the party of interest is a tightly organized and well-defined corporate group or a much more diffuse set of actors with ill-defined boundaries. The latter, for example, may simply cease engaging in the conflict without any formal actions having been taken, whereas this would be virtually impossible in the case of two nations at war.

Conflicts of any complexity and duration will practically always involve multiple parties, some of which may remain technically neutral third parties that may, however, play critical roles in replenishing the resources of the combatants, in serving as mediators, or in limiting the use of extreme means or otherwise regulating the nature and intensity of the conflict. Other parties with interests somewhat different from those of the original contesting parties may be drawn into the fray, and at varying points in time, with the coalitions thus formed serving to increase the total resources available to their partners but also, perhaps, placing constraints on alternative courses of action or increasing difficulties of coordination. Our models must not only allow for the existence of such third parties but must also take into consideration how their existence affects the expectations, tactics, and mobilization efforts of the original parties.

Another type of party that will concern us is the tightly-organized "conflict group" that is specifically oriented to conducting intense forms of conflict, sometimes in close coordination with one of the parties concerned but often in a rather independent manner. In one sense, military forces could be considered as special types of such conflict groups, but we particularly have in mind much smaller, extremist groups such as terrorist cells, guerrilla bands, or secret vigilante groups as for example the Ku Klux Klan or clandestine "death squads" that may operate semi-independently of the official police or other governmental agencies. As we shall note, these small conflict groups tend to have a number of common characteristics and may often have interests that are only partly compatible with those of the general membership of the party of concern.

Our models will be two-party models that allow for the existence of heterogeneity, divergent interests, and leadership and coordination problems within each party. Three- or multiple-party conflicts can come in too many potential combinations and add far too many additional complications to be handled in the present work. Yet, we must allow for the fact that real-world conflict situations are never "closed" in the sense that such third parties or other outside forces can safely be ignored. We shall attempt to handle this lack of closure by admitting that exogenous factors may affect a number of the variables in our theoretical system. For example, each party will have a certain stock of available resources that may have been considerably diminished by prior conflicts or that may have to be withheld from use in anticipation of future conflicts. Among other things, there will be certain unforeseen natural events, such as plagues, droughts, or famines, that may require the diversion of scarce resources or that may give the advantage to one side over the other. And each party may be engaged in several simultaneous conflicts that, for some reason, do not become merged.

An Illustration: The Causes of Social Revolutions

As an illustration of the need for complex and inclusive theoretical models to handle multiple-party power confrontations, we may briefly note an intellectual controversy in the macro sociological and political science literatures on peasant and worker rebellions and social revolutions. Most discussions of these very important types of conflict situations involve comparative studies of from three to five nations, with authors developing rather complex arguments involving far more variables than they have cases on which to test their theories.

As is fairly common in analyses of this sort, each historical case is discussed in sufficiently rich detail that the overall argument must be summarized into some relatively simplified "thesis" that is then challenged by other authors, who choose to emphasize a somewhat different set of explanatory factors. The resulting disputes may then be picked up by those who attempt to boil down the major theses still further. Thus there is a pattern through which authors of the most recent works have the advantage, since they tend to set up straw men by virtue of their oversimplifications of previous theoretical arguments. In reading the original works, however, one gains the impression that the authors' arguments are basically compatible but that in the simplification process they appear to be talking past one another.

Crane Brinton, in his classic *The Anatomy of Revolution* (1938), stressed that all of the four revolutions he studied (in England, France, America, and Russia) involved a period of prosperity and rising expectations that could not be satisfied by a weakened or otherwise ineffective government, and that a dissatisfied segment of intellectuals and other elites formed the spearhead of revolutions that then underwent a roughly similar set of stages. This rising-but-frustrated-expectations thesis was also developed more abstractly by Davies (1962) and elaborated on by Gurr (1970) as being one of the fundamental causes of conflicts in general.[1] Barrington Moore (1966), as well, seemed to endorse the overall thesis that an important explanatory factor is the *gap* between expectations and actuality, rather than the absolute *levels* of deprivation or inequality that may exist in any given society. There also appears to be a general consensus that it is not the most deprived, at the very bottom of a social hierarchy, who are the instigators of revolutions, though they may constitute supporting forces once it is underway and though they may, from time to time, engage in relatively isolated and usually abortive revolts over particular local grievances.

Perhaps because the frustration, expectations-gap thesis seemed so appealing as a generic explanation for conflict, the Tillys (1975) and others rather emphatically attempted to discredit arguments along these lines by claiming, perhaps misleadingly, that grievances and frustrations are ubiquitous and often remain at very high levels for considerable periods of time, so that, as explanatory variables, they are not very helpful in accounting for the timing and location of specific conflicts and rebellions.[2] Protest movements have occurred on a widespread basis in Europe and elsewhere, but only a small fraction of these have resulted in violence or physical conflict. To explain this phenomenon, Tilly and his associates have stressed the nature of the responses by the *targets* of the protests, which in their studies have typically been governmental agents.

Where these responses have been weak, indecisive, or vacillating, but yet have been combined with punitive acts that tended to generate a similar reaction by the protesters, a more violent form of conflict has been encouraged. In many instances, however, there has been extreme repression, accompanied by considerable short-term violence that has successfully suppressed revolt for a prolonged period of time.[3] In considering how rather normal protest movements evolve into more violent forms of conflict, it is therefore critical to understand the nature of the dominant party's responses. The Tillys argue that a theory that places the primary emphasis on social mechanisms that produce frustration cannot adequately (on their terms) explain the frequency or temporal and spatial distributions of social violence.

Theda Skocpol (1979) argues that neither type of approach adequately handles the impacts of outside forces on internal processes. In looking at the cases of the French, Russian, and Chinese Communist social revolutions, Skocpol emphasizes that the *state* is not merely an "arena of conflict," over which contestants are fighting, but an essential actor that must be examined in its relationships with other states, as well as in terms of its internal structure and cleavages.[4] Noting that all three of these major social revolutions took place in relatively "backward" states that had been severely weakened by external struggles with more powerful enemies, Skocpol in effect introduces a set variables that are exogenous to, but not incompatible with, the theories advanced by the other authors under discussion.

Brinton (1938), Davies (1962), and Gurr (1970) stress factors relevant to a subordinate party, which we might refer to as party X. The Tillys and their colleagues stress the nature of the reactions by the target party Y. Skocpol is introducing a third set of factors relating to outside parties Z_i and their impacts on parties X and Y, especially the latter. If a state has been considerably weakened by prior or continued conflict with a more powerful enemy, its response to an internal protest or rebellion is highly likely to be affected. The protest may be ruthlessly suppressed if the state in question remains strong enough but unwilling to tolerate dissent, or it may be tolerated or dealt with inconsistently out of weaknesses brought about by the external conflict.

There are therefore no basic incompatibilities among these three apparently "opposing" explanatory systems—provided that each is not oversimplified by detractors and is expanded or elaborated on sufficiently to allow for variables emphasized in the other theories. In this sense, it seems desirable to synthesize such positions by producing a more inclusive and comprehensive theory of social conflict. In particular instances, such as the three social revolutions discussed by Skocpol, it may be advisable to bring external parties (e.g., other states) into the picture, perhaps as necessary causal agents in influencing the outcomes of the conflict processes in question. In other special cases, perhaps, such outside agents may be safely ignored or simply treated as "givens," while focusing on the internal dynamics of a two-party conflict process.

The state-as-actor versus state-as-arena question, however, becomes important as one considers the nature of the parties X and Y that are the subjects of one's theoretical attention. Should one treat "states" as corporate actors that behave, in effect, as though they are single actors with a definite set of objectives, properties, and strategies? Or should they be treated analytically as though they are composed of separate parts that may or may not act in a concerted fashion? Much may depend, here, on whether or not the possibility of shifting alliances is to be considered. Is the army or police force of a state assumed to be completely under the control of its political leaders, or does it contain factions that support the opposition? Are there factions within the state that are, in effect, coalition partners of the party with which it is in conflict? Some members of the latter party, which may be a quasi-group such as an ethnic minority or a social class, may be supportive of the state apparatus which is under attack. If so, for purposes of analysis it may be more appropriate to consider this latter party, party Y, to consist of a larger corporate group, such as a state, *plus* a number of more loose-knit supporting groups that may or may not shift their allegiances as the conflict wears on.

Our own models will be sufficiently general to leave matters such as these entirely open. Although the distinction between weakly coordinated quasi-groups, on the one hand, and corporate groups, on the other, would seem to be a useful starting point, we shall employ these terms only very loosely to refer to clusters of factors that may distinguish very different kinds of parties to a conflict. Instead, we shall rely on a list of explicit *variables,* such as a party's heterogeneity, degree of consensus on means, centralization of control, or efficiency of mobilization. The essential point in the present connection is that organizational factors will need to be taken into consideration and that they may be far more problematic but yet critical in some situations than in others.

The Causal Modeling Approach

For the most part in the chapters that follow we shall employ a discursive mode of presentation. In Chapter 5, however, as well as in the final sections of Chapters 7, 8, and 10, we shall present several rather complex causal models that serve both as summaries of our previous verbal arguments and as a rudimentary type of formal theorizing. As already implied, the major methodological or metatheoretical assumption made in the present work is that efforts to construct and then test highly parsimonious theories are likely to introduce such serious distortions of realistic conflict processes, via the gross oversimplifications they require, that serious social scientific advances will be hindered by the resulting disputes they then generate. I hope in the subsequent discussion to convince the skeptical reader of the soundness of this perspective on the nature of the scientific enterprise. There are costs in avoiding extreme forms of parsimony, however, and these must be addressed and handled as best we can.

Verbal theories of any degree of complexity become very difficult to follow, even in those relatively few instances where authors provide lists of explicit propositions. One of the reasons for the problem is that most verbal propositions are bivariate in nature, taking a form such as: the greater the X, the greater the Y. Sometimes a third or even fourth variable may be mentioned, as when a list of causes is strung out in a single sentence, as for example: Y is positively influenced by W, X and Z. Or the linkage between X and Y may be conditional on Z, as in the proposition: the greater the value of Z, the steeper the slope linking X and Y.

As a theory becomes complex, verbal theories become increasingly inadequate in a number of respects. First, the linkages among *independent* variables are likely to be neglected. If there are say, 10 purported causes of Y, there will be 45 *pairs* of causes, many of which can be expected to be intercorrelated for a number of reasons. Perhaps X causes Z, or both have a common cause W. Or perhaps there is reciprocal causation among all three. Such interconnections among Y's causes are likely to be ignored by the theorist, and yet they may be critical for an adequate understanding of a complex social process. A causal diagram is much more useful in depicting such complicated causal patternings among supposedly independent variables, as well as in alerting the theorist and reader to missing links in the theory.

Other types of verbal formulations trace out simple causal chains of the form, W leads to X leads to Y leads to Z, but without examining other sorts of complications that need to be considered. Perhaps W affects not only X but V as well, with V also impacting on Y. Perhaps Y or Z feed back to impact on W or X, or even both. It is very likely that there will be a combination of such feedbacks and multiple paths connecting widely separated variables. One variable may affect another indirectly by a number of routes, some of which are, say, positive, whereas the others operate in precisely the opposite direction. If so, the total impact of the one variable on the other may be indeterminate unless the theorist can say something definite about the magnitudes of the relationships involved.

Perhaps the simple six-variable causal model given in Figure 1.1 will be helpful to the reader who is unaccustomed to working with casual models. In this model there is a causal chain running from X_1 to X_2 to X_4 to X_5 to X_6. There are other chains leading from X_1 to X_5 and

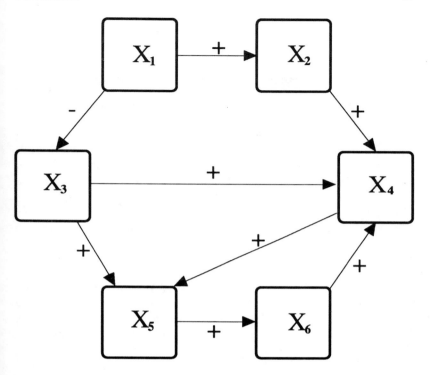

Figure 1.1. Prototype causal model involving six variables

thus to X_6, however, and perhaps the sign of the arrow linking X_1 to X_3 is negative, whereas all other direct paths are positive. If so, we will not be able to predict even the sign of the total correlation between the two end variables X_1 and X_6.

Verbal formulations also may be overly simplistic in terms of the omission of certain causal feedback loops that may involve lag periods of sufficient duration to be detectable and still others that may require one to treat the reciprocal causation as being nearly simultaneous. Frequently, for example, it is assumed that a party's behaviors may be taken as "dependent," whereas a more complete theory would take these behaviors as feeding back to affect some of the supposedly "independent" variables in the theory. In the model of Figure 1.1, for example, such a feedback loop exists among X_4 X_5, and X_6, meaning that there is no clearly "dependent" variable in this set, although all three are either directly or indirectly affected by the first three variables in the model.

Data analyses based on such simplified verbal theories often involve what are called "single equation" approaches that require unreasonable assumptions about the behavior of omitted variables, the effects of which are summarized in disturbance or residual terms. The simple phrase, "other things being equal," is notoriously misleading in this respect. In multiple regression analysis, analysis of variance, and virtually all other types of single-equation approaches it is assumed, for example, that disturbance terms are uncorrelated with the independent variables in their respective equations. This will be totally unrealistic, however, if a "dependent" variable feeds back to affect any of its causes, as is the case for X_6 in the above model. In simplified verbal theories, as well as in conventional data analyses, it is often implicitly assumed that the behaviors of *relatively* powerless actors, such as minorities, deviants and children, do not impact on any of their causes. Yet, certainly when such actors are aggregated, these reverse impacts may be considerable. Children do affect their parents and minorities affect dominant groups. At the macro level, high crime *rates* may feed back to affect subsequent policy decisions.

It is always necessary to omit variables both from one's theory and from one's data analysis, but this does not mean that such omissions are thereby justified. If an omitted variable is a cause of only one of the variables in a given model, then it can be shown that its omission will not produce biases in the estimates of the parameters in that model (Blalock, 1964). In most other instances where variables have had to be omitted, however, the situation will be much more complex. The basic question one must ask is: Without a relatively complete theoretical model, how can one possibly justify the omission of such variables? The mere fact that they are difficult to measure or have not been anticipated is, of course, no theoretical justification for their neglect. If one has simply ignored them in the theory, preferring instead a simplified version that leaves them out, there *can* be no such theoretical justification. One will have no idea of how they would have been fitted into a more complete theory and how they could be expected to influence the disturbance terms that, inevitably, must be included in any empirical tests of the theory.

Therefore if one tries to test separately a series of relatively incomplete theories, with a view to "accepting" the one that explains the most variance, one can be highly misled to the degree that in each instance omitted variables produce biases in one's estimates. Furthermore, where the "independent" variables of one theory are correlated with those in another, there will be no way of sorting things out, short of inserting both sets in a more inclusive theory. What appears to be a shortcut, then, turns out to be much more tedious and potentially misleading than beginning with a more complex and inclusive formulation in the first place. Some of the variables in the one theory may have indirect effects through variables that are contained only in the second theory. There may be reciprocal causation between variables in two supposedly opposing theories, or perhaps the "dependent" variable of both theories feeds back to affect the "independent" variables in the two theories, but to varying degrees or in a manner that is dependent upon the circumstances. All of this will be overlooked unless the more inclusive formulation has been attempted.

Once a complex and more inclusive theory has been formulated, it may then be simplified. This may be possible if empirical results show certain linkages to be negligible, or it may be necessary because certain variables cannot be measured in the particular study under consideration. If the more complete theory is available to the investigator, however, it will be possible to anticipate at least the direction of the possible biases. Future investigators may then be alerted to the advisability of collecting additional information.

Given the general theory it may be possible to delete certain variables which are, by assumption, merely adding frosting to the cake, so to speak. If, for example, there is a simple causal chain from X_1 to X_2 to X_4, as is true in Figure 1.1, then if X_2 were inadvertently omitted, one would still be able to estimate, without bias, the effects of X_1 on X_4. This linkage would now be called "direct," but the slope coefficient linking X_1 to X_4 would be the same as the product of the slopes linking X_1 to X_2 and X_2 to X_4. We would simply have a less "rich" theoretical interpretation of the causal process. The essential point in this connection is that without the more inclusive theory, in this instance the one containing X_2, there is no way of justifying its omission, except on an ad hoc basis.

Causal diagrams represent highly compact ways of stating predicted bivariate relationships, with controls for those variables that appear in the roles of causally prior or intervening variables. If there is no direct arrow connecting any given pair of variables, this implies that, with simultaneous controls for *all* causally prior and intervening variables, the resulting partials are expected to be zero apart from sampling errors. Thus the models imply a whole series of "null" hypotheses. They also imply, however, that there *should* be associations, with proper controls, among pairs of variables that *have* been connected by direct arrows, and in most instances signs representing the directions of these relationships may be inserted directly into the diagram. If a theory contained only 20 variables, there would be 20(19)/2 or 190 possible pairs of bivariate relationships and thus a tremendously large number of bivariate propositions linking such variables.

Our subsequent discussions will imply reciprocal causation or feedback loops between the behaviors of our two major parties X and Y. Causal models may also be used to specify certain reciprocal causal linkages among some of the variables pertaining to a single actor, such as a set of ideological dimensions and subjective probabilities and utilities. To take a much simpler example, suppose X_6 were omitted from the model of Figure 1.1 and replaced by a direct arrow leading from X_5 to X_4, implying a simple two-variable feedback loop between these two variables. With a properly specified system of two simultaneous equations, the coefficients in opposite directions could then be estimated provided that the system did not contain too many unknowns relative to the number of pieces of empirical information.

It should be emphasized that where such reciprocal linkages or even more complex causal loops are involved, one is not justified in pulling out single equations representing each "dependent" variable and then treating each such equation as estimable. Nor is one justified in pulling causal diagrams apart except under very special circumstances. This may be done, of course, but the estimates so derived will contain biases, some of which may be substantial. The more general point in this connection is that an elaborated causal diagram of this nature can represent a large amount of information, which may then be used in empirical investigations to justify a highly complex data analysis, or a much simpler one in the event that the model permits it. If the theory has been grossly oversimplified to begin with, however, there will be no way of assessing where one's problems lie without starting over again and developing the more complex theory. Only *then* should one try to decide which kinds of simplifications can be justified in a given type of setting.

An Overview of the Volume

Chapters 2 and 3 provide discussions of the power framework we shall employ throughout the remainder of the volume and include an analysis of various alternative definitions of power, as well as the notions of resources and their mobilization, mutual and asymmetric dependency, and the subjective expected utility perspective. Chapter 3 focuses more specifically on resource mobilization, the use of selective incentives to reduce free riding, and factors that affect party solidarity.

Chapter 4 deals with reactive processes, through which each party's actions affect those of the other, with the result that conflict either accelerates in intensity or is brought under control. Arms-race dynamic models are first presented and compared. Relationships between dominant and subordinate parties are also given special attention, as is deterrence theory as an alternative to arms-race approaches to the dynamics of social conflict.

In Chapter 5 we attempt to summarize the arguments of the previous three chapters by constructing a rather complex general causal model of conflict processes. This general model, which contains 40 variables, deals specifically with power and mobilization, on the one hand, and reactive and control processes, on the other. Two supplementary submodels are then presented, the first dealing with the impact of a party's heterogeneity on the degree and efficiency of its mobilization effort, and the second showing how this particular submodel may be simplified in instances where the parties of concern are individual persons. In subsequent chapters (Chaps. 7, 8, and 10) three additional submodels are also provided to handle other important kinds of special cases.

In Chapters 6 and 7 there are discussions of various ideological supports for conflict. Fourteen ideological dimensions are delineated and analyzed in terms of their impacts on the degree and efficiency of the mobilization effort, as well as consensus and group solidarity. These dimensions include the degree to which a belief system is highly simplistic, whether or not it is well-insulated from competing ideologies, how fatalistic it is, the degree to which blame is placed on other parties, the extent to which it contains ambiguities and is highly flexible in accomodating new elements, how much it encourages expansive or punitive orientations toward other parties, and several other dimensions that relate directly to relationships it encourages with these other parties. An ideological submodel is then presented at the end of Chapter 7.

Chapter 8 contains discussions of the role of conflict groups in amplifying conflict processes and of the dilemmas encountered in coping with an intractable opponent. An additional submodel dealing with such conflict groups is also provided. The emphasis on dynamic processes is continued in Chapters 9 and 10, which focus primarily on the question of how it is that conflicts are sustained or even intensified in spite of their substantial costs and their differential impacts on individual party members. The role of belief systems and different types of goals is examined, as these change during the course of a conflict and as fatigue factors begin to predominate. Structural factors that may be related to the maintenance of conflict are also discussed.

Chapter 10, which concludes the volume, is concerned with conflict termination processes and opens with a discussion of certain strategic dilemmas encountered when one or both parties begin to search for conflict-reduction mechanisms, and when perceptions of stalemates become increasingly likely. The role of extremists in these processes is also examined. A final elaborate submodel dealing with conflict-sustaining processes is then presented, and some brief concluding observations are made about the implications of our theoretical analysis for those who wish to address policy matters in the context of much more specific forms of social conflict.

A recurring major theme of the book is that most conflict processes are sufficiently complex that the theories or models we use to explain them must also be highly complicated. Simple verbal theories that state a series of propositions in terms of bivariate relationships, or ones that are conditional on only two or three other variables, will in general tend to be misleading and to foster debates among the proponents of supposedly "alternative" theoretical explanations. If we are genuinely interested in the cumulation of knowledge, rather than in merely taking sides in such debates, we must be prepared to construct theoretical models that incorporate the most important features of a variety of simpler theories. Empirical tests of such theories must be correspondingly sophisticated. The kinds of simplifications that are necessarily required in all empirical studies should be explicitly based on theory rather than made on an ad hoc basis. If this does not occur, there will be no systematic way of assessing potential biases in our research or of identifying misleading recommendations made in the policy arena.

Notes

1. According to Gurr (1970) there also have been a very large number of similar arguments made in classic works on revolution, going back at least to Aristotle. See for example Aristotle (1883), Edwards (1927), Pettee (1938), Hobsbawm (1959), and Arendt (1963).

2. For discussions of this point of view see Isaac, Mutran, and Stryker (1980), Jenkins and Perrow (1977), Portes (1971), Shorter and Tilly (1974), Snyder (1975), Snyder and Tilly (1972), and Useem (1980). It should also be pointed out that works such as Gurr (1970) *do* deal with issues affecting the location and timing of conflictful events, much more thoroughly than is often implied by their critics.

3. See Gurr (1970) and Hibbs (1973) for discussions of possibly differing dynamics, depending on whether one is considering relatively minor instances of sporadic revolts or more extensive internal warfare.

4. Giddens (1987) places a similarly heavy emphasis on the importance of the state as actor, rather than as a mere arena of conflict. It should also be noted more generally that political scientists, in contrast to sociologists, usually place a far greater emphasis on the state as actor, so that Skocpol's thesis is by no means unique.

Chapter 2

Power and Dependency

The concept of power is both exceedingly slippery to pin down and yet indispensable in enabling one to analyze a number of important social processes, including that of conflict. As in the physical sciences, power can be defined either as potential or in its kinetic or action form. In physics, power in use is defined as work actually accomplished per unit of time, but it can also be conceived of as a potential for doing work, as for example in the form of a body of a given mass poised a particular distance above the earth's surface or a 200-horsepower engine. In a similar way, one may refer to a powerful nation or political leader as being one that is *capable*, by virtue of resources possessed, of accomplishing objectives or controlling other parties. As an alternative, one may confine the notion of power to actions actually accomplished. In the social sciences, however, the linkage between power as potential and power in action is highly problematic.[1]

In the present work we shall refer to power in its kinetic form or as work actually accomplished, using the term "resources" to refer to the sources of power, or if one prefers, to power as a potential. As we shall see, there will ordinarily be a considerable number of variables that intervene between power resources and power that is actually exerted, so that it will generally require a rather complex model to link the two. By no stretch of the imagination can one assume that a "powerful" party will automatically use its resources to control another actor. Among other things, resources generally are expendable and will need to be replenished. There will be many different and competing purposes for which these same resources may be expended. There are apt to be multiple parties, some of which are of no great interest to the potentially powerful party one is examining. In our society right-handed persons do not attempt to control those of us who are left-handed. Whites do exert power over blacks, however, though not in as concerted or coordinated a form as is used in the Union of South Africa.

Furthermore, there are many possible alternative courses of action or means that may be used in the exercise of power and these will also vary in terms of efficiency. Some means will conserve more resources than others, resources that may be needed for other power confrontations or that may be converted into other things, such as consumption goods. Motives, goals, and beliefs play important roles in determining how and under what conditions resources will actually be employed in a given instance. Our theories of power and conflict will need to take these into account.

Following earlier discussions in Blalock (1967) and Blalock and Wilken (1979), we may take power as exercised (P) as a multiplicative function of three kinds of variables: resources (R), the degree to which these are mobilized (D), and the efficiency of the mobilization effort (E), so that roughly speaking

$$P = kRDE$$

provided it is clearly recognized that none of the three components is likely to be measurable as a ratio scale, though conceptual zero points can be imagined. The implications of the multiplicative model are of importance, however, as the model suggests statistical interactions between any two of the component terms on the right-hand side. In particular, if either efficiency or degree of mobilization were zero, then no effective power would be realized, regardless of the level of the party's resources. Similarly, if there were no resources available, both degree and efficiency of mobilization would become irrelevant. If there were no power potential to be mobilized, there would hardly be any payoff to be expected by improving efficiency. If both R and D were large, however, then minor increments in efficiency could have important impacts on the effective power exerted. If any one term were close to zero, it would take very large values of the other two to bring P to even an intermediate level. Although the multiplicative formulation is crude, it thus seems important to distinguish it from the usual additive one encountered in conventional causal modeling.

Human behavior is goal directed and it is therefore critical to define or conceive of power as implying a directional component. In this connection there have been several different kinds of conceptualizations in the literature. One may define power as the achievement of specific objectives, whatever these may be, thus providing a rather broad orientation that includes much more than power as control over other parties. It has been pointed out, for example, that functionalist definitions of power are likely to stress the achievement of common as well as competitive goals: the power of community leaders to attract new industry, improve the economy, or to develop a central business district.[2] There may be conflict or *dissensus* involved in achieving such common goals, but if so, this may be conceived of as *reducing* or interfering with the efficiency or degree of mobilization effort. The concept of power, as defined in this way, calls our attention to a wider range of social processes than those that are the focus of our own attention. It is perhaps also more compatible with the "work accomplished" definition used in physics.

When referring more specifically to two- or multi-party conflict situations it is more conventional to employ a somewhat narrower definition of power, namely that of control or domination. Dahl (1957, p. 202), for example, employs a common type of definition: "A has power over B to the extent that he can get B to do something that B would not otherwise do." Here we have the notion that power exerted by party X can, ideally, be measured by noting the change in a second party Y's behavior that is due to the actions or threatened actions of X. If Y's behavior is not altered, then X has not exerted power or influence over Y.

The notion of a causal relationship between the actual or threatened behaviors of X and the responses of Y is thus built into this type of definition of power. Herbert Simon (1957, p.5), indeed, almost equates the two notions of power and causation when he says: "For the assertion 'A has power over B,' we can substitute the assertion, 'A's behavior causes B's behavior.'" Needless to say, whenever such a causal process is at all complex, a definitional strategy of this type will inevitably lead to difficulties. But so will the accomplishment-of-goals type of definition if one attempts to separate the power actually exercised by the party in question, here X, from the many other factors that may also have contributed to the achievement of the objective in question. If outcome is simply equated with exercised power, the analytic value of the power concept disappears (Blalock, 1961). If we think of power, as exercised, as an out*put*, then an out*come* will be a function not only of power exerted but of other factors as well, including outputs of other actors and environmental constraints.

A third though less common definition of power involves the notion of overcoming resistances. One may for instance define exerted power as the amount of resistance that has been overcome, taking into consideration forces that are operating on the same as well as the opposing side of the issue in question. Operationally, one would encounter the same kinds of problems in measuring exerted power, however, since a complete listing of extraneous opposing and supporting forces would be needed in order to measure the amount of power actually being exerted by party X. In a power contest between only two parties, X and Y, this would imply that the power exerted by X would have to be measured by a procedure that also required the measurement of Y's exerted power, as well as that exerted by (possibly multiple) third parties *and* by a residual category of forces of a nonhuman nature: such things as physical barriers, unforeseen natural disasters, or events that, though caused by human actions, are in no way controllable by the actors in question.

In special cases it may not matter whether power is defined in terms of the achievement of goals, controlling another party, or overcoming resistances. If, for example, the opponent Y's resistance is the only barrier to goal achievement, then the first and third alternatives will be equivalent. If the goal is simply that of achieving control over Y's behavior, then the first and second will be identical, whereas if the resistance to be overcome is merely that of a resistance to the control effort, the second and third will be indistinguishable.

More generally the three alternative conceptualizations will be somewhat different, with one or the other being more inclusive according to the circumstances. In our very general formulation, it will be assumed that many of the goals desired by both parties to the conflict will be focused on the conflict itself, with the primary resistances to be overcome being those presented by the opposing party. Since we shall need to allow for third-party interventions and a heterogeneity of goals among both parties' members, however, this will not always be the case. Given the difficulties in pinning down causation (and thus power) in reasonably complex conflict situations, however, we shall not restrict the definition of power to a single one of the three types of formulations under discussion, though we shall assume that the *primary* objectives and resistances involved will center on a single opposing party, the control or defeat of which is of central importance to the party on which our attention is focused. If so, there may be little to be gained by restricting the definition to only one of these three alternatives.

There is another distinction made in Blalock and Wilken (1979) that is relevant to the present discussion, though we shall not make use of it in any detail. Party X's resources will depend upon what Cartwright (1959, p. 190) refers to as the "motive base" or the goals of party Y, and perhaps other actors as well. This means that resources should not be equated with a party's objective properties, such as money, weapons, natural resources, or authority. It also implies that resources have exchange values that depend upon the goals of other parties. For example, money alone cannot be counted on to influence other actors unless they value the money and can be "bought" by it or consider its employment legitimate under the circumstances. Authority must be accepted by the other party or at least by another set of actors (e.g., the police) who are willing to follow orders to employ different means to influence Y.

Thus other parties' goals and beliefs will affect the *conversion* (or exchange value) of objective properties into actual resources or sources of power. In many discussions of power, particularly at the macro level, this factor of the "motive base" or goals of other parties may be taken for granted. Sometimes this will indeed be reasonable, as for example when one assumes that men will value their survival above all else. But there will be other circumstances where the conversion of properties into resources will be much more problematic, and so the distinction may become important.

In our very general and content-free conflict models, however, we shall not attempt to exploit the distinction between objective properties and resources, except to point out that X's resources depend upon Y's goals, and vice versa. Emerson's (1962, 1972) discussions of dependency, which we shall take up later in the chapter, will be relevant in this connection. Y may reduce its dependency on X by lowering the values attached to goals that can be blocked or controlled by X, and similarly for X, so that the mutual dependency of the two parties will depend upon their respective goals. As we shall see, Emerson virtually equates low power resources with high dependency, so that the goals of both parties become central to his discussions of power and dependency.

In order to move from resources to power as actually exercised it is necessary to introduce the notions of degree and efficiency of mobilization, both of which will play critical roles in our subsequent discussions. By degree of mobilization we mean the proportion of a party's total resources that are actually mobilized in the power conflict itself rather than being used for other purposes or withheld for later use. Given the difficulties in measuring resource levels, it will of course also be difficult if not impossible to obtain precise measures of degree of mobilization except for very simple types of resources such as manpower or money.

Even so, the mobilization factor is practically always taken into consideration in power analyses and has, indeed, become the label used to characterize an entire orientation to the study of collective behavior, namely the "resource mobilization" literature.[3] One recognizes that parties have varying degrees of success in their mobilization efforts and that many of their members will become "free riders" (Olson, 1965) who choose to let others do the work and make the sacrifices necessary to obtain a common good. Tightly organized "conflict groups" seem capable of mobilizing an extremely high proportion of their total resources, whereas many kinds of potential "interest groups," such as peasants, racial or ethnic groups, or women, may possess considerable potential power that is only rarely and sporadically mobilized. Our causal models of conflict processes will therefore need to address the question of explaining degree of resource mobilization, even though precise measures of this variable will be difficult to obtain in all but the simplest of instances. The following chapter will focus specifically on the factors that impact on the degree and efficiency of resource mobilization, and two of our elaborations on the general model presented in Chapter 5 will also deal with this topic.

Efficiency of mobilization needs to be distinguished from degree of mobilization since some means will have greater impact on the total power exercised than will others, holding degree of effort constant. Here we encounter such factors as coordination and division of labor, leadership rivalries, heterogeneity of goals, knowledge, deception and secrecy, rule breaking, consistency, and a host of other factors that may impact on the outcome of a conflict situation.

Efficiency is defined in physics as the ratio of output to input, with the units of energy being defined so that the upper limit of efficiency is 1.0. In our much more crude usage of the term in the social sciences there is an analogous idea of a ratio, sometimes accompanied by a maximizing assumption to the effect that rational actors will attempt to select among those courses of action that maximize the likelihood of success for a given expenditure of energy. Some means are presumed to be more efficient than others, with it perhaps being advisable to expend a certain fraction of one's total resources to obtain the information necessary to select the optimal strategy. We shall not pursue the subject in any more detail than this in the present chapter, but we shall later introduce into our discussion a number of variables that will be linked to efficiency of mobilization, with the recognition that the parties to a conflict will also take such factors into consideration, though with possible miscalculations that may be influenced by ideological systems, faulty information, or insufficient foresight.

A SIMPLIFIED POWER MODEL

Although our subsequent models of conflict processes will become highly complex, it is advisable at this point to introduce the very simple model of Figure 2.1 in order to indicate the major variables contained in the power framework that will be used to undergird our discussions of conflict processes. The focus of attention in Figure 2.1 is on party X, which may be an individual person, a highly organized corporate group, or a much more loosely organized quasi-group composed of multiple parties in a coalition arrangement. It is assumed that the power confrontation is with party Y but that there may be additional third parties Z_i that may also influence the outcome. A residual set of variables influencing the outcome have been lumped together in the box titled "Environmental Constraints."

In this very general model the resources of X are taken as functions of X's objective properties and the goals of other parties, Y and Z_i, and efficiency of mobilization is taken as a function of X's choices among available means. The three variables, resources of X, degree of mobilization of X's resources, and efficiency of mobilization of X's resources are assumed to multiply to affect the total amount of power exerted by X. This multiplicative joint effect is represented diagramatically by having the three arrows join before they reach the "Power Exerted by X" box (X's output), rather than by three arrows that reach it separately. A similar set of variables, not shown in the diagram, is assumed to affect the power exerted by Y and the power exerted by the Z_i. Outcomes, as distinct from X's output, are influenced by these other actors as well as by a miscellaneous set of environmental factors. No feedbacks are shown in this very simple model, but we may presume that outcomes will affect future levels of resources and mobilization, as well as the goals of all parties.

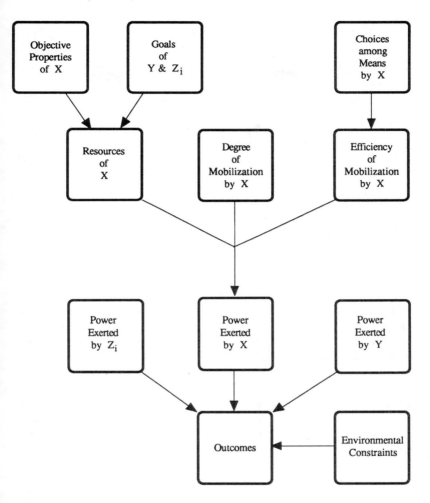

Figure 2.1 Simple power model focusing on party X

A Modified Subjective Expected Utility Perspective

Subjective factors will play an important role in our subsequent discussion, as they do in all human conflict situations. We shall employ a modified "rational actor" framework that allows for considerably more flexibility than do the much simpler versions that have been the subjects of considerable dispute and criticism. It will be assumed that actors have multiple goals, only some of which are directly related to the conflict itself. Thus any "maximizing" that occurs will be far more complex than is implied in discussions of economic decision making where, typically, only one or two goals are assumed by the theorist. Our formulation will therefore be much more compatible with Simon's (1957) notion of "satisficing," or with the idea that rationality is "bounded" by a large number of conditioning constraints, than it is with much more elegant but far more restrictive discussions of strict economic rationality (March and Simon, 1958).

Goal preferences or utilities will not only vary across members of each party to a conflict, but they will also change over time as a result of deprivations, satiation, and modifications in belief systems that link the attainment of some goals to others. Furthermore, since the utilities or values attached to goals are assumed to be subjective, they are not necessarily linearly related to "objective" values. For example, utilities attached to receiving monetary outcomes are typically found to be power functions of actual dollar amounts, with exponents approximately equal to .5, implying a satiation or diminishing returns phenomenon.[4] We shall also allow for actors' subjective probabilities, which may in a few instances coincide closely with empirically determined relative frequencies or "objective" probabilities, but which will more often be subject to distortions, ideological influences, and miscalculations (Barclay and Beach, 1972; Bar-Hillel, 1973; Blalock and Wilken, 1979; Coombs, Dawes, and Tversky, 1970; Coombs and Pruitt, 1960; Lee, 1971; Tversky, 1967; Wyer and Goldberg, 1970).

It will be assumed that a rough sort of maximization occurs through which subjective probabilities and utilities are multiplied and then added, but with various kinds of simplification processes at work. There need not be a "complete" or thorough search among all possible alternatives, for example, as the costs of such a search may be formidable or the temporal constraints prohibitive (Blalock and Wilken, 1979; Coombs et al; 1970; March and Simon, 1958; Simon, 1957). Nevertheless it is assumed that some sort of crude assessment is made of the chances of achieving an objective by a given course of action and that behaviors are based on such assessments. In many instances there may be a lack of agreement among a party's members as to which course of action is most likely to lead to a given outcome and what the expected costs may be.

The basic assumption, then, is that actors make crude calculations, though often very rapid and seemingly "nonrational" ones, based on the following idealized model. Alternative behaviors B_i will be assessed and that alternative selected which maximizes the sum $\sum_{j=1}^{k} P(O_j \mid B_i) \times U(O_j)$. Each outcome O_j is likely to be multidimensional but is evaluated in terms of the goal mixes of the actors concerned, with the total utility attached to that outcome $U(O_j)$ being a weighted average of the utility preferences of the party's membership. In many situations, of course, most members' weights will be only imagined or estimated by the decision-makers involved or may actually be totally ignored by them.

Thus the kind of "greatest good for the greatest numbers" assumption implicit in the above formulation will, in practically all realistic situations, be a subjective factor in the minds of key decision-makers.[5] Being subjective, incidentally, means that neither the actors concerned nor the analyst need to be technically rigid about the inability to make interpersonal comparisons of utilities. If key decision-makers *believe* a party's members hold a given set of utilities, and if they act upon these beliefs, then this is what matters. Certainly, no "calculus" involving well-defined weights is likely to be used in making such decisions, but we do assume that multiple goals and some degree of heterogeneity with respect to goal preferences will be taken into consideration by the relevant actors. Where far more uniform goal hierarchies exist, as we might imagine to be the case in a "battle to the death" between two extremely homogeneous extremist parties, we may always handle the situation as a simplified special case.

GOAL DIMENSIONS AND BELIEF SYSTEMS

A general formulation such as ours must handle the problem of conceptualizing a tremendous number of possible goals in such a way that the specific details of each conflict being investigated do not overwhelm the analysis. Of the many goal classifications that are possible, we shall group goals under three very broad categories.[6]

First there will be those goals, which we shall call G_1 goals, that the two parties share in common in the sense that the attainment of G_1 goals by either party also increases the probability that they will likewise be attained by the other. These goals, then, tend to reinforce cooperation for common objectives and will practically always include a shared objective of ending the conflict and thereby reducing the levels of punishment that each party is receiving. The two parties may also be engaged in exchanges of positively valued goods and services, which may have been interrupted or considerably reduced by the conflict process. They may in addition value each other's well-being over and above the tangible benefits derived from these positive exchanges. Such G_1 goals, which are sometimes ignored in discussions of power and conflict, will tend to dampen or restrain the level of conflict involved. Needless to say, they may be differentially shared by a party's membership, with this possibly leading to important internal cleavages.

Second there will be those goals G_2 over which the parties are in competition or that for other reasons are incompatible in the sense that party X's attainment of these goals will reduce the probability of Y's also attaining them. Objects over which the parties are in direct competition—such things as jobs, rights to control drug outlets, land, natural resources, or the control over third parties—involve such G_2 goals, but so do other objectives that we shall later lump together under the label of "grievances." These may include the desire for revenge, the injury of the other party, or the satisfaction of supposedly "irrational" objectives such as that of imposing one's religious or other type of belief system on the other party or of controlling its members' objectionable behaviors. At the individual level, a husband or wife may each desire to dictate the other's behavior or to gain exclusive possession of their children. Such G_2 goals, like all others, need not be restricted to the much smaller subset of goals used by economists to explain market behavior or conflicts over material objects, and they will also be subject to change during the course of the conflict.

We shall assume the G_2 goals, however diverse they may be, tend to reinforce the conflict process insofar as they remain strong and are perceived to be attainable by conflict-oriented means that are not otherwise too costly. If an outside observer or analyst happens to neglect certain of these goals, or downplays them as being "nonutilitarian," it does not then follow that behaviors based on such goals are "irrational" or that rational-actor theories are ipso facto inadequate. A religious struggle for the souls of the other party's members may be based on highly rationalistic assumptions, provided one holds religious objectives to be more important than economic ones and provided one accepts a belief system that produces subjective probabilities that virtually predetermine a party's courses of action.

Finally, as a kind of residual category, we may distinguish a third type of goal G_3 that is basically irrelevant to the conflict itself but that competes with G_2 goals for scarce resources. Both a husband and wife in a conflict situation may wish to continue to perform well on the job or to maintain outside contacts. Members of two warring nations need food, water, housing, rest and recuperation, medical attention, and other basic necessities that may become increasingly scarce as a conflict wears on. They also have certain personal objectives that cannot be met by the conflict process and that may have to be postponed in order to pursue the conflict to its conclusion. Although selected G_3 goals may be given up altogether or replaced by others that can be satisfied by active participation in the conflict, many others may have been deferred sufficiently long that utilities for these unmet goals increase at accelerating rates.

Although not directly relevant to the immediate conflict process such G_3 goals thus cannot safely be neglected in analyses of conflicts that persist over any reasonable length of time. Indeed, they may become increasingly important in accounting for fatigue processes and the termination of hostilities. They may also contribute to a party's "motive base" or goal hierarchies that, we have argued, affect the other party's level of resources, even where objective properties have remained constant. Frequently, such "irrelevant" goals are simply ignored in discussions of conflict processes, so that deviations from supposedly "rational" strategies then cannot be explained.

All goals can be affected by belief systems or ideologies, and we shall devote Chapters 6 and 7 to discussions of how such belief systems may operate to influence conflict processes. Here it is sufficient to note that beliefs may directly affect subjective probabilities, often by pushing them closer to the limits of zero and unity. If a powerful magic helper in the form of a tribal diety is believed to be on one's side, ultimate victory may be perceived as inevitable. Eternal salvation, if promised as a certainty to those willing to make extreme sacrifices, may serve as a powerful inducement to make such sacrifices, especially if the belief system is capable of persuading true believers that the goal of eternal salvation should outweigh all more worldly and thus short-term objectives. Similarly, beliefs about the capabilities of men and women may affect their individual aspirations and beliefs concerning the adequacies of their partners' behaviors.

Other belief systems may encourage a fatalistic outlook that essentially says that outcomes will be unaffected by behavioral choices, so that subjective probabilities of any valued outcome O_j will remain constant, regardless of the B_i selected. Beliefs may also affect perceptions of how the attainment of one objective (say, a college education) is related to the achievement of another (e.g., a high income). In particular, beliefs may afford actors with very simple causal models or "working theories" that blame other actors for a given state of affairs.[7] By implication they may also suggest that a removal of such actors would also result in a major change for the better. If Jews could be blamed for the defeat of Germany in World War I, their annihilation could not only be justified on punitive grounds but also, presumably, would remove a potential cause of a similar outcome in the future.

Debates over the adequacy of subjective expected utility (SEU) formulations or about "rationality" often do not come to grips with precisely what it is that defines this rationality. If one means by the term a complete listing of all possible alternative courses of action and a highly accurate set of subjective probabilities that correspond very closely to relative frequencies, then rational behaviors will of course never be found in the real world. Actors must inevitably select among a relatively small subset of all possible courses of action, if only because of their limited horizons and unwillingness to expend scarce resources to discover them all, as well as their inability to attach accurate probability values to their expected successes in achieving each and every conceivable outcome.[8] What can be argued, however, is that most actors will attach crude probability estimates to some set of alternative courses of action, as for example whether or not to engage in a conflict with a powerful opponent, how far to carry a bluff, how strong a commitment to make, or what the likely response will be to a peace overture.

Why use rational-actor theories if they cannot be tested and rejected in real-life situations and if they can rather easily be modified by postulating additional goals not considered by the analyst or by allowing for subjective probabilities that are difficult for both the actors and analysts to pin down? The answer is that such an approach constitutes a kind of working tool of the social scientist. If a given sequence of behaviors cannot adequately be explained, perhaps a somewhat different set of goals and utilities needs to be taken into consideration. Simple game-theory orientations, for example, often take payoff matrices as given, the presumption being that actors' utilities are linear functions of objective units, such as dollars or poker chips. Actors are assumed not to have separate utilities for gambling, boredom is disregarded, and the alternatives of rulebreaking or quitting the game are also ruled out by the analyst.[9] Where actors' behaviors then depart from those predicted on the basis of highly simplistic assumptions, "irrationality" or "error" may be invoked as an explanation. According to the tack we are recommending, however, such deviations are to be explained by postulating an expanded set of goals and a set of subjective probabilities that may be only partly affected by the rules of the game or the roll of the dice.

Perhaps it is most sensible to ask why actors should *not* act so as to maximize or at least improve their expected outcomes, given whatever utilities and probabilities they may attach to them. And if one allowed for "nonrational" behaviors, how would one proceed theoretically in predicting such behaviors? One way, of course, is to predict future responses entirely on the basis of prior ones. But from our view this merely presumes that actors are not modifying their goal preferences or expectancies for some period of time. Unless one is willing to assume something more definite about them, it is difficult to provide a theoretical *explanation* for such behaviors.

A NOTE ON HETEROGENEITY AND GOALS

The notion of a party's heterogeneity will play an important role in our subsequent discussions. Heterogeneity, of course, can refer to any number of dimensions, but we shall refer primarily to heterogeneity with respect to values attached to goals and to preferences among means. It would be much simpler to use the term to refer to more readily measured attributes such as race or ethnicity, language, religious memberships, or social status, but these and other factors may not relate at all to whatever conflicts are being analyzed, or their usage may suggest an unwarranted degree of simplicity. Furthermore, it may be difficult to formulate a general theory of conflict in terms of such highly specific kinds of objective factors, some of which may be relevant in one kind of conflict situation but not in another.

For example in the civil rights conflicts between blacks and whites, a number of white liberals aligned themselves with blacks, whereas some blacks remained, in effect, as neutrals. Thus the two parties confronting one another cannot be simply equated with racial membership. Among those blacks and whites who in general sided with blacks in the confrontation, there was considerable heterogeneity in terms of priorities, preferred strategies, and overall commitment. Similarly, in a peasant uprising not all peasants will side with their peers, nor will all members of the elite join attempts to repress them. Some persons on both sides will believe that extreme forms of aggression or repression are necessary, whereas others will attempt to pursue a more moderate course.

One of the critical problems faced by the analyst of any particular power confrontation or conflict situation will therefore be that of delineating the relevant parties concerned, including those that are to be treated as third parties whose behaviors become relevant to the conflict only at certain stages. If a large proportion of whites remained essentially neutral or indifferent to the conflicts that occurred during the civil rights movement, presumably they could be classed as third parties, whose presence may have been taken into consideration by the primary actors but whose actual behaviors could be ignored for most purposes. Using objectively derived status characteristics—such as race—as the principal delineating criteria might give a rather misleading picture of the relative sizes of the two opposing parties. Nor would it be very useful in helping to understand the dynamics of the processes at issue.

Treating heterogeneity in terms of goal hierarchies, differential beliefs and behaviors, or preferred strategies of action also poses greater problems of measurement than would much simpler classifications in terms of objective characteristics, but I am arguing that for the purposes of developing reasonably *general* theories of conflict processes it would seem to make much more sense to think in terms of the former than the latter. In any specific conflict situation, however, there may be a very close empirical correspondence between such objective factors, say involving religious memberships, and the types of subjective variables we shall delineate. Members of one denomination may nearly all adhere to a specific ideological system and have interests that are highly incompatible with those of a second denomination. Perhaps the Protestant-Catholic struggle in Northern Ireland is a case in point. If so, the simple religious dichotomy may be sufficient to distinguish the relevant parties in this particular instance.

Among both Catholics and Protestants, moreover, there may be sharp differences in terms of SES, in which case heterogeneity with respect to class background might become a relevant factor in analyzing the internal dynamics of each party. If, however, SES were totally unrelated to conflict-relevant cleavages within each party, then it

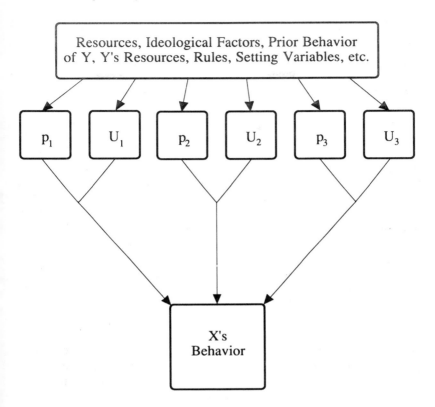

Figure 2.2 Prototype model linking exogenous variables to behaviors via subjective expected utilities

would be much more meaningful to think in terms of heterogeneity with respect to other kinds of variables that will become the focus of attention in our later analysis.

At the level of the individual person, the very simple model of Figure 2.2 represents the argument that a large number of contextual factors (indicated by the large box at the top of the figure) impact on individual behaviors through subjective probabilities and utilities as intervening variables. The separate pairs of p_i and U_i interact multiplicatively, as indicated by the fact that their arrows join before reaching the behavior box. Presumably, if we had a listing of all the actor's p_i

and U_i, a complete explanation of the behavior in question would be possible, though this would of course not account for the values of the p_i and U_i themselves.

Where the party of concern consists of multiple actors, it would then be necessary to find a way to aggregate their responses, taking into consideration their relative power in influencing whatever variable we would want to use to represent the party's "total behavior." In connection with the heterogeneity factor under discussion in the present section, we should also note that a party's heterogeneity, itself, may influence some of the p's and U's of concern. If all members are in total agreement and indicate that they intend to behave in a certain fashion, this will undoubtedly influence individual members' subjective probabilities, if not the corresponding U's as well. There would, however, be a large number of other factors that would influence actors' perceptions and interpretations of the party's heterogeneity, as well as the other contextual factors represented by the box at the top of the figure. Thus the model of Figure 2.2 is grossly oversimplified and will undergo considerable modification in the more complex models of Chapters 5, 7, 8, and 10.

Mutual and Asymmetric Dependency

The degree to which parties X and Y are dependent upon one another will also play an important role in our later discussions. In Richard Emerson's (1962, 1972) terms, party X is dependent on Y to the degree to which Y controls X's access to X's most important objectives, and similarly for Y's dependency on X. To the extent that X is dependent on Y, then we may also say that Y has power over X, and vice versa. In this sense, power (as a potential) has an absolute meaning and not just a relative one, a fact that is exploited in Bacharach and Lawler's (1981) theory of bargaining processes. This means that both X and Y may have considerable power over each other or relatively little, or perhaps Y may have extensive power over X but not vice versa. There is thus both a mutual dependency variable, indicating the average dependency level between the two parties, and a relative dependency variable, indicating the degree to which the power of Y over X exceeds that of X over Y, or of course the reverse.

In his 1962 paper, Emerson points out that X may reduce its dependency on Y by one of two mechanisms: by finding alternative exchange partners to reduce the degree to which Y controls X's access to desired outcomes, or by reducing the utilities or values attached to those goals that are controlled by Y. Similarly, Y may employ the same two strategies, so that there are in all four ways in which the mutual dependency level may be reduced. Giving up or reducing the importance of goals is, of course, a very different kind of strategy from finding alternative sources of supply. Sometimes goal modification may be much simpler, but in the case of "survival" goals this may be virtually impossible.

In relatively simple exchange situations in which only positively valued goods are exchanged, Emerson (1972) argues that positions in social networks may be critical. Imagine, for example, that party Y is located at the hub of a circle, with the spokes containing actors who can conduct exchanges with Y but not with each other. Then Y may bargain with each separate X_i, using the availability of the others to obtain a highly favorable rate of exchange. The other parties, who can only exchange with Y, will be put in a very weak bargaining position, however, unless they are able to form coalitions.[10] Indeed, Y may be able to obtain an extremely favorable or "exploitative" rate of exchange unless the other parties in effect give up the objective of obtaining the previously valued goods that Y controls. Furthermore, Y's advantage is gained solely because of the structure of the situation. None of the X_i need be aware of the network structure or the similarly disadvantageous positions of their counterparts.

Emerson's dependency theory was meant to apply to exchanges of positively valued goods, whereas we are defining conflicts as involving the mutual exchanges of punishments or negatively valued behaviors.[11] Nevertheless, the theory seems appropriate in conflict situations as well, with an important proviso. It has been presumed by Emerson and other exchange theorists that both parties may voluntarily leave the situation if their net exchange rates are unsatisfactory relative to their alternatives. A similar idea was invoked by Thibaut and Kelley (1959) in their reference to alternative "comparison levels" or CL_{alt}. Their idea was that actors will evaluate their potential exchanges in alternative situations and leave the exchange relationship whenever there are alternative partners with whom they can obtain greater net benefits.

In conflict situations it is often not possible to leave the scene, or at least it may be extremely costly to do so. One or even both of the parties' only alternative may be death, which most of us presume to be a highly unsatisfactory state of affairs, Patrick Henry notwithstanding. Furthermore, we may encounter situations in which there is a high degree of dependency for both parties, accompanied by a very inequitable exchange rate. Consider, for example, the master-slave relationship in a setting in which the price of the commodity produced by the slave is very high and where alternative slaves are either nonexistent or extremely costly to purchase. The slaveowner is highly dependent on this slave labor and yet is able to perpetuate a highly exploitative arrangement, though perhaps not quite so exploitative as one in which slaves are more numerous.

How can this come about in a situation in which the bargaining power of each party would presumably be considerable and where we would expect a more equitable rate of exchange? The answer is that the slaves are likely to be prevented from escaping from the exchange relationship, and what are essentially *political* means are likely to be used to control the exchange rate. The slaves' alternatives are effectively reduced to zero. In a sense, so may be those of the slaveholder if we consider only the economic objectives involved. But the owner's life will not be threatened, and there will also be certain less desirable economic alternatives as well, as for example selling the plantation. Those owners who attach high utilities to the humane treatment of their slaves may, indeed, decide to release them and give up the exchange relationship altogether.

What we see from this illustration is that rates of exchange may become very unequal or exploitative even when both parties are highly dependent on each other, with both lacking favorable avenues of escape from the exchange relationship.[12] The situation becomes less puzzling, however, as soon as we allow for the introduction of noneconomic factors, including the use of force to maintain the relationship. In effect, one may extend the notion of "exchange" to include the use of force, in which one party "exchanges" its life for a continuation of a very unfavorable relationship of a nonvoluntary nature. It is "voluntary" only in the sense that the alternative of loss of life or imprisonment carries an even lower utility value, or (perhaps more accurately) because there is an extremely high utility attached to survival. We must, however, recognize that there will sometimes be extreme situations where even death becomes more favorable an outcome than that being experienced. If one gives up the survival goal, dependency on the other party is reduced to zero, and thus in a sense Emerson's basic thesis remains valid.

Another idea that is also implicit in this connection is that exchange relationships and the rates of exchange that emerge depend not only on each party's access to exchange partners and the values attached to the goods being exchanged, but they also depend upon a number of other factors, one of which is the *rules* of the game, which may be partly controlled by one of the two parties involved. Such rules are often treated as givens, not only in exchange theory but also in game theory and other approaches that deal with strategic choices. We must allow for both rule modifications and cheating or rule deviations, however. There will always be a choice as to whether or not to abide by the rules, and the decision made will depend upon the expected costs of doing so, relative to expected benefits.

Those who either control the rule enforcement process directly, or who are in a position to employ sanctions against those who deviate, thus have a distinct advantage and a wider range of viable choices. In particular, it is obvious that many real-world conflict situations are regulated in such a way that one side is favored over the other. A concern for the nature of rules, as well as the relationships of both parties to any third-party rule enforcers, therefore must be incorporated into any reasonably complex theory of conflict processes.

As will be stressed in Chapters 6 and 7, belief systems—as for example ideological constraints on potential courses of action deemed "illegitimate"—must also be taken into consideration for basically the same reasons. Such belief systems may in effect impose high expected costs on those who adopt proscribed behaviors. If one gives up the beliefs in question or finds "loopholes" in them, such expected costs may be reduced or even entirely eliminated. An extremely simplistic and rigid ideological system may make it virtually certain that only a very limited number of courses of action will be pursued, and it may indeed rule out alternatives that would enabie one or the other party to reduce its dependency on the other. If one party controls the belief system of the other, it may thereby increase its power. All of this is to say that there are a variety of factors that may influence the alternatives of each party, so that the control over such factors becomes critical in the power struggle between them.

A simple prototype model, which will be elaborated in our general causal model of Chapter 5, is given in Figure 2.3. Party X's dependency on Y, and Y's dependency on X, are taken as functions of the four variables discussed by Emerson, plus three other factors: the rules under which the exchanges take place, any ideological con-

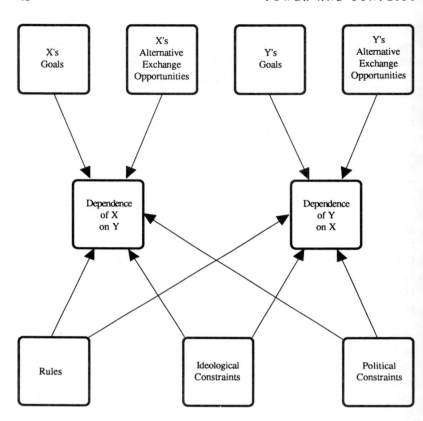

Figure 2.3 Prototype model linking exogenous variables to the mutual dependency between parties X and Y

straints that may be operative, and a set of political constraints—all of which may differentially impact on the two parties of interest.

The Loss-of-Power Gradient

Kenneth Boulding (1962) extended theories of the economic viability of firms to the power arena by discussing the conditions under which nations or small political units can be expected to survive a power struggle. The viability or survival of firms in a competitive contest involving spatially separated business units is taken as a function of a gradient involving the degree of competitive advantage accruing to firms that are spatially proximate to their markets. The competitive-advantage gradient is a function of transportation costs, relative to the cost of the product. Where transportation costs are high, as for example in instances where products are extremely bulky or heavy, such a gradient will tend to be steep, and this in turn will mean that local firms will be protected against distant competitors. If transportation costs decline in relative terms, however, each firm's protected hinterland becomes smaller, and larger firms will tend to swallow up smaller, less competitive ones.

In spatial terms, high transportation costs are likely to mean a large number of relatively small firms, geographically dispersed. Lowered transportation costs will result in a much greater concentration of larger firms, with the limit being zero transportation costs and a single firm that has swallowed up all of its competitors. This assumes, of course, that the rules of the game permit the operation of strictly economic forces that work themselves out in such a simple fashion.

Boulding developed the parallel notion of a loss-of-power gradient, as applied to nation-states engaged in a power struggle in which smaller, less powerful nation-states can be swallowed up by their neighbors and ultimately by much more distant but also more powerful larger ones. The idea is that there is a similar type of power advantage in operating close to home. This may be because of formidable natural barriers that are relatively easy to defend, a greater familiarity with the local terrain, or the logistic support provided by the local population. As in the case of economic firms, there will also be costs of transportation, in this instance of troops, weaponry, and supplies.

The notion of a loss-of-power gradient implies that the steeper the slope that gives the advantage to the local political unit, the more difficult it will be for distant rivals to conquer it. A very gradual gradient, say one that might be expected in a plains region with excellent transportation networks, will mean that political units may become considerably larger in spatial terms than would be the case, say, in an area containing steep mountains and easily protected local valley communities.

This power gradient, according to Boulding, will be a function of the resources that can be mobilized by the attacking party. Other things being equal, the more substantial such resources (relative to the barriers to be overcome), the less steep the gradient, and the more vulnerable each political unit becomes to attacks by distant enemies. In the modern era, where warplanes and nuclear rockets may be sufficient to inflict considerable damage over huge distances, such a loss-of-power gradient may become nearly horizontal, so that only a few "superpowers" come to dominate virtually all other political states.

It must not be thought that loss-of-power gradients are static. Imagine, for example, a situation involving a large number of small political units, each of which is weakened because of continual conflicts with its immediate neighbors. Should any one of these small units be able to dominate its closest rivals and pull them into an effective coalition, however, a snowball effect may be set in motion. Gaining in resources, it will be able to incorporate more and more territory. For any one target, originally situated at a considerable distance from the hub of such a snowballing political power, the loss-of-power gradient may rather suddenly become almost horizontal, given the rapidly expanding resources of its far more powerful opponent.

There have been a number of instances during recorded history where very powerful armies have been created almost overnight through such a snowballing process. Perhaps the successes of Genghis Khan and his Mongol heirs during the 13th century A.D. or those of Alexander the Great are among the most dramatic examples, but Emperor Ch'in's surprisingly rapid unification of China during a brief ten-year period (230–221 B.C.) and Rome's much more deliberate yet steady rate of expansion are perhaps equally dramatic. There may be something to the so-called domino theory of expansion, provided that the dominoes are of a relatively large size as compared with the barriers they may later confront in more distant zones.

The resources needed to capture a given territory may, however, be different from those necessary to retain it, to extract from it other resources over a sustained period of time, and to govern it and suppress rebellions. Often, victorious powers have found themselves overcommitted and unable to devote the resources necessary for a prolonged period of control. In terms of the loss-of-power gradient idea, what this means is that there may be several distinct gradients operative, each having a somewhat different relevant time frame. At a given distance from a political state's center of power, it may be possible to maintain political control for a brief period of time, but at considerable cost in terms of the long-run depletion of resources.

In the economics literature on the viability of firms, there is the notion of conditional viability that may be relevant in this connection (Boulding, 1962). When viability is conditional, this means that a firm's competitors may simply not elect to incorporate it, presumably because of high expected costs relative to benefits. In the case of a nation-state or other political unit, survivability may likewise be conditional on similar cost considerations. Its viability, like that of a firm, may be "secure" if such costs are high relative to benefits, or "insecure" if viability depends primarily on the good will of the other party. Canada's viability vis-à-vis the United States may be "insecure" in this sense, provided we do not read into this notion the idea that Canada is on the brink of being swallowed up by its much more powerful neighbor. Once more, conditionalities of the types under discussion are likely to be subject to changes, depending, for example, on the absence of overpopulation or the threat of serious resource depletion within the more powerful party. A conditionally viable firm or state is, in effect, "up for grabs" whenever it suits the convenience of the stronger party. That party may or may not choose to expend scarce resources in mobilizing for conflict, a subject which will occupy our attention in the following chapter.

Notes

1. For discussions of this and other problems involved in defining and measuring social power see Blalock (1961), Blalock and Wilken (1979), Cartwright (1959), Dahl (1957), French and Raven (1959), March (1966), Nagel (1975), Simon (1957) and Spruill (1983).

2. For discussions of this point see Gamson (1968) and Schermerhorn (1970). For an operational definition of power along functional lines see Hawley (1963).

3. For examples of work in the resource mobilization tradition see Gamson (1975), McAdam (1982), McCarthy and Zald (1977), Oberschall (1973), Tilly (1978), Zald and Ash (1966), and Zald and McCarthy (1979).

4. Magnitude estimation techniques, borrowed from psychophysics, have demonstrated the importance of power functions of the form $Y = a + bX^c$ in characterizing relationships between objective stimuli and subjective responses, with the exponent c typically being less than unity in instances of satiation phenomena. See Galenter (1962) and Hamblin (1971).

5. Bueno de Mesquita (1981), in analyzing the initiation of wars among nation-states, makes the assumption that in each state there is a single rational decision-maker who examines the alliances or commitments among potential partners, but his rational-

actor models do not make explicit allowances for *internal* distributions of utilities and subjective probabilities.

6. For a more inclusive set of goal dimensions see Blalock and Wilken (1979), Chap. 9.

7. This notion of causal "working theories" is highly compatible with, but somewhat broader than, the literature on attribution theory as developed by Heider (1958), Jones and Davis (1965), Kelley (1971), and many others.

8. Particularly when information is costly, or when the behaviors in question are either not especially important to the actors concerned or must be conducted in rapid succession, the strategy of "satisficing" is undoubtedly a more "rational" one than that of "maximizing." See especially Simon (1957), March and Simon (1958), and Blalock and Wilken (1979).

9. For a discussion of this subject see Ofsche and Ofsche (1970).

10. For discussions of coalitions in power-dependence networks see Bacharach and Lawler (1980), Cook and Gillmore (1984), Gillmore (1987), and Oliver (1984). Bacharach and Lawler point out that the social psychological literature on coalition formation tends to ignore *content*, or the nature of the issues and contesting parties and their ideologies, seeing such considerations as "nonutilitarian." This is in contrast with the literature coming from political science, which allows for ideological similarity as a determinant of coalitions. See, for example, Axelrod (1970), Caplow (1956, 1968), DeSwann (1973), Gamson (1961), Komorita and Chertkoff (1973), Leiserson (1970), and Murnighan (1978).

11. For discussions of the problem of extending Emerson's power-dependence approach to the exchange of negative sanctions see Bacharach and Lawler (1981) and Molm (1987).

12. Emerson (1972) argued that power tends to equalize in situations of mutual dependency involving only two parties (the so-called bilateral monopoly situation). This position has been criticized by Bacharach and Lawler (1980), partly on the grounds that Emerson emphasized only relative power, rather than total or absolute power.

Chapter 3

Mobilization, Heterogeneity, and Party Solidarity

Given that most kinds of resources are scarce and will be depleted and therefore in need of replenishment, it should never be assumed that the mere possession of resources will automatically result in their use in a power confrontation. Furthermore, as we have indicated, any reasonably complex party will consist of members whose goals are diverse and not necessarily oriented to any given conflict process. Loosely knit quasi-groups will therefore find it much more difficult to mobilize than will either single parties or corporate actors, which is of course to say that a number of organizational factors will affect the mobilization process.

In the present chapter we shall be concerned with the mobilization process in rather complex and heterogeneous groups or quasi-groups in which organizational and decision-making processes cannot be taken for granted. We shall begin with a discussion of four rather general types of goals that are relevant to conflict processes and that will usually be given different weights by a party's members, who will also attach different subjective probabilities to their attainment. Our discussion will then return to the dispute over the importance of relative deprivation or rising expectations and to the matter of rationality and alienation, as applied to conflict settings. We then briefly discuss the resource mobilization orientation to social movements and the related free-rider problem. Finally, we shall address the important matter of how a party achieves solidarity among its members.

In discussing each of these topics very briefly, our aim is not to develop an exhaustive account of the very extensive bodies of literature on each of these topics, but to help assure that our general model of conflict processes is reasonably complete. Obviously, any study of the mobilization processes at work within a particular complex party would need to specify considerably more detail. It is hoped that in doing so, one would locate additional variables that ideally should be included in a general model. Indeed, after presenting our first general model in Chapter 5, we shall develop an elaboration of this model to deal with some of the variables considered in the present chapter—heterogeneity, free riding, surveillance capabilities, and consensus. In that chapter we shall also indicate how such elaborated submodels can be simplified whenever organizational factors are irrelevant, as in the case of conflict situations involving two individual persons.

Goal Heterogeneity and Subjective Probabilities

We have elected to define a party's heterogeneity in terms of goals rather than objective characteristics that may be only indirectly related to such goals. In particular, we have distinguished among three types of goals: G_1 goals that are held in common with members of the opposing party, G_2 goals that can only be achieved at the expense of the other party, and a residual category of G_3 goals that are basically irrelevant to the conflict itself but that may compete with other goals for scarce resources.

In the present discussion we shall make some further distinctions among goals that refer directly to the mobilization process itself, with the recognition that each party's members will also be heterogeneous with respect to the values or utilities U_i that they attach to these goals. So as to avoid confusion in connection with the three previously mentioned general goals G_i, I shall refer to the following four utilities with the symbols U_i:

U_1: the utility attached to the goal of attaining some specific objective relating to the other party (e.g., obtaining its territory, gaining freedom from exploitation, protecting against invasion, dominating a spouse, or even winning an argument);

U_2: the utility attached to aggression or to injuring the other party;

U_3: the utility attached to avoiding injury, punishment by the other party, or other costs associated with the conflict; and

U_4: the utility attached to gaining status or recognition as a result of participation in the conflict.

With each U_i we may associate a corresponding p_i representing the subjective probability of achieving, through conflict, the respective goal to which the U_i has been attached, as compared with the probability of achieving it in the absence of a conflict or a mobilization effort. Notice that we are attaching the utilities and subjective probabilities to *individual actors* at this point, assuming that they can be aggregated in some fashion to determine a "mobilization potential." Once a party has become reasonably coordinated we would want to simplify the analysis by shifting units of analysis, either to corporate actors or to quasi-groups characterized by varying degrees of heterogeneity, coordination and efficiency of their mobilization efforts.

We expect U_1 and U_2 to be positively associated, in general, if only because a wish to injure the other party is likely to result from a series of grievances based on past hostilities, exploitation, or fear of aggression by that other party. The desire to aggress may also result from envy of the other party's possessions, organizational position, or superior standard of living. We must, however, allow for the possibility that the two kinds of motivations may be only weakly correlated. Some of a party's members may attach higher values to the one goal than to the other. The relative magnitudes of U_1 and U_2 may also affect rates of satiation and thus the dynamics of a conflict process, once it is underway. We may anticipate, for example, that U_2 will tend to increase as a function of the amount of punishment inflicted by the other party, so that if this utility is initially low as compared with U_1, there may be considerable room for an increase in the total utility attached to continuing the conflict.

Similarly, we need to distinguish between the goal U_3 of avoiding injury or personal risks and that of achieving status or recognition from participation. Some actors may join a conflict primarily because they attach a high premium to the kinds of "selective incentives" that the party may provide for leaders, heroes, or loyal participants. Where such personal benefits are either not forthcoming or become subject to satiation, these individuals may no longer continue to participate as extensively as they did initially. Those who are hesitant to join a conflict out of a fear of injury or because of other personal costs of participation may ultimately become convinced that, perhaps because of the anonymity of large numbers, the risks associated with active participation are no greater than those expected by nonparticipants.

The p_3 and U_3 components are likely to be especially important in the case of weak or dominated parties that are held in this position by force or the threat of extreme negative sanctions. Blacks in the Deep South prior to World War II, for example, lived in constant fear of reprisals for even very minor infractions of enforced patterns of "etiquette." Similarly, we hear of a sufficient number of instances of the "battered wife" syndrome in contemporary America to make us believe that the pattern is a common one. In such cases, there may be what amounts to an obsession with avoiding punishment at any cost, which implies that the p_3U_3 term dominates all others. Presumably, it is a consequence of the combination of high dependency and weak resources and, by implication, the perception that escape from the situation is either virtually impossible or would be extremely costly.

In the case of macro parties that are fairly heterogeneous, in our subjective expected utility formulation we must deal with a combination of different utilities and subjective probabilities that will vary across individuals, as well as across time as a conflict evolves. At any given point in time, such heterogeneities will result in different threshold levels for participation. Granovetter (1978) discusses such thresholds in terms of the single criterion of numbers of prior (or expected) participants. He argues that some individuals may be willing to join a riot or other type of social movement if there are only a very small number of prior participants, whereas others may only join once there are considerably more. He then makes the important point that one needs to look not only at *average* threshold levels but also at the *distributions* of thresholds within a group.

More generally, heterogeneity in threshold levels, which we are assuming result from heterogeneity in goal preferences and expectation levels, may be of critical importance in determining not only mobilization strategies and efficiency but also outcomes as well. If participation threshold levels are uniformly moderately high, except for a few isolated individuals, a mobilization effort may never get underway. But if threshold levels have a more rectangular distribution, a snowballing effect may occur, as persons with increasingly high threshold levels are gradually brought into the fray.

It should also be noted that it may make a considerable difference whether intermediate values of the product terms p_iU_i are based on (a) moderate levels of both terms, (b) extremely high p values but very low U's, or (c) near-zero p's but high U's. This is the case because, in dynamic models, the various p's and U's can be expected to change, perhaps because of satiation or deprivation in the case of the U's or responses by the other party in the case of the p's. As we shall later discuss, a consistent and harsh punitive response by a powerful opponent may have an opposite effect on the p's and U's, with the numerical value of the product term then depending very heavily on their initial values. For example, if the utilities attached to gaining revenge or overcoming domination were already high and the p's attached to these moderately low, a very harsh response by the dominant party may marginally increase the U's but reduce the p's to such low levels that the mobilization effort collapses. But if the U's were already high and the p's extremely low, a vacillating response may increase the latter sufficiently to encourage a substantial increase in the mobilization effort.

As noted, we need to compare conflict-related behaviors with those alternatives, including cooperative ones, that are not directed toward punishing an opponent. In particular, one alternative will be that of maintaining the status quo or not changing one's behavior. Presumably, such an alternative will involve a lower risk of a punitive response by the other party, so that p_3 of avoiding punishment will be greater for the status-quo alternative than the conflictual form of behavior. Whenever the alternative behavior is expected to result in approximately the same p_1 and p_2 values as the conflict behavior, or whenever both p_1 and p_2 are extremely small—implying that there is little expectation that conflict will help satisfy the U_1 or U_2 values— then it will generally be this difference in risk of punishment factors that determines p_3 and thus the behavioral outcome *unless* p_4 can somehow be manipulated so as to favor the conflict-oriented behavior. This would then place a premium on so-called "selective incentives," a matter that we shall discuss in more detail below. In contrast, whenever either or both of the products p_1U_1 or p_2U_2 for the conflict alternative are reasonably high relative to nonconflict alternatives, such selective incentives may be much less needed to counterbalance the expected costs factor.

In all these instances it is the *multiplicative* or statistical interactive effects of the subjective probabilities and utilities that are critical. As a general rule we expect that subjective probabilities will be functions of each party's assessments of relative resources and the goals or motive base of the *other* party, whereas U's will be functions of past grievances (especially in the cases of U_1 and U_2), as well as numerous other factors that may be considered exogenous to the conflict process itself. The p's will also be functions of a party's alternatives and the expected responses of third parties. As we shall discuss in Chapters 6 and 7, ideological factors may likewise play important roles in affecting both utilities and subjective probabilities. The general point is that an explicit separation of the two kinds of components facilitates a more precise analysis of the causal factors that may influence mobilization processes.

THE RELATIVE DEPRIVATION AND RISING EXPECTATIONS DISPUTE REVISITED

We have already noted that there has been considerable dispute concerning the impact on conflict processes of rising expectations that are subsequently unrealized and that lead to frustration and aggression as a result of the growing gap between expectations and reality. Perhaps the most succinct version of the rising expectations argument is presented by Davies (1962), who suggests that expectations tend to increase linearly, whereas actual levels of satisfaction are more likely to take the form of a "J-curve," as indicated in Figure 3.1. If so, there will at some point be an increasing gap between the two curves, giving rise to frustration and thus to the *motivation* U_1 to engage in conflict so as to reduce the obstacles to continued improvements.

Therefore it is suggested that a period of steady improvements, say in living conditions, will foster rising expectations, which become frustrated once one enters a period of relative decline. Much the same would occur if stability were followed by a period of absolute decline.[1] Davies attributes to Karl Marx this kind of "relative deprivation" thesis, which could also be applied to situations in which one party witnesses a period of gain for a rival party, coupled with a much smaller gain or even a slight absolute decline in its own position (Gurr, 1970). In either case, the differential between expectations and reality becomes augmented, with an increased utility for change in the reverse direction.

Davies also indicates that his J-curve argument is compatible with the thesis that revolts often occur whenever highly repressive governmental policies are altered in the direction of more moderate or vacillating ones. This latter thesis, it seems, pertains much more specifically to the subjective probability factor. Presumably, highly repressive policies produce very large utilities for change on the part of the oppressed party, but also very low subjective probabilities of achieving objectives through conflict as well as substantial probabilities of

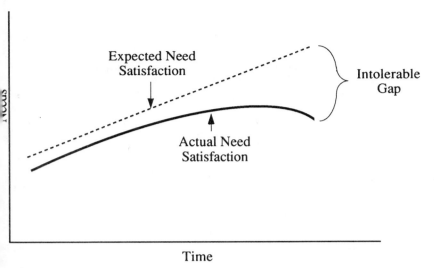

Time

Figure 3.1 Davies' J-curve hypothesis showing a growing gap between expected and actual need satisfaction

Source: Adapted from Davies (1962, p. 6).

high costs of such conflict. If the repression is either moderated or made less certain to occur, such subjective probabilities may be drastically changed. Given the very high U values associated with them, the product terms may then be considerably altered in the direction of increased subordinate-group mobilization.

One of the ambiguities, at least in the Davies formulation, is that "rising expectations" may be a function of changes in either or both of the p and U components. A period of increasing overall prosperity, for example, can modify actors' utilities in the direction of their *desiring* more material goods, but it can also alter their subjective probabilities of attaining them, given a simple continuation of the current behaviors. If conditions begin to become less favorable, the thesis suggests that the utilities will not be subject to such drastic changes but may indeed follow a linear trend for a relatively long period of time. Subjective probabilities, however, may more readily be altered according to the "working theories" or attribution process of the relevant actors. Are the changes thought to result from "impersonal" macroeconomic trends, or are they attributed to the policies of villainous actors? If the latter, aggrieved parties may rather rapidly alter their subjective probabilities, perhaps concluding that desired changes can only be brought about by concerted actions of some kind. If the p_3U_3 term is not too large, they may decide to attack the "guilty" party.

At least if one is concerned with explaining a wide variety of conflict situations, it seems unwise to reject arguments that, like those of Davies and Gurr, place a premium on notions such as rising expectations, relative deprivation, and frustration-aggression. It may, however, be an empirical fact that many kinds of social rebellions and revolutions have involved situations in which utilities for change have been rather uniformly high over prolonged periods, so that rather sudden changes in protest or conflict levels must be explained by other factors. Among the relative deprivation theorists, Gurr (1970), in particular, has discussed a wide variety of factors that help determine how a mobilization *potential*, based on relative deprivation, is actually translated into actions directed at specific targets, as for example a given political regime.

Theorists in the resource mobilization tradition have generally played down explanations involving rising expectations and frustration-aggression in favor of these other kinds of causal factors. In the case of the McCarthy-Zald (1977) perspective, for example, Perrow (1979) argues that it has tended to adopt a rational-actor orientation that is highly compatible with that of economists, in general, and Mancur Olson (1965), in particular. From this perspective, problems of resource mobilization are analyzed as though social movement organizations (SMOs) are much the same as business firms, and participants are primarily motivated by the desire to minimize costs whenever opportunities to "free ride" are present. Fireman and Gamson (1979), among others, point to the neglect of solidarity concerns in this type of literature.

Other scholars associated with the resource mobilization school, including Gamson (1975) and Tilly (1978), also tend to take certain kinds of utilities as givens. In particular, factors that affect grievance levels (here represented by our U_1) may be downgraded by simply assuming such grievances to remain at high levels over the relevant time period. If so, the thesis that "there are always grievances" becomes reasonable, though it may tend to neglect important variations in degree. Such assumptions may indeed be realistic for, say, blacks during most of American history or European urban masses during the 18th and 19th centuries. They may not apply, however, to conflict situations involving rival criminal gangs, a husband-wife dyad, or certain recent kinds of labor-management conflicts such as those brought about by changes in international markets.

There is thus no necessary incompatibility between theories that stress grievances, competitive goals, or frustrations brought about by recent changes and those that either give primary attention to factors that influence subjective probabilities or that deal more directly with resource mobilization processes. One must keep in mind that some explanatory variables may work best in explaining *changes* in behaviors, whereas others may be more appropriate in explaining (possibly stable) *levels* of these same behaviors. High overall levels of internal or domestic conflict within nation-states may, for instance, characterize certain kinds of social systems, whereas variations in these levels may have to be explained by a different set of factors. In particular, if we assume that subjective probabilities are more volatile than their corresponding utilities, the former may be more useful than the latter in accounting for short-term fluctuations in behaviors, including periodic outbreaks of violence or other forms of overt conflict. As we shall emphasize in the following chapter, responses by the other party may be critical in influencing these subjective probabilities.

A NOTE ON RATIONALITY AND ALIENATION

Perhaps because of a reaction to theoretical orientations that have dominated the literature for prolonged periods, there is sometimes a tendency not only to overstate an alternative theory but also to confound several ideas that need to be distinguished. The resource mobilization literature in sociology developed, in part, as a counter to a collective behavior orientation that placed a heavy emphasis on explaining social movements in terms of the breakdown of social control and the behaviors of rather irrational, alienated individuals. Le Bon's (1896) theories of "crowd behavior" epitomized this literature which was reinforced by somewhat later breakdown theories that depicted "mass society" as lacking in effective intermediate-level secondary organizations capable of linking more or less isolated and alienated individuals to the larger social order.[2] Certain kinds of mass movements, characterized by contagion-type diffusion processes and exemplified by the urban riot, were then seen as basically irrational responses to such anomic situations. Rioters, for example, were seen as both isolated and alienated, rather than as "rational" actors engaged in rather more organized forms of social protest.[3]

As a reaction to this admittedly overdrawn prototype explanation of mass social movements, certain of the resource mobilization scholars began to emphasize the more rational aspects of social movements, including the so-called "rational actor" assumptions of the traditional economist. Unfortunately, the rational actor model—which I am taking as a reasonable starting point—became rather narrowly conceived and limited primarily to the self-interested actor with very restricted (and largely economic) goals. Olson's (1965) analysis of the free-rider problem and the necessity of providing selective incentives is a case in point. So too, the notions of "rationality" and of "utilitarian" behaviors have come to have the connotation of being limited to a rather narrow definition of self-interest and a very restricted set of goals. Indeed, if actors happen to attach high utilities to goals that have been ignored in the highly simplified analyses of some rational-actor theorists, such actors may be pronounced "irrational" or as having "nonutilitarian" goals.

According to our view, most actors will have a large number of goals and rather complex though necessarily oversimplified "working theories" as to the causal factors influencing desired and undesired outcomes, and thus the most reasonable courses of action to follow. If some actors attach extremely high utilities to certain outcomes—such as gaining eternal salvation—that have been neglected by the analyst, then indeed it may be difficult for that analyst to explain the extremist behaviors they may undertake. In no way does this make them "irrational," however.

We shall take goal preferences as given in the short run, though subject to modification as the dynamics of a conflict situation unfold. If the term "rational" is to be used at all, we prefer that it be applied to the actor's thought processes in evaluating alternative courses of action, given the actor's utilities and an initial set of subjective probabilities. Does the actor make a reasonable attempt to maximize expected outcomes, given whatever mix of p's and U's he or she happens to have? Somewhat more "rational," in this sense, will be the actor who permits subjective probabilities to be modified according to the empirical evidence, such as the observation of relative frequencies or as a result of a search for new information. We do not want to impose the assumption that some *goals* are more "irrational" than others, however, unless the actor conceives of them as merely means to other ends and then continues rigidly to hold onto an easily falsified working theory linking such means to these desired ends. Even in such an instance we must admit that there may be no genuine consensus concerning the many kinds of evidence needed for falsification, so that the rejection of, say, "scientific" evidence may not, in itself, imply irrational thought processes on the part of the actor.

In the case of the utilities we have been discussing, certain actors may have very high utilities for injuring the other party, perhaps because they believe it is the pathway to eternal salvation. Others may "rationally" place a premium on obtaining so-called collective goods, even at the expense of their own personal welfare. They may have a strong commitment to an ethnic or religious group and its collective interests, so much so that selective incentives are not needed to motivate them to participate. In Hechter's (1987) terminology, there may be a strong *obligation* to the group, in the sense that its members are motivated to contribute to it without a corresponding recompense or quid pro quo. Such an obligation may, indeed, become an important *goal* of a rational actor and may be closely tied to the U_1 of our prior discussion.

The isolation or alienation of individual actors is a separate issue from that of rationality. Actors may be mutually isolated, generally alienated from others in the group, and yet entirely rational. Such alienation may possibly result in a high utility attached to the injury of another party. If so, any resulting aggression against that party would be rational, provided that it was expected to satisfy that actor's objectives and not result in the blockage of other more important goals. For such actors, a calculus of expected costs and benefits might involve, primarily, the U_2 and U_3 values and their corresponding subjective probabilities.

Participation in a riot might be quite rational for such alienated or isolated actors and have little to do with social protest. Merely characterizing a riot participant as "irrational" because he or she wishes to destroy property or gain vicarious excitement may simply indicate that the analyst has a very inadequate understanding of that actor's goal hierarchy. By the same token, actors who are highly attached to others and who follow their instructions without thought of the consequences may not be engaged in a highly "rational" search process in selecting among alternative means. Similarly, those who score high in

terms of their obligation to a particular group may or may not be
highly rational actors and may, as well, score either high or low on
general measures of alienation.

Solidarity, Selective Incentives, and Surveillance

The problem groups face in mobilizing resources is closely bound
to the notion of solidarity, especially if the most important resources
needed for the conflict situation are possessed by individual members
and must be extracted from them at some cost. Most certainly, this
will be the case where so-called manpower issues are involved, as for
example in the case of military forces. Much the same applies to
organized forms of social protest conducted by quasi-groups: strikes,
demonstrations and boycotts, the nonpayment of taxes or deliberate
violations of the law, or even the political organization of voters
opposed to existing policies. Citizens may be urged to make financial
contributions to a particular cause or to devote their energies to a
social movement that is presumed to act in their interests. How can
individuals be persuaded or otherwise induced not to free ride, especially in those instances in which they could be expected to benefit
from any collective goods gained as a result of the successful outcome
of a conflict? Where the expected costs of participation are high, how
can actors' other utilities be exploited to the advantage of the larger
party?

As we have previously noted, Fireman and Gamson (1979), among
others, have inveighed against a narrowly conceived rational-actor
analysis that presupposes that self-interested individuals require selective incentives to induce them to participate. They note that one may
define such selective incentives so broadly that arguments become
tautologous: any mechanism by which persons are induced to join a
movement becomes, by definition, a selective incentive for them.
They prefer, instead, a more specific but narrower usage of the term
which, they argue, is more consistent with Olson's (1965) actual illustrations of the concept: such things as added financial benefits to
participants, offices and other forms of recognition, or other very
tangible benefits. They would exclude from the category of selective
incentives such things as psychic rewards from participation, the gain-

ing of new friendships or increased self-respect, and presumably expected rewards provided by supernatural powers.

Yet, as we have just argued, actors' own goal hierarchies may include such "intangible" rewards as important personal objectives. If these are excluded from the notion of selective incentives, this does not then imply that they cannot be used to motivate actors to participate or to turn over individually possessed resources, such as income, to the larger party in question. Given this ambiguity in connection with exactly what belongs under the rubric of selective incentives, we shall use the term only very loosely to refer to those inducements that a party offers to its present or potential members that appeal to the individual motivations of such actors. As Fireman and Gamson note, parties vary considerably in terms of their ability to offer highly tangible individual incentives. Loosely organized quasi-groups, which are often the bases for important social movements, will generally have to rely much more heavily than, say, business firms on such things as loyalty, commitment and solidarity, than on tangible economic or status rewards.

Michael Hechter's (1987) work on group solidarity is highly relevant to this matter. Hechter actually defines solidarity in a manner that nearly equates it with our notion of degree of mobilization. Although stated as an empirical proposition, he defines solidarity in the following way: "The greater the proportion of each member's private resources contributed to collective ends, the greater the solidarity of the group" (p. 18). He also takes a group's solidarity as a function of two independent factors: the extensiveness or inclusiveness of its corporate obligations and the degree to which individual members actually comply with these obligations. The extensiveness or inclusiveness of these obligations, and thus the premium or "tax" they are willing to pay in contributing to the attainment of collective benefits, is in turn a function of their dependence on the group.

Hechter's analysis calls attention to the need for distinguishing between an entire party's dependence on its opponent (e.g., X's dependence on Y), and each party's *members'* dependence on their own group and, in some instances, on the other party as well. If the membership of one party, say X, is heterogeneous with respect to its members' relative dependencies, we may expect solidarity to be weakened as a result of differing sets of priorities that such members may have. Also, such heterogeneity is likely to result in *dissensus* over the choice of means or alternative courses of action so that certain possibilities may effectively be ruled out and, perhaps equally likely, certain mutually incompatible means may appeal to different population segments.

Consider, for example, the situations of household versus field slaves within a plantation economy such as existed in the antebellum South. Both types of slaves might benefit from achieving freedom, but household slaves were much more likely to develop close dependency ties and affective bonds with their masters and their families. In contrast, individual field hands may have, in a sense, been dependent on the slave *system* as a means of livelihood, but they were far less attached to their specific masters and, as well, tended to find their support networks among other field hands. Given this heterogeneity of interests and differing degrees of dependency on their individual masters, it is no wonder that solidarity among slaves, as a group, was weakened and that incipient slave revolts were often thwarted by informants among the household slave category. In such an instance one might even say that it was the opposition group, here slave owners, who provided selective incentives to their household slaves so as to undermine their loyalty or attachments to the larger group of fellow slaves.

A high degree of dependence of X's members on the larger party will also be a function of exit costs, as Hechter suggests. A critical but usually drastic form of selective incentive open to most groups is that of expulsion from membership. To the degree that individuals possess few alternatives to membership in the group of concern, these exit costs will be high and thus the threat of expulsion will imply a considerable cost. Where group boundaries are sharply delimited, as for example is true of nation-states, racial groups, and linguistically determined ethnic groups, the dependence of individual members on the larger group will also tend to be extreme. A rejection by the larger group can, in effect, lead to their virtual isolation from nearly all forms of social contact. By the same token, however, expulsion is rarely invoked in such closed-boundary situations except as an extreme measure.

Hechter also points out that the probability of an individual's compliance depends on the surveillance and sanctioning capabilities of the group. Since both will be costly and may require special agents who have their own individual concerns, the *efficiency* of a group's monitoring mechanisms may also be critical in affecting its solidarity level or its degree of mobilization. Hechter discusses a number of mechanisms for increasing such efficiency: by making sanctions public, by decreasing individuals' privacy and increasing their mutual visibility to one another (say through living arrangements), and by encouraging members to monitor one another through gossip. There may also be application of sanctions to an entire subgroup whenever its individual members violate important norms. Hechter points to effective control mechanisms in the Japanese type of organizational system, which in many different spheres involves the hierarchical arrangement of small groups so as to increase competition among those at the same level and to encourage reporting upward in the control hierarchy.

Anthony Giddens (1987) also stresses the importance of surveillance of a party's members, claiming it to be the major distinguishing feature of modern nation-states as compared with earlier societies—even including major empires and kingdoms. He argues that in earlier times it was, at most, the urban populations close to the political center of the society in question who could be subject to close surveillance, owing to the ineffectiveness of surveillance technology in controlling more remote or rural populations. To be sure, records were often kept so as to improve the efficiency of taxation and wartime conscription, but this did not affect the day-to-day activities of the vast majority of the peoples residing within the boundaries of the society. It is only with the vastly improved communication and control techniques of modern nation-states that a more total form of surveillance becomes possible. Thus, Giddens argues, the situation we are facing today is historically unique and helps to account for the magnitude and scope of major conflicts, such as the two world wars of this century, as well as the very close linkage between the industrial and military sectors in contemporary societies.

Although Hechter does not discuss conflict processes per se, his arguments, as well as those of Giddens, imply that parties that are engaged in long-term or endemic conflicts are very much in need of attaining high degrees of solidarity and will therefore strive to achieve greater efficiency in their monitoring and control mechanisms. Some parties will be much more effectively organized to do so within short periods of time, however, and this will then affect their overall ability to mobilize resources efficiently.

There are additional factors that also need to be discussed in connection with motivating individuals to contribute to a collective effort designed to produce a collective good, and more specifically to take part in a conflict effort against another party. Klandermans (1984) uses a subjective expected utility perspective to discuss the question of how it is that social movements are able to persuade potential participants to join the cooperative effort. He argues that expectancies play a critical role in this process, since individuals must often make decisions at a point where it is unclear as to how many others will also participate. In effect, there will be three distinct kinds of expectancies: (1) those pertaining to the numbers of others who will also participate; (2) those concerning one's own contributions to changing the probability of success, and (3) the probability of success itself, even if large numbers participate.

As Gamson (1975) and Yamagishi (1986), among others, have also stressed, a critical factor in all three of the above expectancies will be the nature of the activity concerned and whether or not success is heavily dependent on having a large proportion of the potential membership who are actual participants. If this proportion is very high, then individuals may be discouraged from participation, not so much because of free riding as their fear that their own contributions will be useless because of a lack of support from others. Why join a costly strike that requires almost total participation if even half of the others refuse to do so?

Unfortunately, whenever large numbers of members participate, as is often necessary for successful mobilization, it becomes both difficult and expensive to supply tangible kinds of selective incentives. If there are only a small number of nonparticipants, *negative* selective incentives may of course be applied. As Hechter notes, however, it may in general be much more difficult for large parties to make use of selective incentives than is the case for much smaller ones, where monitoring is also much easier.

In addition to the size factor, the degree of spatial separation or mutual isolation of members will not only affect ease of communication but also monitoring efficiency as well. A party's ability to protect its members against punitive actions by the other party, and thus to reduce the p_3 component, is also likely to be affected by both the spatial and social isolation of its members. Where party X is characterized by large size and a relatively compact locational pattern, its members not only can communicate more effectively but they also gain a certain anonymity and thus protection from individual punishment by the opponent.

By the same token, anonymity can also enable them to avoid detection as deviants from their own party's norms, however. Their ability to free ride is increased, while their risks of punishment by the other party are also reduced, so that the net result will depend upon the relative utilities involved. If, however, free riding can be controlled by a hierarchical monitoring system similar to that which Hechter describes as being typical in Japanese society or that operates in mainland China and a number of other communist societies, it may be possible for the party concerned to locate and control its own members while simultaneously protecting them from detection by the other party.

Free riding can also be reduced by "manufacturing" or augmenting genuine grievances against the other party, so that values of U_1 and U_2 are also increased, thereby providing additional incentives for members to participate. Sometimes this can be accomplished by locating vulnerable and therefore cost-free local targets who are symbolically linked to the real opponent and who therefore can serve as convenient scapegoats. Japanese-Americans, many of whom were American citizens and virtually none of whom had displayed any signs of disloyalty, were singled out immediately after Pearl Harbor and were placed in "detention" camps. Media campaigns on the West Coast had previously whipped up strong anti-Japanese sentiments which served to motivate many white Americans in the region to direct their hostilities to these innocent symbolic "representatives" of Japan, persons who were of course much easier to attack at minimal cost.

In other instances certain kinds of persons may be singled out as potential traitors or sympathizers with the opponent on the basis of supposedly deviant attitudes or behaviors. Thus liberals are easily confused with socialists and "radicals," and therefore with Communists. They may then serve as rallying points to mobilize those party members who are encouraged to believe that the threat is very close at hand and that aggressive actions taken toward such individuals are also necessary to defeat the opponent. Utilities linked to aggressive psychic needs or the goal of injuring another party can thus be tapped, while simultaneously providing a very safe alternative to that of actually entering a conflict with a powerful enemy. The symbolic nature of the local "opponent" may then become useful in enabling certain leaders to capitalize on manufactured fears and to build a following that is subsequently motivated to direct its energies toward the "real" enemy.

As we shall emphasize in Chapters 6 and 7, parties may also construct elaborate ideologies or belief systems that grossly oversimplify the real world, that blame the opponent for nearly everything, and that justify punitive action taken toward it. Not only may this tend to allay the possible guilt of its members, but it may also make certain goals highly salient by calling attention to threats to their realization. Members' working theories concerning social causation will undoubtedly be influenced by such ideological systems and, in terms of the p's and U's we have been discussing, are likely to push relevant p's closer to the extremes of zero and unity, while also selectively influencing utilities in the direction of creating a higher degree of consensus on both ends and means.

A party's "history" may also be rewritten so as to emphasize those periods of the past during which grievances toward the opposing group were extremely high. This may involve pointing to a glorious past, during which the enemy was totally defeated and its territory occupied. Or it may stress a history of continued exploitation by the other party and severe grievances against it, with such grievances continuing until the present. Some ideological systems will of course be more effective in these regards than others.

Before we consider belief systems in greater detail, we need to supplement the present discussion of mobilization processes that occur within a single party with an analysis of two-party interactive processes. We shall examine how the actions of party X may affect those of party Y and vice versa, and how the resulting stimulus-response patterning may result either in an accelerating conflict process or the eventual stabilization at an equilibrium level that may favor the one party over the other. In Chapter 5 we shall then pause to develop an elaborate causal model representing the arguments of Chapters 2, 3 and 4.

Notes

1. Gurr (1970) distinguishes between three special cases of the more general relative deprivation situation. In the case of what he calls "decremental deprivation," value expectations remain level, whereas value capabilities (or what is actually possible) decline with time. In the case of what he refers to as "aspirational deprivation," value capabilities remain constant but value expectations increase, perhaps at an accelerating

rate. The kind of situation depicted by Davies and represented by our Figure 3.1 is referred to by Gurr as "progressive deprivation."

2. For illustrations of the "mass society" orientation see Arendt (1951), Fromm (1945), Kornhauser (1959), and Nisbet (1953). For a critique of this orientation see Gusfield (1962). The more recent resource mobilization literature tends to assume that the mass society tradition has been in large part discredited, though actual empirical tests of the implicit theory involved would be exceedingly difficult to construct.

3. For discussions of riot behaviors in the sociological literature, for example, see Berk and Aldrich (1972), Killian (1984), Lieberson and Silverman (1965), Morgan and Clark (1973), Paige (1971), and Spilerman (1970, 1976).

Chapter 4

Reactive and Control Processes

In the previous two chapters we examined power and conflict processes from the perspective of first the one and then the other party, but we did not really address the question of how the two parties interact. In this chapter we shall look more closely at how the behaviors of one party affect the responses of the other and how the resulting interactions can be analyzed as a dynamic process. Do the sequences of stimuli and responses escalate so as to produce ever increasing conflict levels or do they begin to stabilize? Under what conditions can stability be expected, and at what *level* of conflict? What if both parties wish to avoid an escalating situation but simultaneously attempt to be in a dominant position if and when stabilization occurs?

We shall begin the chapter with a brief discussion of a classic in the field, Richardson's mathematical models of the dynamics of arms races. Certain elaborations on the so-called Richardson process models will then be presented, followed by a discussion of a social control model that is more appropriate to relationships between dominant and subordinate parties. This will then lead us to a discussion of deterrence theory and the circumstances under which punitive responses may or may not escalate the level of conflict.

Richardson Processes

In a book titled *Arms and Insecurity*, published posthumously in 1960, Lewis F. Richardson developed a mathematical model designed to explain arms races among two or more nations. Such "Richardson process" models, as they have been referred to in the literature, are far more general in nature than references to arms races would seem to suggest and may be used to explain the dynamics of conflict processes in a variety of different kinds of parties. For convenience, however, we shall refer to the arms race illustration that was Richardson's focus of concern. We shall also limit our discussion to the two-party situation, although Richardson actually devoted considerable attention to multination arms races.

Richardson's two-nation model, expressed in differential equation form, is as follows:

$$dX/dt = kY - aX + g$$
$$dY/dt = mX - bY + h$$

$$(1)$$

where X and Y represent the levels of armaments in the two countries; where k and m represent "defense" or "sensitivity" coefficients; where the feedback coefficients a and b represent "fatigue" coefficients; and where the constants g and h represent what Richardson referred to as "grievance" terms. It is assumed that the defense or sensitivity coefficients k and m, as well as the fatigue coefficients a and b, are all positive, with negative feedbacks being implied by the negative signs preceding a and b.

The basic idea is that nation X reacts to increases in Y's armaments levels by increasing its own arms, this in turn leading to an increase in Y's levels because of the second equation showing that Y, in turn, will increase its arms in response to the change in X's levels. Each nation is also subject to certain limitations on its budget, however, and there also may be other internal factors within each nation that affect its level of "fatigue," which is taken to be a function of the actual level of arms that exists in the nation of concern.

The differential equation format involving dX/dt and dY/dt expresses *rates of change* in one variable as a function of the *levels* of arms that exist at any given moment. In effect, this allows for gradual and continuous adjustments in each nation's level of arms, as it reacts to the new levels in the other nation as well as internal factors whose aggregate effects are represented by the fatigue coefficients. With all coefficients assumed positive, the necessary condition for stability is that the product of the fatigue coefficients must be greater than that of the two sensitivity coefficients, that is $ab > km$.

To see what this stability condition implies, suppose that the product of the fatigue coefficients were approximately zero. There would then be no effective mechanism for dampening the arms race. An increase in Y's arms would increase *the rate of increase* in X's arms, and this would in turn increase the acceleration rate in Y's arms. The total levels of arms in both nations would accelerate upwards at an ever-increasing rate until an explosive outcome invalidated the model. Notice that it is the *product* of the two fatigue coefficients that is critical in preventing such an accelerating movement. If one nation is subject to moderately high fatigue, whereas the other's fatigue coefficient is near zero, then the product ab will be very small and the dynamics of the situation will lead to an accelerating arms race unless one of the two sensitivity coefficients is also close to zero.

In Richardson's very simple formulation, grievance terms do not affect the stability condition, though they will be important in determining equilibrium levels if and when stability has been reached, and this may have considerable importance in terms of which party ends up dominating the other. Grievance terms may be either positive or negative and constitute a kind of residual category in Richardson's formulation. According to Richardson (p. 16), such grievances could include "deeply rooted prejudices, standing grievances, old unsatisfied ambitions, wicked and persistent dreams of world conquest, or, on the contrary, a permanent feeling of contentment."

As the model is formulated, it should be noted that such grievance terms would produce constant *rates* of change dX/dt or dY/dt, which could be either positive or negative depending on the signs of g and h. Such constant rates would then contribute to the shifting of *levels* of arms, being upward if the coefficients were positive and downward if they were negative. A nation with positive grievances, let us say a recently defeated nation, might be increasing its armaments at a constant rate that is not dependent upon what the other nation is doing or its own internal arms levels. A satisfied, pacifistic nation with a negative grievance term would be shifting its arms levels downward at a constant rate.

Armaments involve only resources or potential sources of power that may not actually be employed against another nation. As will be discussed in a later section, those who subscribe to "deterrence theory" formulations argue that increases in arms levels serve to deter actual aggression, so that arms races by no means should be equated with accelerations in actual conflict levels. Here we are interested in the general implications of Richardson process models, however, and will therefore conceive of X and Y more broadly as the level of actual punishment that one party inflicts on the other. Thus we may also treat dX/dt as representing the rate of change in the level of party X's punitive behavior toward Y, taking this as a response to Y's punitive response to X and X's own internal fatigue level. Rather than thinking in terms of "defense" coefficients, we may therefore treat the coefficients k and m as representing the *sensitivity* of the one party to changes in the punitive behaviors of the other. A large (positive) value of k means that a very small increase in Y's punitive behavior toward X will result in a substantial increase in the *rate* dX/dt at which X's punitive responses will increase.

Possibly these sensitivity coefficients may be negative, as for example in situations in which a subordinate party submits to a dominant one by actually lowering its punitive responses whenever aggressive acts by the more powerful party are increased. A powerful but largely indifferent party may attempt to conciliate a hostile weaker party by lowering its level of punitive acts in response to aggression by that weaker party. The more general point is that the Richardson model is in principle capable of handling a wide variety of special cases and that the variables X and Y may be conceptualized far more broadly than the notion of arms races seems to suggest.

In the case of interpersonal conflicts, for example, fatigue may be conceptualized in terms of physiological exhaustion or of psychological satiation, whereas the notion of sensitivity would connote both a high degree of salience of the other party's actions and a tendency to react very quickly and attentively to any changes in that party's behaviors. Intensive interpersonal relationships involving high degrees of mutual dependency, as for instance in a marital dyad, would be predicted to involve high sensitivity coefficients for both parties. In a relationship entailing asymmetric power relationships, as for example that between a supervisor and a subordinate, we might expect a higher sensitivity coefficient on the part of the subordinate, if only because of that actor's greater dependency on the behaviors of the supervisor.

Returning to the arms race illustration, we may examine a few of the interesting propositions that Richardson is able to derive from the model of equations (1) or some relatively simple modifications of them. He notes, for example, that unilateral disarmament cannot by itself produce stability. Suppose that the level of armaments in nation Y (but not X) were reduced to zero, giving the momentary results

$$dX/dt = -aX + g$$

and   (2)

$$dY/dt = mX + h$$

If country X were relatively satisfied, g might be numerically small, and the right-hand side of the equation for dX/dt could be negative. With the level of X still positive, however, the right side of the second equation would ordinarily be positive, unless Y were a truly pacifistic nation with m and h both zero. There would then be pressures to increase the level of Y to a positive value. This, in turn, would reintroduce a positive term into the first equation, and another arms race would be under way. We see that mutual disarmament—setting *both* X and Y momentarily equal to zero—would likewise not produce stability if the two grievance terms were positive. Richardson concludes that without mutual satisfaction and trust mutual disarmament will not necessarily produce stability. An analogous point could be made in connection with many types of interpersonal conflicts.

Richardson also considers the interesting case of what he refers to as "rivalry" between two nations, where each nation is motivated primarily by the *difference* between the levels of armaments. That is, nation X increases its arms in proportion to the degree that Y exceeds X, and similarly for nation Y. He then represents this kind of rivalry situation by the pair of equations

$$dX/dt = k(Y - X) - aX + g$$

(3)

$$dY/dt = m(X - Y) - bY + h$$

The grievance coefficients g and h again do not enter into the necessary stability condition, which is

$$(k + a)(m + b) > km$$

and which is automatically satisfied since we are assuming that all four coefficients are positive. Thus we reach the conclusion that "rivalry," in this specific sense, always implies that the necessary conditions for stability are met. Such a model is, of course, unrealistic in a number of respects, including the fact that it requires one to assume accurate knowledge of the X and Y levels by both parties. If one nation believes that the other possesses secret armaments of unknown potential, the model is obviously inappropriate. Indeed, it may work better in instances of conflicts involving more intimate personal relationships, where it may be much more difficult to hide or disguise one's own resources vis-á-vis those of the other party.

Nations will not only be concerned about the conditions under which arms races can be expected to stabilize, but they will also generally wish to be in dominant positions if and when stability has been attained. At least they will not want to be placed in a clearly subordinate position or perhaps even one in which they are overly dependent on powerful coalition partners in the kind of balance of power arrangements that have, historically, proven to be highly unstable. It therefore becomes important to assess the expected equilibrium *levels* for both nations. Assuming the necessary stability conditions have been met, these can be obtained by setting both dX/dt and dY/dt equal to zero and solving for the equilibrium levels of X and Y, which we may represent as X_O and Y_O respectively. These are

$$X_O = (bg + hk)/(ab - km)$$

and
$$(4)$$

$$Y_O = (mg + ah)/(ab - km)$$

Noting that equilibrium requires that ab be greater than km, we see that the denominators of both expressions must be positive. Nation X will of course desire that its own equilibrium level be greater than that of Y. This will imply that it will be to its advantage to have high positive grievance levels, a small fatigue coefficient relative to that of nation Y, and also a larger sensitivity coefficient. Nation Y, however, will desire the reverse. If both nations attempt to manipulate their coefficients so as to attain such a state of affairs, then the product of the fatigue coefficients will be reduced and that of the sensitivity coefficients increased, thereby working against stability. Therefore even though both nations may desire stability, if they both also wish to be in the dominant position once stability has been attained they will attempt to influence the coefficients under their own control in such a way that instability will result. The arms race will accelerate into an exploding climax.

Much the same may apply, say, in terms of the dynamics of conflict escalation within a marital dyad. If both parties attempt to dominate the other, while simultaneously trying to shield themselves from dominating behaviors of the other, it may be extremely difficult to avoid an escalating spiral. Sensitivity coefficients, in particular, are likely to increase to the point that their product is considerably greater than that of fatigue coefficients. The more general point, of course, is that it may be nearly impossible for such parties to have it both ways: to hold down conflict and simultaneously to achieve certain mutually incompatible goals. The saving grace in the case of many types of interpersonal relationships is that common goals, or mutual interests that can only be met through cooperation, are also likely to be high enough to work to reduce such sensitivity coefficients and to hold grievance levels within tolerable limits. The relative utilities attached to the different types of goals will obviously be of considerable importance in such instances.

GOALS AND OPTIMIZING STRATEGIES

Richardson-type process models are obviously incomplete in a number of respects, only some of which we shall stress. One of these is that they treat responses in a rather mechanistic fashion, without paying explicit attention to the goals of either party. Such goals may be implicit in the notions of "grievances," "fatigue," and "sensitivity" but are preferably handled explicitly by incorporating them directly into the models used. Although we shall not pursue formal dynamic models of the type Richardson proposed, it seems advisable to call the reader's attention to one proposed line of attack which, with suitable modifications, might be used to extend Richardson process models in this direction.

Gillespie, Zinnes, Tahim, Schrodt, and Rubison (1977) suggest the application to this kind of process of optimal control theory, as developed by systems engineers. Let us suppose that one party, say Y, adheres to a Richardson-type reactive process, whereas the other, here X, reacts so as to optimize two possibly incompatible goals. The first is to achieve a balance of power situation or a high degree of security in which nation X's arms levels are sufficient to offset those of Y, so that Y does not attain a clearly dominant position. The second is to maintain the arms race within bounds, so that stability (at some level) is achieved. By plugging these two goals into nation X's equation, and then noting the implications of a strategy designed to optimize both simultaneously, Gillespie et al. are able to show the implications of the model. Their theoretical results are basically consistent with what we would expect, as they observe (p. 230) that if nation X "increases its armaments to satisfy its desired level of national security—hence meeting the first part of its objective, it also increases the total amount of armaments possessed by the two antagonistic nations—hence not meeting the second component of its objective." Any effort by nation X to reduce its own arms levels in order to achieve stability will tend to endanger its own security.

These conclusions to the effect that these two specific goals are basically incompatible are perhaps not surprising in view of the previous discussion of the stability conditions for Richardson's equations. It is the *strategy* of the optimal control theory approach, however, that is worth emphasizing. Presumably, one could examine the implications of very different pairs (or larger sets) of goals to assess their mutual consistency or compatibility, given certain assumptions about the behavior of the other party, here nation Y. Where the mathematics of such models becomes too complex to derive an analytic solution, computer simulations can be used to obtain insights about the expected dynamics of two or even multiparty conflict situations. The method thus provides a means by which assumptions about goal priorities can be introduced into equation systems that retain certain features of Richardson process models while modifying others.

ABELSON'S AGGRESSIVE REACTION MODEL

Starting with what might appear to be a very different perspective, Robert Abelson (1963) derived exactly the same set of equations as Richardson's, a fact that is both informative and disturbing theoretically. In doing so, Abelson has also increased our understanding of the psychological assumptions that may be used to generate conflict models with more general applicability than Richardson's theory of arms races. Abelson considered the case of two parties, each of which reacts to the responses of the other with intensities that tend to decay with the passage of time. Since there may be a whole series of responses by both parties, however, these must be summed over time.

Suppose party X acts with intensity A_1 at time T and that party Y continues to respond to this action, with the magnitude of this response at any later time t being given by

$$A_2(t) = e^{-b(t-T)}mA_1(T) \qquad (5)$$

The fact that party Y is assumed to forgive the original act of party X as time progresses is represented by the exponent of the natural constant e. The coefficient b is called the "forgiveness" coefficient of party Y. The greater the difference between t and T and the greater the forgiveness coefficient, the greater the product $b(t-T)$ and therefore the weaker the response at time t, since e has been raised to the *negative* power of this product term. We thus see that the rapidity of the decay depends on the size of the forgiveness coefficient. The factor $mA_1(T)$ determines the magnitude of the initial response by Y and consists of a coefficient m, representing the "sensitivity" of party Y to the acts of party X, multiplied by the intensity or magnitude $A_1(T)$ of party X's act at time T.

This equation only applies to a single act of X at time T. If we imagine a whole series of such acts at different times, we might assume that the magnitude of the response by Y at any particular time t would be obtained by summing its reactions to all the various acts of party X at different times in the past. Of course, given the decay factor, the most recent behaviors of party X should be the most prominent determinants of Y's behavior at time t. If we assume a very large number of acts over a continuous period of time, we should use an integral sign, rather than a summation sign. Assuming that the initial act of X took place at time 0, this would give for the *total* magnitude of the response by party Y at time t the value

$$A_2(t) = \int_o^t e^{-b(t-T)} mA_1(T)dt \qquad (6)$$

By a similar argument, the responses of party X to the numerous actions of party Y would be given by

$$A_1(t) = \int_o^t e^{-a(t-T)} kA_2(T)dt \qquad (7)$$

where a and k represent the forgiveness and sensitivity coefficients of X. These two equations are what are called integral equations, but they can readily be transformed into differential equations of the form introduced by Richardson. When this is done we obtain the following familiar pair of equations

$$dX/dt = kY - aX$$

and $\qquad\qquad\qquad\qquad\qquad\qquad\qquad\qquad\qquad\qquad\qquad$ (8)

$$dY/dt = mX - bY$$

which are exactly the same as Richardson's equations except for the omission of the grievance constants.

INTERPRETATIONS OF "CONSTANTS" IN EQUATIONS

Both Richardson's and Abelson's approaches make use of sensitivity coefficients representing the intensity of the one party's reactions to behaviors by the other, and we shall employ a similar variable in our subsequent discussions. The essential point to note in this connection is that such sensitivity coefficients are treated as *constants* in both systems, though X's and Y's coefficients may differ from one another. This allows for a possible asymmetry that may depend on other factors, such as the dependency of one party on the other or belief systems that affect the subjective interpretations that are given to the other party's behaviors. Both parties are assumed to be characterized by constant sensitivity coefficients, but that of X may be much greater than that of Y, or vice versa.

The Richardson and Abelson approaches differ in a very important respect, however. Whereas Richardson refers to "fatigue" coefficients, Abelson's formulation is in terms of "forgiveness" or what amounts to a memory decay factor. In both models the rate of change in X (or Y) is taken as a constant multiplied by the level of X (or Y), but the interpretation given to the causal mechanisms involved is very different. Fatigue invokes the notion of diminishing resources and goals that may compete with one another. It involves a diminishing returns phenomenon that operates to slow down the rate of growth in, say, X's armaments if the level of that variable becomes too great. The illustrative example of guns versus butter comes to mind. Forgiveness, however, refers directly to the temporal dimension. A party that forgives readily is one with a relatively short-term memory that relies much more heavily on the current behavior of the other party than on the past. Indeed, when we consider X's forgiveness of Y, the focus of attention is placed primarily on psychological factors internal to X, rather than on constraining factors that contribute to X's "fatigue."

We note a very important point in terms of this illustration of two theoretical formulations that, apart from the grievance constants, result in exactly the same pair of equations. Mathematical models of this type rely heavily on the interpretations one gives to the so-called "constants" that inevitably must be invoked, in this instance as multipliers of the X and Y terms. The verbal theory or substantive interpretation one gives to such equation systems is thus not automatic, given the equations, but remains problematic. The difficulty we encounter here is that our two mathematically equivalent theories are deceptively simplistic and are equivalent only because the "constants" they employ are not explicitly treated as variables. It represents a definite limitation imposed by the implicit parsimony criterion being invoked by users of such models. The causal modeling approach we shall later employ is designed to complicate matters by examining such "constants" and replacing them with a series of additional variables.

Why should a constant that is multiplied by X in the equation for dX/dt be interpreted as "fatigue," rather than as "forgiveness" or perhaps some other concept? In the case of two nations in an arms race, for instance, there may be factors internal to party X that actually operate to *increase* rather than decrease dX/dt as X increases. Perhaps "fatigue" is decreased by internal factors that support additional arms in proportion to the numbers that already exist, say through the operation of the vested interests of munitions firms that have grown increasingly powerful. Indeed, certain critics of Richardson process models have invoked such internal processes to argue that arms races may actually be accelerated by vested interests that exert pressures that are basically independent of the behaviors of the opposing party.[1]

The basic issues here are at least twofold. One is that of treating such coefficients as constants, rather than as variables that themselves need to be explained. The other is that of labeling such coefficients in such a way as to avoid overly simplistic interpretations. When one uses the labels "fatigue" and "forgiveness," many of the possible causes of such "constants" may be overlooked. In both the Richardson and Abelson formulations what we have are sets of coefficients that are multiplied by first degree terms in both X and Y. Such coefficients may be composites of many parts, each of which is affected by a different set of causal factors. Some of these may be sources of fatigue. Others may contribute to forgiveness or memory decay.

When one treats these coefficients as constants one thereby sidesteps a host of difficult questions that surface once the supposed constants are treated as *variables* to be explained in their own right. This is a general shortcoming of overly simplistic mathematical models containing a small number of constants. The simpler the models and the fewer the constants, the more likely it is that there will be two or more plausible equation systems that are mathematically equivalent, thus leading to interpretive difficulties of the sort we have just encountered. The "constants" in the two theories under discussion refer to four (and possibly more) kinds of conceptual variables that we shall include in our subsequent discussion: grievances, fatigue, forgiveness, and sensitivity. Once we conceive of these as variables rather than as constants, our models must become far more complex. This is one among several reasons why we prefer structural-equation or causal modeling approaches to theory construction.

A PARTIAL MODEL

By way of summary it may be helpful at this point to provide a partial model of the causal processes involved, as represented in Figure 4.1. Unfortunately, differential-equation formulations such as those of Richardson and Abelson are not easy to diagram so as to represent the implied temporal sequences involved. We may, however, think in terms of discrete time periods t, t + 1, t + 2, and so forth and then take the behaviors of party X at time t as affecting the later responses of Y, and vice versa. In the diagram of Figure 4.1, as well as later figures, we shall make use of only two time periods t and t + 1, it being understood that the process may continue for further time periods t + 2, t + 3, and so forth.

If we examine only the first two lines of boxes in Figure 4.1 we see that the *rate of change* in X's behavior (or level of arms) at time t is a function of (1) X's grievances at t, (2) X's fatigue level at t, (3) X's sensitivity at t, and (4) X's forgiveness at t. A similar set of four factors influence the rate of change in Y's behavior at time t. As we have just noted, each of these factors is taken as a constant in the Richardson and Abelson formulations. The implication of a dynamic model, however, is that these factors may themselves be altered at the later point in time, t + 1, as a result of changes in X's and Y's behaviors at time t.

Some of these effects are represented by the arrows connecting these behaviors to subsequent levels of the four supposedly "independent" variables that have been treated as constants in the equations. For example, X's behaviors may affect Y's subsequent grievance, sensitivity, fatigue, or forgiveness levels, which of course means that certain of the coefficients in either equation system may themselves be altered by prior events. The model of Figure 4.1 is intended to be merely suggestive, however, as there may also be a number of addi-

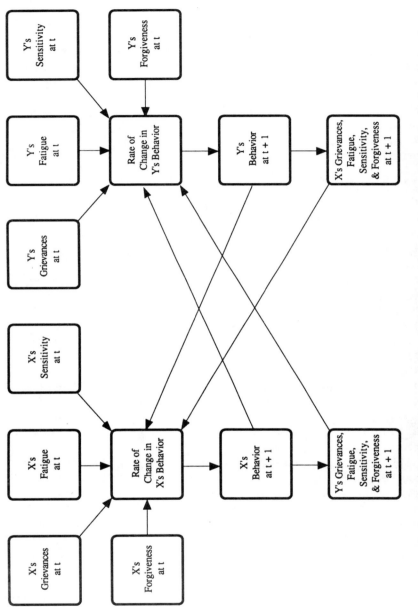

Figure 4.1 Partial model for Richardson and Abelson processes

82

tional variables that likewise affect these coefficients. Some of these latter variables will be included in the more complete general model provided in the next chapter.

It may be advisable, at this point, to comment on certain differences between macro-level conflicts, such as wars between two nation-states, and micro-level conflicts, such as interpersonal conflicts between coworkers or perhaps a husband-wife pair. Our variables are intended to be generic in scope, but they will obviously have somewhat different meanings as the type of conflict shifts. For instance, at the individual level, the notion of "fatigue" connotes a physiological tiring process, an exhaustion of the body often accompanied by certain attitudinal characteristics: a strong desire to avoid the situation, to be by oneself, or to engage in various forms of escapist activities. In contrast, "fatigue" among nations suggests resource depletion and, perhaps, a high *average* level of biological fatigue among its members, or at least among key actors. Similarly, although we can readily imagine a wife "forgiving" her husband or having important grievances against him, in precisely what sense can a nation-state "forgive" another? Perhaps its leaders, as persons, do so, or perhaps there is an "average forgiveness level" among its members.

Clearly, the kinds of general models we shall present and discuss in the remainder of the work cannot handle complications of this nature. Precise operational definitions of the most important concepts or variables will therefore have to be somewhat peculiar to the setting concerned, as well as to the nature of the conflict being analyzed. Problems of measurement comparability will naturally arise and be closely intertwined with issues relating to the generalizability of the theory (Blalock, 1982).

Much of our subsequent discussion will entail illustrations taken from the macro level, involving nation-states at war or conflicts among quasi-groups such as racial or ethnic groups. Readers will therefore not only have to make needed "transformations" to conflict situations of more direct interest to themselves. Sooner or later, they will need to reformulate special cases that more adequately handle complications that are appropriate to those cases. We shall illustrate certain types of complications of this nature in several of our submodels, as discussed in Chapters 5, 7, 8, and 10. Researchers, of course, will need to wrestle with problems of operationalization and dimensionality. Is "fatigue" a unidimensional concept in this particular context? What kinds of grievances are most relevant to the conflict at hand? What properties constitute resources? What specific goals must be taken into consideration, and which can be ignored? Needless to say, we cannot hope to address questions of this degree of specificity in a general work such as this.

Social Control Processes

Not all reactive process models need be symmetric in form. Hamblin, Hout, Miller and Pitcher (1977) propose a model in which the nonlinear dynamic models for two parties are slightly different, depending upon which party has lesser power. As we have seen, Gillespie et al. (1977) assume that one party adheres to a Richardson-process type of equation whereas the other attempts to maximize the joint satisfaction of two goals. In the present section we shall consider a social control model proposed by Salert and Sprague (1980), in which the subordinate party's behaviors can be characterized by an equation allowing for a diffusion process combined with a reaction to punitive responses by a more powerful party, whereas the latter's responses are oriented to locating an "appropriate" level of punitiveness so as to maintain social control.

Salert and Sprague are concerned with race riots and police responses, but their model can readily be generalized. It seems most appropriate in those situations where the subordinate party is a very loosely coordinated quasi-group, the members of which can be characterized by high grievance levels. There is thus a substantial potential for conflict, with members perhaps having different thresholds or tolerance levels for joining the conflict (Granovetter, 1978). Once a riot begins it initially spreads via a diffusion process, building up rather rapidly at first, as news of the riot starts to spread. Later, however, the number of additional participants begins to diminish, either because nearly everyone has learned of the conflict's existence or because only those with very high threshold levels remain as nonparticipants. At some point the effects of fatigue begin to take over, as exhausted or satiated persons drop out and few others remain to take their places. So the participation rate subsides, and the riot or other form of conflict comes to a gradual end.

The police or other control agents also play an important role in such a process, and their behaviors may involve an entirely different dynamic process. Here it is not so much a matter of fatigue or shortage of replacements, though in a more complete model such factors would also need to be considered in all instances in which the supply of control agents is inadequate. According to Salert and Sprague, the dynamic from the standpoint of control agents involves the problem of settling upon an "appropriate" level of punitive response. A response that is too weak may create the impression that there is lack of resolve or a basic weakness that signals a willingness to make substantial concessions. It also means a low average level of punishment, and thus lowered expected costs for the average potential participant within the subordinate party and perhaps an altering of threshold levels in favor of increased participation. Given the obvious psychic and possible material benefits in joining an open rebellion, there will be little incentive to remain out of the fray.

In contrast, an overreaction on the part of control agents may produce a further set of grievances added to the preexisting ones, with the possibility that those grievances stemming from the conflict itself may also reduce threshold levels of nonparticipants and gain sympathy among third parties, who may enter on the side of the subordinate party or at least act to constrain the control agents. The kinds of "police riots" discussed by Stark (1972) are a case in point. Indeed, since control agents may themselves be poorly trained and only loosely coordinated, there may be a comparable "threshold" level beyond which given agents' behaviors go out of control, and where contagion models could also be employed to help explain the differential responses of such control agents.

Critical in all of this is the question of the degree to which both parties can be considered sufficiently unorganized and poorly coordinated that individualistic diffusion-type explanatory models would be needed to help explain the dynamics of the conflict. If, for example, the police have been well trained and disciplined to avoid police riots, then perhaps a simple model involving a more or less rational search for an "appropriate" response level will be sufficient. Under such a model, if a given level of punishment is found to be insufficient a greater amount will be employed. If this overshoots the mark, a fine-tuned adjustment can be made until the optimal response level is located.

We surmise that few if any actual riot processes can be approximated by this kind of idealized model, and indeed Salert and Sprague note that it may be extremely difficult for police or other control agents to locate such an appropriate response level. Yet it does seem likely that in other more highly organized forms of conflict, as for instance limited wars among nation-states, both parties may be seeking to locate appropriate response levels so as to avoid escalation while at the same time controlling the opponent's punitive actions.

Clearly, much of this assumes a reasonably accurate appraisal of the other party's motivational structure, including its heterogeneity with respect to threshold levels. Here it is important to note Granovetter's point that it is not only average threshold levels that are important, but their *distribution* as well. If a given level of punitive response "sets off" a counterresponse among a small segment of the opposing party who have low threshold levels, this, in turn, may be sufficient to encourage others with somewhat higher thresholds to join them. It will indeed be difficult to estimate such threshold levels in advance of the conflict, nor will it be a simple matter to adjust one's punitive actions downward once the conflict is underway.

The above arguments are compatible with the Tilly's (1975) previously discussed thesis that rather ordinary protest activities may or may not result in violence according to the nature of the responses by control agents. Thus, they argue, it is primarily the *political* process, rather than changes in grievance levels or economic factors, that determines the nature of the outcome. A weak or vacillating response, or one that is too punitive, is likely to result in violence, with most of the violent behavior being perpetrated by the dominant or controlling party (Gurr, 1970). In the case of much more significant uprisings such as major social revolutions of the sort discussed by Brinton (1938), Moore (1966) and Skocpol (1979), outcomes may also depend upon actual weaknesses or internal dissension among members of the dominant party. Genuine grievances, when coupled with repressive actions that are also ineffective in preventing the spread of open revolt, may then result in a cumulative or accelerating process that ultimately produces a major revolution.

Compatible kinds of arguments have been developed by Gurr (1970), Lichbach and Gurr (1981), and Gurr and Lichbach (1986), who distinguish between more or less spontaneous forms of conflict, such as protest and turmoil, and more prolonged and organized forms, such as internal revolt. In his study of mass political violence in 108 nations, Hibbs (1973) similarly developed a series of alternative causal models designed to account for patterns of collective protest and internal warfare. In the case of collective protest movements of the sort discussed by Salert and Sprague, Hibbs argued that such

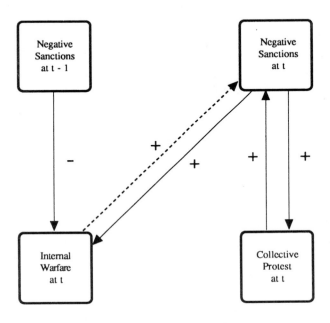

Figure 4.2 Portion of Hibbs' model linking lagged and nonlagged negative sanctions to collective protests and internal warfare

Source: Adapted from Hibbs (1973, p. 181).

processes are more likely to involve spontaneous, short-term actions and reactions. In the case of more highly organized internal warfare, however, there may be more pronounced lagged effects of repression that work in the opposite direction. In his best-fitting model (p. 181), which we may represent by Figure 4.2, Hibbs inferred positive and immediate feedbacks (of approximately the same magnitude) between the use of collective protest and the application of negative sanctions, suggesting the sort of causal mechanism depicted by Salert and Sprague in the case of police overresponses.

The overuse of punishment is thus presumed to have an almost immediate effect of increasing the extent of collective protest. In the case of internal warfare, which requires a much higher degree of organization on the part of the subordinate party, Hibbs inferred an important *negative* and delayed impact of the use of negative sanctions. In other words, past punitive actions tend to inhibit future internal warfare. Thus by distinguishing spontaneous forms of behaviors from more organized ones, and by also allowing for both simultaneous and delayed impacts of repressive responses, Hibbs provides a more refined type of explanation for the phenomena of interest to students of revolutions or other lesser forms of internal warfare.

In terms of goals and utilities it seems likely that repression will usually have an almost immediate impact on the utility for revenge or the desire to aggress against one's opponent (Gurr, 1970). Over time such a revenge goal may diminish in magnitude, especially if the "forgiveness" coefficient is large. Other grievance factors may remain more or less constant, but the memory of prior costs brought about by a repressive response may inhibit more organized forms of protest, though not spontaneous ones. Among other things, repression may increase the fear among potential participants that they will not be joined by sufficient numbers of others to increase the probability of ultimate success. Thus punitive responses may inhibit rationally-oriented future behaviors but have the opposite effect in the immediate present. If such reasoning is correct, it is important to determine the nature of factors that influence the lag process, as well as those that help maintain or reduce the impact of the memory decay factor. Ideological variables of the sort to be discussed in Chapters 6 and 7 will undoubtedly also be relevant in this connection.

The approach used by Salert and Sprague could also be modified so as to make it appropriate for use in connection with interpersonal conflicts in which one, or perhaps both, of the parties attempt to control the behaviors of the other by finding an appropriate level of response. Of course the diffusion-type argument, as applied to riot situations, would have to be modified but perhaps the threshold notion retained. If one looked at the behaviors of, say, the subordinate party as constituting a sequence, with thresholds varying according to the occasion, what constituted an "appropriate" level of response at one moment might be defined either as a weak or overreactive response at another, depending on such a varying threshold. The resulting dynamics would of course be difficult to model, and one would

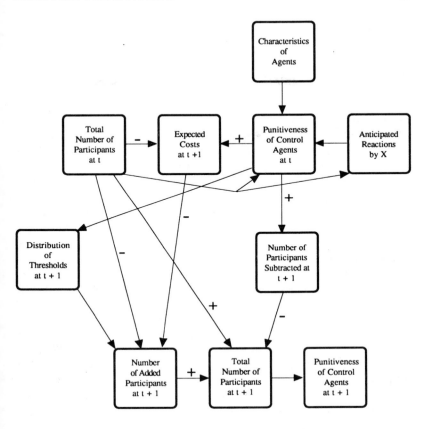

Figure 4.3 Partial model for Salert and Sprague control processes

need to be especially concerned not to impose prematurely too many restrictions in the form of supposed "constants." It might be hoped, however, that important parameter values would change in some lawlike fashion. Perhaps one party's sensitivity levels might become progressively larger, thereby lowering threshold levels or tolerances for a given level of response.

A simplified model depicting the Salert and Sprague argument is provided in Figure 4.3. The total number of (riot) participants at time t + 1 is taken as a function of (1) the prior number of participants at time t, plus (2) the number of added participants at t + 1, minus (3) the number who have dropped out as a result of a combination of fatigue/satiation and the prior punitive responses by the other party (e.g, the police). The number of added participants at $t + 1$ is taken as a function of the prior number of participants, the distribution of thresholds at $t + 1$, and the expected costs (at time $t + 1$) to participants, relative to the expected gains. These expected costs will, of course, also be a function of the other party's prior punitive behaviors. The latter behaviors, in turn, will depend on various characteristics of the agents, including their prior training and individual threshold levels, as well as anticipated reactions to the control efforts. Since the total number of participants at $t + 1$ is assumed to affect future expected costs and punitive behaviors of the other party, it will also indirectly affect the number of participants at these later times, either to increase these numbers or to reduce them via the previously discussed mechanisms.

Deterrence Theory Versus Richardson Processes

Arms races involve the power resources of several parties, but merely because each party reacts to the level of resources of the other by increasing its own arms level does not mean that the two parties will necessarily engage in actual conflict. Indeed, party X's *ability* to harm Y, and vice versa, may tend to inhibit the outbreak of violence through the mutual fear of punishment. Thus an arms buildup may actually inhibit conflict rather than encourage it. From the perspective of, say, party X, its accumulation of arms is likely to be seen as a deterrent to other parties, with its own weapons being perceived internally as strictly "defensive." Party Y, however, is likely to perceive X's weapons as "offensive" and therefore X's arms buildup as constituting a threat. A reverse process occurs, of course, in the case of Y's weapons, with X being sensitive to Y's arms level and thus tending to respond to Y's increases in a positive feedback loop.

Deterrence theory suggests that under such circumstances both parties may be inhibited from the actual *use* of their potential because of a fear of punishment.[2] The rather optimistic conclusion may then be reached that neither side will elect to initiate conflict, so that the arms buildup actually reduces rather than increases the likelihood of conflict, though not necessarily its destructiveness once underway. Is such a deterrence process more likely to occur under some conditions than others? And what subjective factors will be at work?

As Bacharach and Lawler (1980) point out, the deterrence argument depends very heavily on the assumption of credibility: that each party will actually employ its potential power under clearly defined conditions but will withhold it under others. Therefore a reasonably high degree of rationality on the part of both parties is presumed. Each will know where to draw the line and will stop just short of provoking an all-out, mutually damaging overt conflict. If one party threatens a given line of action and the other threatens to retaliate in response, the latter threat must be credible, which means that the first party must believe that the second party is indeed willing to undergo a punitive conflict situation. If each side has set up a trip-wire mechanism, in Schelling's (1966) terminology, the other side must be extremely careful not to violate it. Miscommunications, bluffing and bluff-calling, and "brinkmanship" must be avoided for deterrence to work satisfactorily. In effect, each party must be willing to assume that its opponent is sufficiently rational not to take undue risks.

Bacharach and Lawler (1980, 1981) also point out that "face saving" is critical in connection with deterrence theory. Where the parties have approximately equal power, so that one does not clearly dominate the other, the capitulation of the first party to the second is likely to be perceived—both by the second party and by outsiders—as being caused by "internal" weaknesses, such as a lack of resolve, rather than by external exigencies. Bacharach and Lawler base this argument on attribution theory and findings in the social psychological literature to the effect that persons tend to attribute behaviors of strong parties to internal causes and those of weaker parties to external ones.[3] Therefore a party that is initially perceived as strong vis-à-vis its opponent is relatively more vulnerable to loss of face than is a weaker party. Presumably, then, a stronger party will be more inclined actually to use its potential power when challenged to do so, rather than risking a loss of face. Where both parties have approximately equal potential power, each will be likely to use it and deterrence is less effective.

In a closely related argument, Nieburg (1969) notes that in many kinds of "underdeveloped" control systems a simple retribution process is likely to operate. By this he means that an "eye-for-an-eye" or "push-push" mentality will be at work, through which parties of approximately equal power respond almost automatically to a given act with a corresponding one that closely matches it. Such a process is especially likely to occur whenever there is no more powerful third party capable or inclined to inject itself to stop the process. Nieburg cites as illustrations numerous instances involving tribal societies, clan warfare (such as occurred among Scottish Highlanders or the notorious Hatfields and the McCoys), Sicilian Mafia clashes, frontier-society conflict, and underworld gang-warfare.

Nieburg's argument is that such retribution processes can continue for very long periods of time until overarching control mechanisms are created to dampen and regulate them. As an example of such a regulatory practice he cites the organization of top crime families into a powerful syndicate composed of leaders of all major factions and capable of meting out almost certain punishment to those who insist upon breaching its regulations. In order to end such a chain of retributions, a member of the offender's own group is often selected to conduct the "final" act against the guilty party, an act which presumably is designed to satisfy the opposing faction.

Nieburg also points out that whenever the simple "push-push" retribution process results in a "push-shove" or "push-kill" response, domination is implied. That is, if party Y responds to party X's act with an even more severe one, and if party X does not respond by upping the ante, then Y has in effect staked and earned a claim to dominance. If X then wishes to extricate itself from a subordinate position it must accelerate the level of conflict, much as occurs in the classic Richardson-type process. On the other hand, if X decreases its response level a hierarchy of dominance is created, much as occurs among male animals of the same species. A lesser member may on occasion challenge the dominance hierarchy but is likely to be met with a counterresponse that reestablishes the superiority of the attacked party—unless and until the latter becomes sufficiently weakened that the attacker gains the superior position.

According to Nieburg, conflict situations of this sort are endemic to both animal and human social organizations. Where differences in potential power are rather obvious, as for example among males of the same species but of differing sizes, levels of overt conflict are likely to be confined to occasional sparring for position or to bluffs that are successfully called. In such situations deterrence, when based on considerable power differentials, may work to inhibit the actual use of punitive behaviors. As Bacharach and Lawler (1980) point out in this connection, where substantial inequality of potential power exists and is obvious to all concerned, there is less likely to be a loss of face on the part of the weaker parties.

TIT-FOR-TAT STRATEGIES AND COOPERATION

A strategy that has many features in common with Nieburg's push-push response pattern is the so-called tit-for-tat strategy discussed in the game theory literature.[4] Both strategies may be considered as forms of deterrence, or as means of inhibiting punitive responses by the other party. In contrast to the push-push pattern, which does not really deal explicitly with positive or cooperative response patterns, the tit-for-tat pattern returns nearly identical responses, whether positive or negative.

The most extensive discussion of this latter game strategy is contained in Robert Axelrod's book, *The Evolution of Cooperation* (1984), which is heavily based on analyses of alternative strategies used in iterative Prisoner's Dilemma games (iPDG) characterized by repeated plays of the PDG by two players capable of monitoring and recalling each other's response patterns in prior games. It is assumed in Axelrod's discussions that payoff matrices remain constant throughout the series of games, that players may possibly discount the values of future payoffs, and that they generally cannot accurately predict when the series will terminate. It is also implicitly assumed that they are not in a position to alter these payoffs in any way, deceive their partners as to which courses of action they have actually taken, modify game rules, cheat, or leave the game prior to the termination of the entire sequence of plays. It also assumed that they both know and agree upon the date of the initiation of the series, so that the first party to defect can be identified.

If we assume that parties X and Y each have only two options on each play of an iPDG, either to "cooperate" or "defect" (or employ a punitive response), we may represent an illustrative PDG payoff matrix as follows:

		Party X's Behaviors	
		Cooperate	*Defect*
Party Y's	*Cooperate*	R = 3, R = 3	S = 0, T = 5
Behaviors	*Defect*	T = 5, S = 0	P = 1, P = 1

where party Y's payoffs are listed first and party X's listed second in each cell. The symbol R represents the rewards both parties receive if both cooperate; T represents the temptation to defect when the other party cooperates; S represents the "sucker" payoff for cooperating when the other party defects; and P represents the punishment allocated to each party when both select the noncooperative alternative.

As Axelrod and others have noted, if the PDG is played only once with a given opponent, it will always be rational to defect, thereby earning either T or the punishment payoff P. But if the game is played an indeterminate number of times, the question then becomes that of finding a set of strategies that will succeed (against most opponents) in inducing a cooperative response. In a "tournament" involving a number of different competing strategies, Axelrod found that the very simple "nice" strategy of "tit-for-tat" received the highest scores even when contestants were told of this strategy's success in a prior round and were challenged, specifically, to present more successful alternatives. By a "nice" strategy, as compared with a "nasty" one, Axelrod means one that begins with the cooperative choice and does not defect until the other party does so. The simple tit-for-tat pattern, which is similar in some ways to Nieburg's (1969) "push-push" strategy, involves the notion that cooperative responses by the other party are met with cooperation, but defecting responses are countered by defections on the very next move. Thus the tit-for-tat strategy is "provocable" but also "forgiving" in the sense that the response is determined only by the immediately prior action of the other party. If Y returns to a cooperative response, X reciprocates until the next act of defection.

One of the fundamental problems with Axelrod's simple analysis is that in many real-life situations actors cannot count on payoff matrices remaining stable. Indeed, one or both actors may be acting to *modify* the matrix so as to achieve a more favorable strategic position, say by reducing the other party's T value relative to its expected R, or by increasing its punishment P whenever both parties defect (or engage in a mutually punitive conflict spiral). Indeed, one party may be attempting to do away with the second party altogether, or to place it in a clearly subordinate position, say by taking away some of its resources or ability to impose future sanctions. The iPDG setup generally presupposes a set of inviolate rules which predetermine payoff matrices once and for all, and this—in turn—seems to require a dominant "rule enforcer" capable of holding the payoff matrix constant throughout the duration of the interaction. Yet Axelrod argues that no such superordinate actors are required for the argument to hold. It seems unlikely that, in the absence of such third parties, it is at all reasonable to assume a fixed matrix that cannot be impacted by the outcomes of previous encounters. Indeed, the matrix may be so transformed that a PDG setup no longer obtains. The payoffs P in the situation where both parties fail to cooperate may, for example, become greater than the rewards R when they both cooperate, in which case conflict will become highly likely, and especially so whenever T is also substantially greater than R for both parties.

It must also be remembered that it is actually a set of *expected* payoffs that really constitutes the relevant parameters. Such expected payoffs may be functions of those that have been received in prior encounters, but once we admit to the possibility that payoffs may be altered as the iterations proceed, then there will be an additional set of uncertainties involved. Not only will each party not know how the other will act on the next sequence, but the payoff matrix itself will also be in doubt. In other words, subjective probabilities will be even more difficult to calculate, leaving additional room for ideological and other distorting factors to enter the picture. In part, the question becomes "Who will provide the payoffs?" Will they be taken from the other party, say as a result of one's own victory, or will they be supplied by a third party? If it is the former, then clearly the relative power positions of the parties X and Y at the end of a given iteration will be critical. And this, in turn, may provide an additional incentive to enter into conflict or to engage in an escalation of armaments that, in turn, results in conflict.

In game-theory analyses in general, as well as the PDG literature in particular, participants are made aware of whether or not a zero-sum setup characterizes the payoff matrices. In the PDG, for example, it is presumed obvious that a non-zero-sum payoff matrix is being used, so that there are potentially greater payoffs for cooperation than defection. If they cooperate, then both players can win, presumably at the expense of some third party that is footing the bill. In real-life settings, however, one or both parties may perceive a zero-sum setup even where a more "objective" observer may be aware of the very high costs of conflicts involving the mutual exchanges of negative sanctions, as compared with the benefits of cooperation. As we have suggested, such a perception by the parties to a conflict may be a function of whether or not they expect that rewards can be taken from the other party, once it has been defeated. Clearly, then, in order to induce a cooperative arrangement, the nature of the positive-sum game must be made evident to both parties.

As Axelrod has noted, a tit-for-tat strategy does not yield a "win" over the other party, and indeed he suggests that its use depends upon having a "nonenvious" orientation. Those who employ this strategy must therefore depend on the anticipated mutual cooperation yielding a higher average reward R than would have been achieved under alternative strategies. If, instead, the objective is to best one's "opponent" or to end up in a dominant position, the implication is that the actor concerned is trying in an iPDG to maximize some quantity other than its own absolute rewards. If it defines "success" as entailing ending up in a position superior to that of the opponent, or of maximizing the difference between the two parties' outcomes, then it is more likely to define the situation in zero-sum terms and to reject cooperation. Once more, it becomes critical for third parties to emphasize the advantages to both X and Y of defining the situation in non-zero sum terms. If Bacharach and Lawler (1981) are correct in arguing that situations involving high total power or mutual dependency are more likely to result in positive-sum game orientations, then in order to induce cooperation, or to make the tit-for-tat strategy successful, it also becomes important to attempt to create situations in which not only is such mutual dependency high, but both parties are motivated to keep it that way.

Another problem arising from the extreme simplicity of iPDG set-ups involves the assumption that both parties recognize the same starting point for the series, so that the party that defects first can be clearly identified. Otherwise, Axelrod's distinction between "nice" and "nasty" strategies breaks down. In many real-life conflict situations, however, each party may select its own (perceived) starting point. Depending on ideological and other factors, we would generally expect each party to select out certain points in the history of prolonged conflicts in which the *other* party could be shown to have engaged in an especially treacherous or heinous act that "required" retaliation as well as justifying a suspicious orientation and belief that it had been the "victimized" party. Whenever two parties have been in contact over a prolonged period, it will doubtless be rather easy for each to select a different starting point so as to argue that it indeed was the other party that first defected.

Axelrod stresses that it is the immediacy of the defecting response in the tit-for-tat strategy that is important, so that a clear signal is sent to the initial defector. In his concluding discussion, he also points out that, perhaps because of the ambiguities involved, it may be wise for the employer of this strategy to provide a somewhat weaker retaliatory response, so as to help prevent the initiation of a destructive conflict spiral or, in Nieburg's terms, a tendency for both parties to employ a push-shove response pattern. If, for example, party X responds to Y's punitive behaviors by punishing Y only .9 as much as Y has punished X, and if Y in turn also employs a somewhat diminished punitive response, then this particular sequence of mutually punitive responses could be expected to decay to the point where more cooperative responses might take over. Needless to say, it becomes critical in employing this strategy that both parties can readily perceive and agree on the fact that the other party's responses are, indeed, becoming increasingly restrained.

DETERRENCE, RISK-TAKING, AND TRUST

Deterrence theory is posed with a serious problem in those instances where one or both parties are highly prone to risk-taking as a deliberate strategy. Schelling (1966) points out that if a party has made a commitment to a particular line of action, and in effect has challenged the other party to violate a trip-wire mechanism, this places that other party in the disadvantageous position of having to decide whether or not to take the final step in instigating a conflict. Likewise, if a party gains the reputation of being willing to take considerable risks that are dependent on events that are beyond its own control, it may be in a position to bluff the other party into giving ground and thereby losing face. The game of "chicken" immediately comes to mind.

Suppose both parties recognize that conflict will result in a disastrous outcome through which each will lose considerably more than would be the case under a no-conflict situation. Both will be motivated to avoid conflict, but one party may be more willing than the other to take a calculated risk, especially if it can communicate to the other party that it is committed to a conflict response even where it cannot control "chance" factors. This highly risky choice may be sufficient to encourage the other party to back off and thereby give ground. Similarly, an opponent that is perceived as highly irrational or unpredictable may gain a substantial advantage over a more predictable, "rational" opponent. Indeed, in this sense it would be rational to appear irrational!

One supposedly "irrational" form of behavior is for a weaker party to attack a much stronger one. Bruce Bueno de Mesquita (1981), however, points out and uses data to confirm that weaker nation-states often initiate wars, on very rational grounds, in instances where it may be expected that stronger parties will be brought into the fray because of their prior commitments to such weaker parties. Therefore, nations may be "trapped" by their commitments into losing the initiative to more reckless ones that have relatively less to lose by taking risks of this nature. In a sense, the more "rational" actor may be the smaller risk-taking state, rather than the more powerful one that has made an irrevocable commitment to it. Bueno de Mesquita's argument thus lends support to those, such as Morgenthau (1948), who take a skeptical position regarding the efficacy of balance-of-power strategies in serving as a deterrence to warfare.

In such instances the assumptions required by deterrence theory would seem to break down. The mere fact that both parties possess sufficient resources to inflict considerable damage on the other party therefore does not mean that both will be inhibited from using these resources. Yet deterrence theory is appealing, especially when examined from the perspective of a single party that may have a number of potential adversaries rather than merely one. A nation-state surrounded by hostile countries would be rational to increase its armament levels, since a mutual disarmament arrangement with a single neighbor would leave both countries vulnerable to the others. A nation-state or other party that possesses substantial potential power and that simultaneously communicates clearly and credibly the conditions under which it will employ its resources may thus protect itself against attack, provided it does not permit itself to get into the "war trap" kind of situation analyzed by Bueno de Mesquita.

Unfortunately, such a country's neighbors are likely to perceive its arms or other resources as more offensive than defensive, and they may therefore find it rational to increase their own armaments levels. An arms race will then be underway. Any miscalculations or "irrationality" on the part of a single party may then lead to the temptation actually to use one's power, perhaps in a preemptive strike or in an effort to outmanuever what is perceived to be an unpredictable or intractable opponent. Over the long term, moreover, few parties may be willing to assume that a potential opponent that is presently well behaved will always remain so.

Critical here is the notion of trust and each party's subjective probabilities concerning the behavior of its opponent. If by trust we mean that party X has an unconditional belief that the other party Y will always act in such a manner as to protect X's interests as well as its own, then it will be unnecessary for X to respond at all to resource buildups by the other party. Relationships between the United States and Canada, for instance, suggest this form of unconditional trust on the part of both parties, at least in the foreseeable future.

Under such circumstances one may usually anticipate a clear-cut dominance hierarchy, where the weaker party really has little choice but to trust the stronger one in this unconditional sense. Somewhat more realistically, the weaker party's trust may derive from the fact that the stronger party has little or nothing to gain through conflict or domination. Circumstances may change, however. American Indians have learned through bitter experience that such a trusting relationship is basically conditional on their having virtually nothing to "exchange" that is valued by the far more powerful white colonial powers with which they have had to contend. Whenever the "useless" land they occupied suddenly became valuable to white settlers, they were either slaughtered or removed to still more distant territories and eventually onto reservations on marginally productive lands.

For rather obvious reasons, then, conditional forms of trust are far more common. Such a trusting orientation may be based primarily on a party's own deterrence resources, a faith in the other party's current leadership, a belief that powerful third parties would intervene to protect it, or the perception that its own resources and possessions are so inadequate that no other party will either perceive it as a threat or be inclined to take its meager resources away. Clearly, in the last instance any efforts to increase an extremely weak party's resource base will tend to make it increasingly vulnerable to attack.

In the cases of the second and third of the above bases for trust the party concerned will be highly dependent on developments that are beyond its own control, and thus the conditional trust that it develops is likely to be both short-term in nature and also subject to divisive internal processes. Some members who stand to gain from a high dependence relationship with the stronger party may develop such a trusting orientation, whereas others are likely to attempt to undermine it. Where such a conditional trust is in the process of being undermined for whatever reasons, members of the weaker party may find themselves in an ambivalent position, sometimes supporting conciliatory movements and at other times feeling pressured to build up a stronger deterrence base or to employ threat tactics to extract concessions from the more powerful party. Where vacillation among such drastically different approaches occurs, the level of trust within the opposing party may be adversely affected and the risk of a preemptive strike increased.

Dynamics Involving Threats and Intractable Opponents

Examined from the standpoint of a single party, say X, it can be argued that there are a number of important advantages to be gained through the use of threat tactics, provided these are periodically validated so as to remain credible. To change the status quo it is often useful to employ threat tactics. As we have noted, a party that gains the reputation of being more willing to take risks than its opponent, or one that is in a position to make irrevocable commitments that in effect challenge the opponent to take the final step, may thereby be able to extract concessions from a more cautious party with equal resources.

Bacharach and Lawler (1980) link the toughness of a party's bargaining stance to its degree of dependence, arguing that a high degree of dependence will lead a party toward a more conciliatory bargaining stance, involving fewer threats of punishment. Therefore a higher level of *mutual* interdependence will tend to dampen conflict tendencies, as well as reducing the probability that "push-push" dynamics will lead to "push-shove" conflict spirals. As previously noted, they make the important distinction between the "absolute" power within the dyad (which they define in terms of the level of mutual dependence) and "relative" power (or the degree to which there is power inequality between the two parties). In this instance, a high level of absolute power or mutual dependence will tend to soften bargaining stances and thereby reduce the risk of an accelerating conflict-spiral.

One must be cautious in applying such an argument, however. Consider master-slave relationships in a setting in which there is a high degree of mutual dependence of each party on the profitability of a plantation system. The master is highly dependent on *some* body of slaves to produce a valued commercial product, but this very dependence is likely to induce the master not only to employ punitive measures but also to seek and use outside political forces (e.g., the police) to reduce the slaves' escape options.

In such instances one must distinguish between dependence on a system, such as slavery, and dependence on a specified set of actors, such as one's own slaves. For instance if the price of the goods being produced is increased relative to alternatives, the slaveholder's dependence on the system itself may increase. If so, the owner may or may not become increasingly dependent upon a particular set of slaves, according to the supply of alternative slaves. If such a supply has become restricted, say by the end of the slave trade, this may result in improved bargaining power for individual slaves and, presumably, better treatment and less master-slave conflict. Such an increase in the value of slave labor might, however, result in even harsher treatment, as the owner attempted to extract more and more labor from them, with a view to rather simply replacing them with others, once their production levels became sufficiently low. These increasingly harsh demands could generate higher conflict levels and perhaps even open rebellion.

One can certainly imagine, then, a number of situations in which increased mutual dependence results in increased, rather than decreased, levels of tension. The Bacharach-Lawler thesis, as well as arguments based primarily on *positive* exchanges, may require modification in instances where the exchanges are either exploitative in nature or involve many fewer common or cooperative interests. Where one party attempts to reduce the other's alternatives by force, and thus to increase its dependence, this very act may increase the level of conflict.

THE INTRACTABLE OPPONENT

As implied in our earlier discussion, one or both of the parties to a conflict may be extremely rigid, prone to a high degree of risk taking, and not easily put off by a strong deterrence policy. In Chapter 8 we shall deal, specifically, with what I shall refer to as "conflict groups" as a special type of party of this nature, but it seems appropriate to discuss in more general terms the problems that arise for an opponent of such a party. In a prisoner's dilemma situation, for example, one party may continue to select a competitive or punitive alternative, regardless of the apparent "irrationality" of such a stance in terms of both parties' long-term interests.

A nation-state may be led by a fanatical leader who, against all odds, is willing to take on much more powerful opponents or expose a very high percentage of his or her own party's membership to extreme risks. A state that is characterized by a rigid belief system may be able to mobilize its true believers into a powerful fighting force that succeeds in defeating much larger states with considerably greater resources. In all such instances the more moderate opponent may face a dichotomized choice situation: either capitulate entirely or adopt the same course of action. Bargaining may be out of the question, and threats against such intractable opponents may be useless or may even intensify their determination to engage in conflict at any cost.

Let us suppose that the intractable party is Y and that it has been subjected to prolonged exploitation or is a defeated enemy that has undergone what it defines as a humiliating and extremely punitive experience at the hands of party X or its allies. The degree of punitiveness or the unfairness of settlement terms will, of course, be subject to Y's interpretation and may be highly exaggerated or experienced as especially humiliating if X is defined by Y to be inferior or unjustifiably vengeful. The case of post World-War I Germany comes to mind, as does the postbellum South during Reconstruction. Toward the end of the civil rights movement in the late 1960s, certain black-power extremists acted in a similar fashion, though in retrospect their words may have been much more bluff than implying a concrete plan for open rebellion.

In such instances we expect that legitimate grievances will also be exaggerated and simplistic ideological systems invented or invoked, so as to increase Y's mobilization to an unusual degree and to blot out from memory any of X's responses that may be incompatible with these grievances or beliefs. Thus genuine communication between the two parties may be effectively cut off, so that Y's responses are no longer contingent on X's verbal or nonverbal cues or even on X's current level of resources. In Richardson's terms, Y's "grievance coefficient" completely dominates Y's responses. Neither fatigue nor a sensitivity to X's behavior shifts will be relevant to predicting Y's behaviors.

Any acts by X to right previous "wrongs" are likely to be interpreted by Y either as token gestures that are to be ignored or as signs of weakness and a lack of resolve. If they happen to appeal to some segment of Y's population, they may immediately be interpreted as attempts to buy off that segment. This may or may not be a realistic interpretation on the part of Y's members, but regardless of its accuracy, the most likely outcome will be accelerating demands on the part of Y, resulting in X's (correct or incorrect) interpretation that Y's demands are insatiable and that they will sooner or later become totally unreasonable. There may be internal disagreements among X's members as to the point at which Y's demands should be resisted, but we may anticipate that if X continues to make concessions that are then met with expanded demands, the position of moderates within X will be undermined, with the result that X, as well, will become increasingly intractable.

Shortly before the immediate confrontation, it is sometimes the case that a relatively moderate leadership within party Y may have attempted to obtain minor concessions from X, only to be rebuffed. This occurred, for example, in many Southern communities during the 1940s and early 1950s prior to the major civil rights eruptions of the late 1950s and 1960s. Discussions between white and black moderate leaders seldom produced tangible results during this earlier period, with the result that so-called "compromise" black leadership became discredited and their requests interpreted as "tokenism" or as expedient moves to improve their own status as white-sponsored leaders.

More generally, unless such leaders are in a position to extract increasingly important concessions, their positions become undermined and untenable in the eyes of more militant members of a subordinate party. Once they have become discredited, it then becomes exceedingly difficult for the dominant party X to rely on them as a moderating force, at least until more extremist elements have also failed in their own efforts to extract significant concessions.

A similar kind of dynamic may occur within the superordinate party X, as well, if moderate leaders have been unsuccessful in reducing tensions. Any concessions they may have granted during the early stages of the confrontation may be interpreted by other party X members as having been misguided and as signaling to extremists within party Y that continued concessions can be extracted with relatively few costs. In Great Britain the moderate leader Neville Chamberlain became a symbol of the "betrayal" to Hitler at Munich once it became clear that Hitler's demands were basically insatiable. In such instances there is an obvious positive feedback loop linking the intractability of one party with that of the other, and a Richardson process—with major grievance components on both sides—will be well underway. If the subordinate party Y is the initial intractable party, we may also anticipate a growing sensitivity coefficient on the part of X. Perhaps X will be tempted to employ a preemptive strike tactic as well.

An important implication for the analyst is that it may be necessary to examine leadership struggles within both parties and to recognize that actions by party X may undercut or reinforce leadership policies in party Y and vice versa. Often, the partisans themselves fail to give sufficient attention to such dynamic processes within the opposing party, as well as their own responsibility for changes in that other party's actions. They may simply *assume* that extremists are—and always have been—in control of the other party, or perhaps oppositely that extremists could never come into positions of power if moderates are presently in negotiating roles vis-à-vis themselves.

Thus if party X stalls in negotiations or makes only very minor concessions, this may undercut the position of moderates in party Y, so much so that they may be almost totally cut off from influencing later developments. Those leaders of party Y who become labeled as "sponsored" or as "puppets" may become scapegoats and, as symbolic representatives of party X, may suffer extreme forms of aggression or even assassination. They may also remain as symbolic pegs on which to hang a continued hatred or distrust of party X.

All of this suggests that controlling or dampening conflict processes often requires a number of favorable conditions, as well as a degree of tractability on both sides. In particular, G_1 and G_3 types goals must be reasonably important among a sizeable segment of both parties. High mutual dependency and a prior history of mutual exchanges of positively valued goods and services will also facilitate conflict-termination processes, a topic that will occupy our attention in the final two chapters.

Our verbal arguments have by now become sufficiently complex that it seems desirable to summarize them by means of a set of much more succinct causal diagrams. In the following chapter we shall present our primary general causal model, along with two submodels intended to supplement it by making a set of elaborations that will be relevant in more specific kinds of conflict situations. Additional submodels will be presented in later chapters.

Notes

1. For example see Cusak and Ward (1981), Ostrom (1978) and Rattinger (1975).

2. For discussions of deterrence theory see Bacharach and Lawler (1981), Bueno de Mesquita (1981), Huntington (1958), Morgan (1977), Singer (1958), and Wallace (1979).

3. See references to attribution theory and deterrence theory cited in Bacharach and Lawler (1980). See also Jones and Davis (1965), Jones and Nisbett (1971), Kelley (1971), Schopler and Layton (1974), and Tedeschi, Schlenker, and Bonoma (1973).

4. There is an extensive body of conflict-resolution literature examining alternative strategies that can be used in the PDG and other mixed cooperative-competitive setups to induce cooperation on the part of an opponent, as well as implications for outcomes whenever one party consistently employs a competitive (or punitive) strategy. See especially Axelrod (1980, 1981), P. Bonacich (1972), Gruder (1971), Kelley and Stahelski (1970), Kelley and Thibaut (1978), Pilisuk (1984), and Wagner (1983).

Chapter 5

The General Causal Model of Conflict Processes

The arguments of the previous three chapters have been complex and have involved a large number of variables. Furthermore, only a relatively small proportion of the potential interrelationships among these variables has been discussed. In our introductory chapter it was pointed out that this is a very common shortcoming of complex verbal or discursive theories and that causal diagrams can be used to present considerably more information in a compact manner. The accompanying brief discussions of such diagrams also provide convenient summaries of prior arguments. The diagrams themselves may also serve as a basis for empirical analyses, provided that a reasonably high percentage of the variables they contain can actually be measured. At that level, a series of additional considerations must also be confronted: whether or not to introduce auxiliary measurement theories so as to allow for measurement biases, whether or not to allow for nonlinearities, which of the many joint effects on a given variable are possibly nonadditive, whether or not discrete lag periods are to be used, how many data points need to be considered, and so forth.

Three causal models are presented and discussed in the chapter. The first is our general model of conflict processes. Our subsequent models will consist of elaborations on this general model, as illustrative of further complications that may need to be introduced to handle important kinds of special cases. The second model in the present chapter constitutes one such special case dealing with complications relating to mobilization processes. This second model specifies how a party's heterogeneity, ability to supply selective incentives, and surveillance capabilities may impact on its degree and efficiency of mobilization. The third submodel presented in the chapter constitutes a simplification of the second and is appropriate for micro-level conflict situations, as for example a husband-wife conflict, in which a number of complicating factor such as a group's heterogeneity and surveillance capacity, can be deleted from the model. This third model thus serves to illustrate the process through which a more complex model may be simplified in special cases.

The General Model

The general model to be discussed in the present section contains 40 variables—and therefore 780 pairs of variables—and is thus sufficiently complex that it may be difficult for the reader to spot the forest because of the trees. Therefore it may be easier to examine the much simpler schematic diagram of Figure 5.1, which indicates the causal flow of the argument without the accompanying details. This schematic diagram is keyed, by means of numbers near the bottom of each box, to the four general categories of variables discussed in the subsections that follow. These are:

1. goals, resources, and dependence;
2. rules, constraints, fatigue, and vulnerability;
3. trust, forgiveness, and sensitivity; and
4. motivation, constraints, and actual punitive behavior.

The general flow of causation is from constraints and objective characteristics of party X, to a set of subjective factors that are relevant to the other party Y, and finally to X's actual behaviors and their consequences for Y. As was true for Figure 2.1, which represented our power model discussed in Chapter 2, the focus in the general model is on the characteristics and behaviors of party X. It is assumed that a similar set of variables will be needed to analyze behavior of party Y. It is *not* assumed, however, that the parameters are the same for both parties, that they have equal power or inclination to use it, or that even the lag periods are the same for both parties.

Simplifications that can be made in the model accounting for party X's behaviors may not be justified in the case of party Y, and vice versa. One party may be a loose-knit quasi-group and the other a corporate actor, for example. By allowing for consequences at the later time period t+1, the model implies a sequence of behaviors through which each party responds to the other, sometimes almost

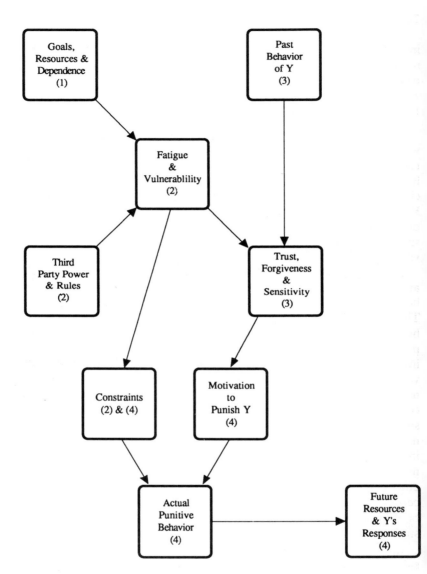

Figure 5.1 Causal flow of general model

Source: Adapted from Blalock (1987, p. 18).

immediately but possibly with considerable lags as well. Thus the model is potentially dynamic, although many important features of truly dynamic models have not been incorporated.

1. GOALS, RESOURCES, AND DEPENDENCE

The variables under discussion in the present section appear toward the top and the very left of the diagram of Figure 5.2, which represents our general model. Although as a general rule it is not legitimate to split a larger model apart except under very special circumstances, for the sake of ease of presentation the diagram of Figure 5.2 will be decomposed into four parts so as to make it less difficult for the reader to grasp the model in its entirety. The first such simplified model is given in Figure 5.2A, which contains only the variables to be discussed in the present section.

In the general model, and also in Figure 5.2A prior conflicts with Y are taken as predetermined and as causes of X's grievance levels, both of which have been placed at the extreme left of both figures. These two variables are assumed to be among the many variables that help to determine X's ideological system, with ideological variables possibly feeding back to influence grievance levels. For the time being, such ideological factors are otherwise treated as being exogenous variables that are not affected by the remaining variables in the model. Such an assumption is reasonable as long as the parties in conflict are micro units, as for example the member of a family or small local organization, but not in instances where the parties are macro actors, such as entire nation-states or even reasonably large interest groups. As a conflict evolves, macro parties may actually modify aspects of a belief system and thus turn ideological factors into endogenous variables that, themselves, must be explained in terms of certain other variables in the model. Complications such as these will be discussed in Chapters 6 and 7 and summarized in the ideological submodel provided in Chapter 7.

Grievances among party X members will play a critical role in our subsequent discussion and are here taken as functions of prior conflicts with Y. For present purposes we are using the notion of grievances in a somewhat narrower sense than in the Richardson formulation but one that is compatible with lay usage of the term. By grievances we are referring to attitudes that relate directly to Y's actual or imagined prior aggressive or exploitative actions. Such grievances are

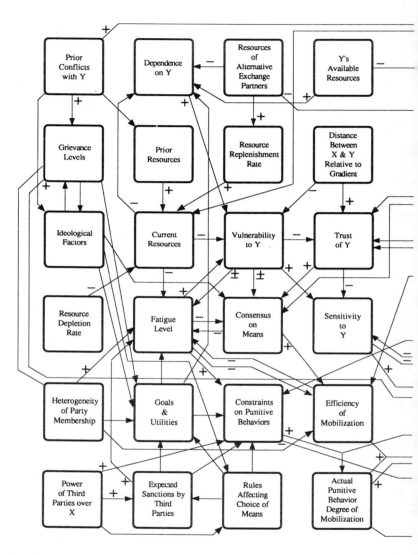

Figure 5.2 General model

Source: Adapted from Blalock (1987, pp. 20–21).

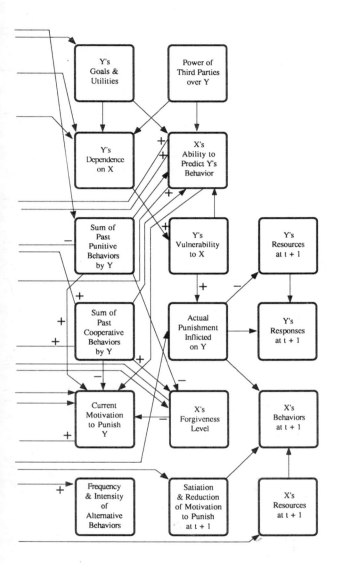

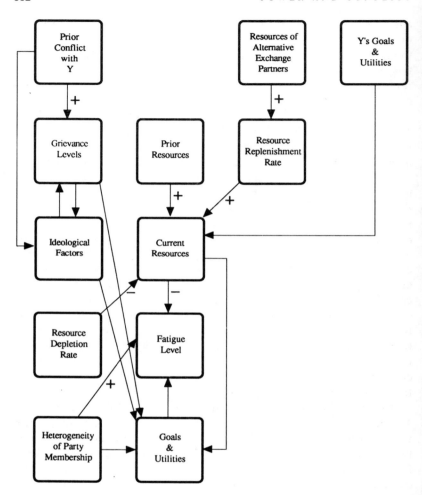

Figure 5.2A

assumed to affect the goals and utilities of X's members, which are
also taken as functions of ideological variables as well as certain
characteristics of the party in question, here party X. Such characteristics cannot be specified in such a highly general model but may include a number of objective "background" variables, as for example,

age, sex, race and ethnicity, occupation or other SES characteristics, or group memberships. As noted earlier, we are using the notion of the heterogeneity of a party's membership to refer not to such objective characteristics themselves but to the heterogeneity of *interests* as represented by goal and utility mixes, as well as preferred strategies of action.

The arrow drawn from the box labeled "Heterogeneity of Party Membership" to that designated as "Goals and Utilities" is intended to represent the argument that any reasonably complex party will contain members with diverse goals and interests. In particular, there will be "mixes" of G_1, G_2, and G_3 goals representing, respectively, goals that are shared with Y, those that are likely to be opposed by Y, and those that are basically irrelevant to the conflict itself but that may compete for scarce resources and thus impact on the ultimate course of the conflict. In the diagrams, both heterogeneity, and goals and utilities are assumed to affect the fatigue level and ultimately both the efficiency and degree of resource mobilization. This linkage between heterogeneity and these and other subsequent variables will also be discussed in more detail later in this chapter in conjunction with a submodel represented by Figure 5.3. It should specifically be noted that X's members may be differentially exposed to the conflict situation so that they may have diverse mixes of costs and benefits derived from the conflict, with these possibly changing over the course of the conflict. In our most general model, these and possibly other complications are subsumed under the heading of "heterogeneity."

It is important to recognize that goal incompatibility among party X's members is likely to be a function of the amount and nature of the resources that are available. If such resources are sufficient, for example, it may be relatively easy to satisfy members' G_3 goals without having to divert essential resources from the conflict effort. As the conflict wears on, however, and as resources become depleted, such "irrelevant" goals may have to be deferred or renounced. If so, *dissensus* may result and the efficiency of the overall effort impaired. We shall examine this kind of situation in Chapters 9 and 10, where we discuss the factors that affect the conflict process as it unfolds.

Therefore, one must not think of goal incompatibility in an absolute or fixed sense, since the degree of incompatibility may depend upon the circumstances. There may be a few instances, however, in which an actual logical inconsistency exists between two goals, or there may be an apparent inconsistency that has not been effectively rationalized by the ideological system accepted by X's membership. The incompatibility may possibly be well recognized and form the basis of a major internal cleavage between those who wish to pursue the conflict and those who are opposed to it. A detailed analysis of the specific goals, operative belief systems, and available resources would then be needed to expand on the highly general model of Figure 5.2.

Current resources are assumed to be affected by prior resource levels, the resource depletion rate and also the replenishment rate. In our discussion of Chapter 2 we noted that X's resources are a joint function of certain of X's objective properties (such as money, natural resources, weapons, and position within a hierarchical structure) combined with Y's and other parties' goals or "motive bases." Specifically, we are taking X's resources to be a function of the goals of Y and possible third parties. There is an additional complication not dealt with explicitly in the model, however. Certain of X's resources will depend upon the goals of its *own* members, which for example may have affected the resource depletion rate, as we have implied in the case of G_3 goals. Leadership authority, as well as the ability of leaders to "tap" internal objective properties (such as grain or money), will obviously require a degree of cooperation on the part of the party's membership, and this will in turn depend upon their goal mix. For the most part, however, we shall be dealing with those resources of party X that are directly applied to influence Y's behavior, in which case we shall be primarily concerned with the goals of party Y members.

It is important to distinguish between resource depletion rates and replenishment rates since, in most specific applications of the model, these variables will depend upon very different causal processes. We are focusing primarily on those objective properties (such as food, weapons, and money) that are expended during the course of the conflict, partly to apply negative sanctions to Y and partly to satisfy the ongoing needs of party X's members. Such expenditure rates are functions of the prior levels of efficiency and degree of mobilization, as well as the duration of the conflict up to the present. Actors may, of course, project or try to estimate future depletion rates on the basis of past experiences and the expected duration of the conflict.

We also need to recognize that some kinds of resources, such as food or money, are expended in such a way that rates of depletion are easily measurable, so that extrapolations can readily be made. Other resources, such as authority, may not deplete in the same sense, however, and therefore loss of authority may not become recognizable until after the fact. This means that some kinds of resources may remain taken for granted or assumed nondepletable by the actors concerned, even where outside observers may conclude that they are in fact subject to change. In a more complete submodel one therefore might want to distinguished between actual and perceived depletion rates, as well as actual and expected replenishment rates.

Replenishment rates are likely to depend on very different social processes, including the organizational efficiency of those group members who are not, themselves, directly engaged in the power confrontation—farmers, munitions workers, medical personnel, and so forth. Replenishment rates may also depend on the actions of third parties and the resources they are able and willing to supply over some specified period of time. Depletion and replenishment rates may therefore follow very different time paths during the course of a conflict, and one may be much more predictable or subject to control by either X or Y than is the other. As a conflict wears on and fatigue levels become increasingly critical, replenishment rates may come to play a more important role, especially where the duration of the conflict has been underestimated. Although it may be the difference between the two rates that is critical in determining the level of either party's current resources, it therefore seems wise to treat them as conceptually and empirically distinct variables in the general model.

Although our models take note of third parties in this simplified two-party formulation, we must keep in mind the kind of point that Skocpol (1979), among others, has emphasized. Third-party interactions may have depleted either X's or Y's stocks of resources or may require that they set aside a substantial portion of their total resources to be used in a potential conflict with such other parties. Thus, Y's responses to X may be inconsistent and vacillating or perhaps primarily defensive in nature because of the actions, real or threatened, by these third parties.

In one sense this type of complication may be handled by treating such third parties as though they had formed a coalition with, say, X, as long as we do not imply that such a coalition has necessarily been planned or entered into explicitly. Party X may simply take advantage of a prior conflict between Y and another party, as Skocpol argued actually occurred in the cases of the French, Russian, and Chinese social revolutions. Our formulation thus allows for third-party influences that operate *through* one or another of the explictly included boxes in the diagram, even though we have not attempted to provide a large number of additional boxes representing the explanatory mechanisms needed to account for third-party interactions with the two parties that are the direct focus of attention in our general model.

2. RULES, CONSTRAINTS, FATIGUE, AND VULNERABILITY

In this section we shall be concerned with that portion of the general model that deals with (1) the relationships between vulnerability and dependence; (2) relationships among rules, third-party power, and constraints upon means; and (3) how all of these factors relate to fatigue and, ultimately, the degree and efficiency of the mobilization effort. Boxes representing these variables are located near the top-center and lower-left portions of the general model of Figure 5.2 and have also been pulled out, for presentational purposes, and used in the simplified model of Figure 5.2B.

As we have indicated, the notion of X's dependency on Y is central to Emerson's approach to power and is a function of Y's available resources needed by X, the availability of alternative suppliers to X, and X's goals and utilities. Dependency is distinguished from the notion of vulnerability, which is assumed in the model to be caused by dependency *and* a number of other factors. Vulnerability, as the term is used here, is a somewhat more general notion than that of viability, as discussed by Boulding (1962), since we do not want to imply that actual survival is necessarily at stake. Party X may be vulnerable to Y without its survival being threatened, though indeed survivability as a distinct entity may be at issue in some specific applications of the model.

A party may be highly vulnerable to another party without being dependent on it in Emerson's sense of the term. A small nation may, for example, be almost entirely self-sufficient economically and yet be a "sitting duck" for a possibly remote larger nation, should the latter wish to attack it. In this sense it is "conditionally viable" in Boulding's usage of that term, but we shall refer to it more simply as being vulnerable to Y. In the general model, vulnerability to Y is taken as a function of the loss-of-power gradient and the spatial distance between the two parties, as well as X's current resources and fatigue level. The dependency of X on Y is assumed to be a function

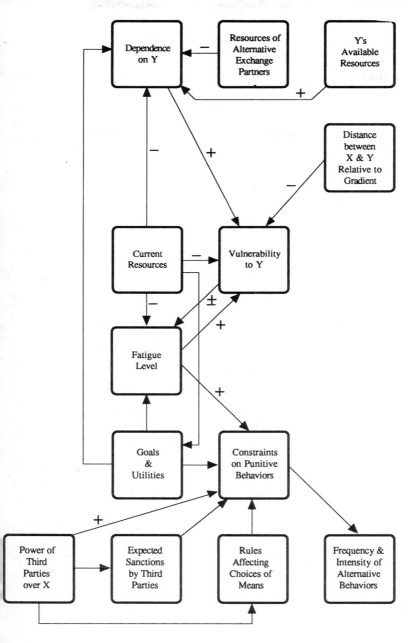

Figure 5.2B

of X's current resources and its own goals as well as the availability of alternative suppliers.

Although not explicitly incorporated in the general model of Figure 5.2 it should also be noted that actors may misperceive their own and the other party's dependency, vulnerability, and the loss-of-power gradient. In a more detailed submodel it might therefore be advisable to insert *perceived* values of these variables as intervening between their "true" values (if these could be identified and measured) and factors such as fatigue levels and mobilization variables. Members of party X, for example, may feel unjustifiably secure if they overestimate the effectiveness of their defensive barriers and thus the steepness of the loss-of-power gradient.

The case of France in World War II immediately comes to mind. Once its Maginot Line had been bypassed, France's mobilization efforts almost immediately collapsed, much to the surprise of nearly everyone. Quite possibly a party that has made one or more recent mistakes of this nature may on subsequent occasions misperceive the situation in the opposite direction, in this instance believing that the gradient is nearly horizontal and, thus, defensive resources practically useless. The general point is that both parties will tend to act on the basis of their perceptions of such variables, with these perceptions being only partly a function of the objective features of the setting.

There may be special cases where it is reasonable to simplify the model by treating vulnerability and dependency as interchangeable. Specifically, this kind of simplification may be appropriate whenever the loss-of-power gradient and spatial distance separating the two parties can be ignored or when it can safely be assumed that party Y will automatically choose to take advantage of X's dependency. As noted, there may also be instances where it is reasonable to assume that behaviors can rather simply be predicted without recourse to analyses of sources of perceptual distortions or detailed analyses of conflicting goals and party heterogeneity. Since we believe such factors to be operative in a very large proportion of real social conflicts, however, it is our position that general models of conflict processes need to take them explicitly into account.

The relationship between vulnerability and fatigue is likely to be complex and, as the diagram implies, may involve reciprocal causation. A party that is highly vulnerable to another may take steps to reduce its dependency by modifying its goal structure so as to achieve a higher degree of internal consensus and to renounce those goals that require resources that are controlled by Y. If so, its fatigue level may be reduced. On the other hand, if there is already a high degree of *dissensus* regarding the desirability of reducing such a dependency (and thus vulnerability as well), this may result in internal cleavages that distract from the mobilization effort and increase the overall fatigue level. The indeterminacy of the sign of the net impact of vulnerability on fatigue is represented in the figure by a " ± " symbol.

In the opposite causal direction, a high degree of fatigue may weaken the party's defenses and, thus, reduce the steepness of the loss-of-power gradient, thereby increasing its vulnerability to Y. Submodels appropriate to different kinds of conflict situations would be needed to spell out the detailed mechanisms expected in these special cases. It may turn out that a party's heterogeneity may *interact* nonadditively with vulnerabilty in their joint effects on fatigue levels. For simplicity, this possibility has not been represented in the diagram. We should note, however, that any applications of Richardson's model that treat fatigue as a constant multiplier of X's (or Y's) level of armaments are undoubtedly gross oversimplifications of real conflict processes.

In the bottom-left corner of Figures 5.2 and 5.2B we have introduced another exogenous variable, the power of third parties over X, which is taken as a cause of expected sanctions by third parties and the rules affecting the choice of means used by X. We cannot take such rules as givens, as is common practice among game theorists, because both parties X and Y may help to shape these rules and may, under certain conditions, elect to violate them. We assume, however, that when third parties have strong interests in preserving such rules and when they are in a position to sanction X (and Y) for rule violation, then such rules will place certain constraints on the means that X and Y choose to employ.

Specifically, these constraints are likely to include constraints on punitive behaviors, hence the arrows drawn to this box from the two boxes pertaining to third parties and the box referring to rules. Of course there may be multiple third parties, some of which elect to sanction some rule violations but not others, but such complexities are not incorporated into our general model. Actually it is the *expected* responses by third parties to rule violations that are critical, and we suppose that these, in turn, are based on the previous behaviors (and warnings) of such third parties. A more detailed model would thus allow for misinterpretations and miscalculations by X, as well as a possible lack of consensus among X's members with respect to the expected responses by third parties. None of these complications is included in the model.

Toward the bottom-right side of Figures 5.2 and 5.2B we have included a residual box titled "Frequency and Intensity of Alternative Behaviors," which is taken as caused by constraints on punitive behaviors and, of course, other factors that have not been included in the model. Here we shall not consider what these alternative behaviors may be, but they certainly include an attempt to escape from the conflict situation, perhaps by conceding defeat or giving up valued resources such as land, fortifications, property rights, or claims to Y's possessions. Or they may include behaviors that are oriented to achieving G_1 goals that are held in common with Y, with a view to increasing the proportion of positive exchanges as compared with negative ones. Obviously the election of one or another of such alternative behaviors will depend upon the goal mix of X's members, as well as the internal distribution of power among them. Once more, complications such as these have not been incorporated into the figures.

3. TRUST, FORGIVENESS, AND SENSITIVITY

The variables discussed in this section appear near the right center of the diagram of Figure 5.2 and focus on the subjective factors of sensitivity, forgiveness, the predictability of Y's response, and trust, all of which affect X's motivation to apply negative sanctions to Y and thus to engage in conflict. For the reader's convenience, these variables have also been represented in the simplified model of Figure 5.2C.

The immediate causes of trust, forgiveness, and motivation to punish Y are assumed to be Y's past punitive and cooperative behaviors toward X. Except for the arrow drawn from prior conflicts with Y to past punitive behaviors of Y, these past behaviors on the part of Y are treated as predetermined (or uncaused) in the model but will obviously depend on past values of many of the same variables that also appear in the model. Thus, although this part of the model is technically recursive since it involves lagged values of endogenous variables, it would also be reasonable to consider this entire subsystem as being nonrecursive or as involving nearly simultaneous reciprocal causation or feedback loops. In the special case where definite lag periods can be specified, and whenever data collection points coin-

The General Causal Model of Conflict Processes

121

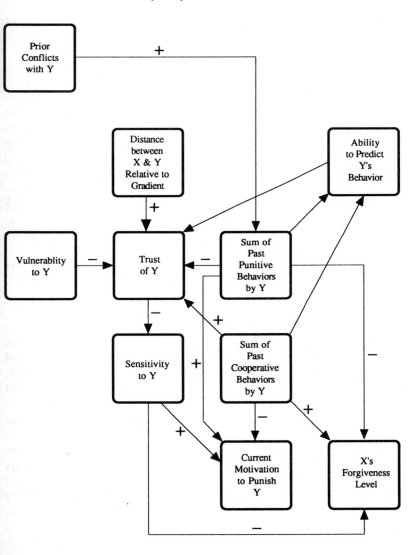

Figure 5.2C

cide with these lag periods, such a nonrecursive setup can more simply be treated as recursive, as is the case in Figures 5.2 and 5.2C. What we have not included in the figures, however, is the notion that the coefficients representing the effects of Y's past behaviors may become smaller and smaller as one goes backward in time, as modeled in Abelson's (continuous time) formulation and his notion of forgiveness coefficients.

Party X's forgiveness level, which was treated as a constant in Abelson's model, is taken as a function of these past behaviors of Y, both cooperative and punitive. It is also assumed to be partly determined by X's sensitivity and thus indirectly by X's vulnerability to Y. The presumption is that ordinarily the greater X's sensitivity (and vulnerability), the less willing X will be to forgive and forget Y's previous punitive behaviors. Party X's memory with regard to Y's previous *cooperative* acts may be less directly affected by sensitivity, however. At least it seems less plausible to attempt to predict the direction of the relationship between these two variables. Of course, X's forgiveness of Y will also be affected by other variables not included in the model, factors such as the vested interests of leaders who may wish to "use" Y's transgressions to consolidate their own power or to distract members' attention from internal problems. Although they have not been incorporated into either figure, ideological factors may also be at work. In particular, the prevailing belief system may be highly simplistic and one that tends to place blame on outside parties, in this instance Y. If so, X's forgiveness coefficient may be small.

Party X's ability to predict Y's behavior will also be affected by Y's past behaviors, particularly if X perceives the relationship between the two parties as being basically unchanged. The *sequencing* of Y's actions is not included in our general model, however, though more specific submodels might be constructed to take this into account. As noted in the previous chapter, one strategy for inducing cooperative behavior from a potential opponent is to apply a positive tit-for-tat sequence in which X initially tries cooperation and continues to respond in this manner until Y employs a competitive or punitive response, in which case X reciprocates with a similar response. If the two parties come to "understand" one another in this fashion, the future behaviors of each may be predictable, regardless (or perhaps because) of the actual empirical frequencies of the two types of responses. The model assumes that predictability will impact on X's expectations concerning Y's responses.

We have implied that the notion of "trust" is a bit slippery. There is a sense in which we may say that X trusts Y to the degree that Y's response is easily predicted, even though it may be a punitive one. If so, then "trust" and "predictability" would be virtually synonymous. In the layman's usage, however, trust seems to involve not simply predictability but also the anticipation of a highly favorable mix of Y responses in the direction of positive ones. The idea is that Y is expected to behave in a manner that is highly compatible with X's own interests, which will usually imply cooperation and a minimal use of negative sanctions. If there is a high degree of trust involved, then whenever Y in fact does employ negative sanctions these are interpreted by X to be merely temporary and motivated by a desire to restore a cooperative relationship or to benefit X over the long run.

Thus X's trust is assumed to incorporate both high predictability and a large proportion of cooperative or at least nonpunitive acts on the part of Y, as well as a recognition by X that whatever punitive acts have been employed by Y have been for justifiable reasons. In our own simplified model, trust is taken as a joint function of predictability and the mix of previous punitive and cooperative acts, without incorporating such interpretive cognitive processes. A more complete model focusing on cooperation as well as conflict processes could obviously be developed.

Our model also takes trust as a function of the distance between the two parties, relative to the (perceived) loss-of-power gradient. The assumption is that a party, especially a weak one, can be more safe in trusting a distant party because of the fact that it will be more costly for it to engage in conflict. Neighboring countries or ethnic groups, for example, are notoriously distrustful of one another, undoubtedly because of their relatively higher vulnerabilities as well as the likelihood of a history of past conflicts, the memories of which have been kept alive so as to maintain potential mobilization efforts.

Since more remote countries (or other parties) may also border on a given country's immediate neighbors, and thus have had similarly hostile encounters with them, there may develop higher degrees of trust among such remote parties than among their much closer counterparts. Indeed, there have been numerous historical instances where temporary coalitions have formed among nations or city-states that have adjoined a particular rival but that, themselves, have been safely distanced from one another. Of course much more than trust has been involved in such coalition-formation processes, but at least the temporary level of trust must have been great enough to permit such cooperative arrangements.

Boulding's notion of "conditional viability" may also be useful in accounting for such arrangements. If party X is threatened by an immediate neighbor, party Y, it may form a coalition with one of Y's other neighbors, say Z, even where Z may be even more powerful than Y. From X's standpoint, although Z may constitute a potential threat, the assumption may be that Z will not choose to employ its power against a more remote party such as itself. At least Y is assumed to be a more immediate threat than Z.

Party X's sensitivity to and trust of Y will also depend on X's perceptions of Y's goals, as implied in the above comments concerning spatial proximity. It is not Y's *actual* goals that are at issue here, but rather how these are filtered through X's cognitive processes. Here such things as secrecy and deception may play important roles. Party Y may attempt to convince X that its own intentions lie in a given direction, whereas X may interpret Y's statements in view of Y's previous actions. A bluff or promise by Y may or may not be taken seriously. Party Y's reputation for risk-taking or reckless behaviors may also be critical in shaping X's expectations, as well as X's level of trust.

For reasons of parsimony, none of these variables appear explicitly in our general model. Here it is sufficient to point out that it will generally be to each party's advantage to increase the other party's level of trust, and that for this reason potential future encounters may need to be considered by each party. If Y has rather consistently behaved in the past so as to lower X's trust level, then this may serve to place X "on guard" and to increase its sensitivity coefficient in Richardson's (1960) sense of that term. In our general model, we have simply drawn in a direct arrow from trust of Y to sensitivity to Y to represent such a possibly highly-complex process. Likewise, a direct arrow has been drawn from X's sensitivity to Y to X's motivation to punish Y.

4. MOTIVATION, CONSTRAINTS, AND ACTUAL PUNITIVE BEHAVIOR

Toward the bottom center of Figures 5.2 and 5.2D we have taken party X's current motivation to punish Y as a function of grievance levels, Y's previous punitive and cooperative behaviors (which also

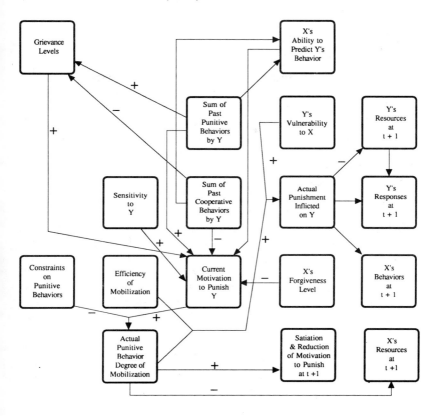

Figure 5.2D

affect grievances but do not completely determine them), X's sensitivity and forgiveness levels, and X's ability to predict Y's responses.

Of course it is actually X's *perceptions* of Y's past behaviors that are the critical factor which helps to determine X's motivation to punish Y. We have implicitly included this notion by referring to a *summation* of such past behaviors, with the weights attached to each distinct behavior being a function of X's memory decay factor. It is very possible, for example, that X may have a very long memory with respect to Y's punitive actions but a much shorter one in connection with Y's previous cooperative behaviors. Except for showing a direct link between X's forgiveness level and X's motivation to punish Y, we have not dealt with such added complications in the general model. These could be incorporated into a more detailed submodel for this portion of the overall process.

We are also distinguishing between current motivation to punish Y and X's grievance levels. Grievances refer to attitudes stemming from X's interpretations of Y's prior behaviors. Outside observers may or may not take such grievances to be "legitimate," since such attitudes may be filtered through an ideological system that may distort Y's actual past behaviors or interpret them in the light of X's own peculiar interests, perhaps ignoring X's own role in the process. In addition, X's current motivation to punish Y will depend upon certain other variables, as already indicated. Again, in special applications of the model it may be reasonable to treat past grievances and current motivation to punish as interchangeable, making it possible to simplify the general model. Such a simplification may be particularly appropriate if one is analyzing conflicts of rather short duration, where distinctions between past and current values are relatively unimportant and where it may also be difficult to distinguish empirically between grievances and motivation to punish the other party.

It is assumed that the variable labeled "Actual Punitive Behavior: Degree of Mobilization" is a multiplicative function of the two variables, constraints on punitive behaviors, which already been discussed, and X's current motivation to punish Y. This nonadditive joint effect is represented diagrammatically by having the two arrows join before they reach the dependent variable, rather than showing separate arrows into it. The implication of a multiplicative joint effect is that if constraints are extremely high or if motivation is virtually zero, there will be virtually no actual punitive behavior regardless of the level of the other independent variable. If the constraints are low and motivation high, however, the joint impact is expected to be greater than in the case of an additive or compensatory model.

The amount of punishment actually inflicted on Y is taken to be a somewhat more complex interactive function of the three variables labeled "Actual Punitive Behavior: Degree of Mobilization," "X's Efficiency of Mobilization," and "Y's Vulnerability to X." The arrows coming from the first pair of these variables join, indicating a multiplicative relationship between them. The idea is that even if X exerts a large quantity of punitive behavior toward Y, it will not have any actual impact if the efficiency is near zero, since efficiency is assumed to interact multiplicatively with degree of mobilization to affect the amount of power actually exerted. Likewise, efficiency will be of little importance if there is virtually no punitive behavior employed. With both efficiency and actual punitive behavior high, however, the product of the two will mean that the total power delivered will be considerable.

There is, however, the matter of Y's vulnerability to X. If this vulnerability is close to zero, then even though there have been extensive punitive actions, efficiently delivered, the actual punishment inflicted on Y will be negligible. By the same token, if there is either near-zero efficiency or very minimal punitive action taken by X, then even though Y may be highly vulnerable, the actual punishment inflicted on Y will also be negligible. If all three variables—actual punitive behavior delivered, efficiency, and Y's vulnerability to X—have high levels, however, the actual punishment inflicted is expected to be substantial.[1]

Finally, there will be impacts on later values of a number of variables, which means that there will not only be implications for the continuation of the particular conflict in question but for possible future conflicts as well. A high level of actual punitive behavior by X will tend to deplete its own future resources at time $t+1$ and perhaps also satiate or even reduce X's motivation to punish Y in the future. This latter effect will ordinarily be amplified to the degree that X believes that Y has actually been injured in the process, though it is possible that under some circumstances guilt mechanisms may operate to intensify X's motivation to punish Y, a possibility that is ignored in the model, where we have indicated a positive relationship between X's punitive behavior and satiation levels, and thus its motivation to punish Y at a later time.

The model also implies that the actual level of punishment inflicted on Y will affect Y's future resources, presumably negatively—at least initially. It will also lead Y to reassess the damages and thus may modify Y's response at later times. Party X's own future behaviors are also presumed to be affected by the amount of actual punishment inflicted on Y, but we have not allowed explicitly in the model for misperceptions or miscalculations on the part of X. Nor does the model specify the nature of Y's response, which may be either in the direction of intensifying the conflict by attempting to inflict even greater damage on X or in the direction of reducing its own level of punitive actions.

By implication, the general model allows for repeated cycles of stimulus-response behaviors by X and Y. We may next use the model to try to account for Y's responses by reversing the roles of the two parties and tracing out the consequences of Y's responses for X. Ideally, by moving through a sequence of such behaviors by both X and Y, one could treat the model as nearly recursive. In practice, however, it may be advisable to formulate simultaneous-equation systems that allow for different parameters for the two parties but that do not explicitly deal with the temporal sequences involved.

Our general model is already sufficiently complex that there seems little point in formulating such a two-sided model unless and until the one-sided one has been more completely specified. We have already suggested a few ways in which progress might be made in this regard. The submodels that follow also deal with several different kinds of elaborations on the basic general model.

A Submodel Linking Heterogeneity and Mobilization

Whenever the party of concern is sufficiently complex that members' interests are likely to diverge and mobilization cannot be taken for granted, an additional set of variables will need to be considered. These include the party's heterogeneity, the degree of consensus on means, the party's surveillance capacity and ability to supply selective incentives, and the effectiveness of such selective incentives in affecting both the degree and efficiency of mobilization. The submodel provided in this section is intended to deal with complications of this nature.

In the submodel of Figure 5.3, ideological factors are taken as exogenous and are simply lumped together in a single box in the top-left corner. These ideological factors are assumed to affect directly only three kinds of variables in the model: heterogeneity of membership, the need for selective incentives, and consensus on means. Obviously, then, a more complete model might be constructed by combining features of the present model and the ideological submodel to be discussed in Chapter 7. Recall that we are conceptualizing the party's heterogeneity in terms of goal preferences or utilities, as well as the subjective probabilities associated with each. Belief systems obviously impact on such utilities and subjective probabilities and thus also on the degree to which party members are homogeneous or heterogeneous with respect to such preferences and expectancies. Apart from this impact of ideological factors, however, heterogeneity is also treated as exogenous to the model under consideration.

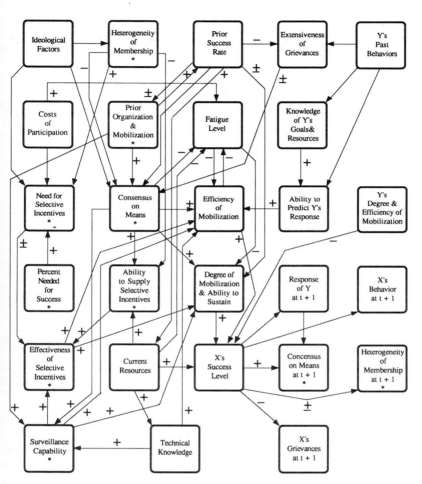

Figure 5.3 Heterogeneity submodel

Source: Adapted from Blalock (1987, p. 31).

The notion of selective incentives plays an important role in the model, but we must distinguish between the need for selective incentives, the party's ability to supply them, and their effectiveness in affecting the mobilization effort. Therefore we have provided three separate boxes to represent these variables, all of which appear toward the middle of the first two columns. We leave open the exact definition of the term "selective incentive" but presume that in many instances one would want to include more than strictly material rewards and punishments.

A party's need for selective incentives is taken as a function of four kinds of variables: ideological factors, heterogeneity of membership, the (expected) costs of participation to individual members, and the percentage of the party's membership that is actually needed for success in the mobilization effort. Heterogeneity, per se, may in some instances not be as critical as the relative importance of G_2 as compared with G_1 and G_3 goals, but we assume that heterogeneity will generally create problems for the party and that it will result in the need for a variety of incentives to appeal to such a diversity of interests. We have also drawn an arrow, with an associated negative sign, from heterogeneity to consensus on means, with consensus in turn affecting the party's ability to supply needed selective incentives.

In accord with Hechter's (1987) argument, we have drawn an arrow from surveillance capability to the effectiveness of selective incentives, with this latter variable also being affected by both the need for selective incentives and the party's ability to supply them. Surveillance capability, in turn, is assumed positively influenced by the availability of technical knowledge, consensus on means, and the party's prior level of organization and mobilization. Surveillance capability is also assumed to have direct positive effects on both the degree and efficiency of mobilization, thereby recognizing that it does not necessarily operate on them through selective incentives alone.

Another critical variable in the model is consensus on means. This is assumed to be influenced not only by ideological factors and heterogeneity, but also by the party's prior level of organization and mobilization, its prior success rate in dealing with party Y, and the extensiveness of X's grievances. Not shown in the figure is the *heterogeneity* of grievance levels among X's members, or of their relative power in impacting on subsequent variables, including both degree and efficiency of mobilization.

All of these prior causes of consensus on means appear at or near the top of the figure. The linkage between grievances and consensus is taken to have an indeterminate sign, as it may not be at all obvious to members how to cope with an opponent in spite of the level of grievances against it. In general, we would expect such a *dissensus* to be greatest in the case of weak parties having a long history of exploitation or conflict with a very powerful opponent whose past behaviors have been difficult to predict.

Consensus on means is then taken as a cause of a number of other variables in the model. These include a negative impact on fatigue and positive effects on surveillance capability, ability to supply selective incentives, and both the degree and efficiency of mobilization. The party's current resources are treated as predetermined in the model except for their being affected by X's prior success rate. They are assumed to have positive impacts on the availability of technical knowledge and the ability to supply selective incentives but negative effects on the fatigue level. Other possible effects of this variable are taken as indirect.

Most of the remaining linkages in the model are straightforward. Prior successes are assumed to impact negatively on the extensiveness of grievances, which is also affected by Y's past behaviors. There is a presumed positive feedback loop between fatigue and efficiency (since both signs are negative). Efficiency is also assumed to be positively affected by X's ability to predict Y's responses, with this variable in turn being affected by Y's own past behaviors and X's knowledge of Y's goals and resources. Degree of mobilization is impacted by many of the same variables plus X's prior success rate.

Finally, X's level of success is affected not only by X's degree and efficiency of mobilization but also by X's current resources in accord with our previously discussed multiplicative model. Because of their peculiar locations in the diagram, however, we have drawn three distinct arrows from these variables, rather than having them join before reaching the box labeled "X's Success level." Success level is, of course, also affected in a similar fashion by Y's degree and efficiency of mobilization. Not shown in the diagram are the impacts on success coming from the behaviors of third parties or from exogenous forces that are not under either party's control.

Level of success is then assumed to influence a number of other factors at a later time $t+1$. These include X's heterogeneity and consensus levels, its grievances and its behaviors at later times, and of course Y's responses as well. These variables in turn affect subsequent values of variables that appear elsewhere in the model.

A Mobilization Submodel for Interpersonal Conflicts

The previous submodel contained 27 variables, many of which are certainly not relevant in instances where one is dealing with micro-level processes where the parties concerned are persons or very small homogeneous groups. There may even be a few instances involving conflicts between tightly controlled corporate groups where a party's heterogeneity, free riding, and related coordination problems can be ignored or considered to be of such minor importance that it is not necessary to complicate the model with their inclusion. In all such instances, it may be advisable to simplify the model by dropping a number of variables.

For the sake of specificity, let us assume that we are dealing with an interpersonal conflict situation, say between two coworkers or perhaps a husband and wife. Certainly, third parties, rules and norms, and other situational factors will need to be taken into consideration. Each party will have "surveillance" problems regarding the behaviors of the other, but it will obviously be meaningless to refer to the surveillance of a party's own members. Nor will consensus on means, internal heterogeneity, free riding, or the use and effectiveness of selective incentives need to be included in the model. Indeed, it would only confuse matters to retain them. Of the 27 variables included in our heterogeneity-mobilization submodel, the 10 that have been marked with asterisks in Figure 5.3 may therefore be omitted in models of interpersonal conflict. If we do so, we arrive at the simplified submodel given in Figure 5.4.

In simplifying any model, the first step, as implied, is to delete whatever variables do not belong in the simplified model and to connect the remaining as in the original model. In other words, one should (at least temporarily) retain all those arrows that link the retained variables. The next step is to examine those arrows that connected the retained and omitted variables, looking especially for instances in which an omitted variable served as an intervening variable between two of the retained variables.

It now becomes important to ask, "Why was the variable dropped?" If it was dropped merely because information was missing, or because the intervening variable could not be measured, one assumes that it continues to affect the dependent variable. If, for example, $X \rightarrow Y \rightarrow Z$, and if Y has been dropped, the revised model would show a "direct" link between X and Z, since it remains true that a

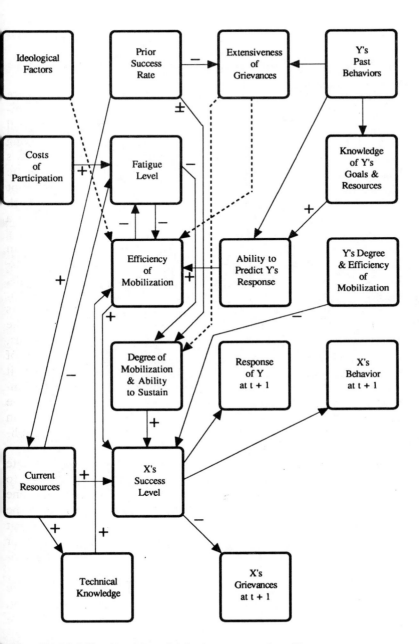

Figure 5.4 Mobilization submodel for interpersonal conflicts

133

change in X is expected to produce a change in Z, even though it has not been possible to measure Y. We have a less "rich" model for interpretive purposes, however, since we cannot specify the mechanism through which X affects Z.

The case at hand is somewhat different, however. For interpersonal conflicts, notions such as the party's heterogeneity and consensus on means make no sense. Or, one might consider heterogeneity (within a single person) to take on a fixed value of zero, and consensus a maximum value of, say, unity. If so, then a factor that affects heterogeneity could not indirectly affect a subsequent variable "through" heterogeneity, if heterogeneity retained a fixed value of zero for all interpersonal conflicts. We have drawn in three dashed arrows in Figure 5.4 to represent this sort of situation. One of these connects ideological dimensions to efficiency of mobilization. In the more complex model of Figure 5.3, the idea was that certain aspects of a belief system (to be discussed in more detail in Chapters 6 and 7) will have impacts on the degree to which a party's members think alike, with this in turn impacting on the efficiency of their mobilization. But what if the party consists of a single person? Can ideological factors impact on efficiency of mobilization, apart from their effects on "heterogeneity"? If the conclusion is in the affirmative, then the dashed arrow should be replaced by a solid one, indicating that in the original model as well it would have been appropriate to link ideology to efficiency of mobilization with a direct arrow. This would then imply that ideological factors may impact on mobilization through alternative paths that do not pass through heterogeneity.

Thus, by examining the simplified model, additional insights may be obtained regarding the more complex model. Perhaps, even though the party's "heterogeneity" is taken as zero in the simplified model, there is a somewhat analogous variable appropriate at the micro level. This might be the individual actor's "confusion" or "inconsistency" or "ambivalence" about various courses of action, with these in turn affecting efficiency of mobilization. If so, one or more of these variables might be added to the "simplified" model, thereby making it somewhat more complex. One obvious implication of such an intellectual exercise is that no causal model should be treated as "final" or "complete." As we have implied in several places, our very general models will undoubtedly have to be modified as soon as one attempts to apply them to important special cases.

A similar type of argument might be made in the case of the other two dashed arrows in Figure 5.4, both of which lead out of the box titled "Extensiveness of Grievances." In the more complex submodel of Figure 5.3, one of these went from consensus on means to efficiency of mobilization and the other went from this now-omitted intervening variable to degree of mobilization. One would once again ask whether or not a micro party's grievance level would be expected to affect either its degree or its efficiency of mobilization. Perhaps it will be taken to affect degree of mobilization but not efficiency. If so, one would want a direct arrow from grievance level to degree of mobilization, both in the micro model of Figure 5.4 and the more general submodel of Figure 5.3.

In the interest of simplicity we have not inserted other dashed arrows into the reduced model of Figure 5.4, but readers should examine the linkages involving all omitted variables to discover and then analyze possible modifications that should be made in Figure 5.3 in the special cases of whatever types of micro-level conflict situations they are attempting to analyze.

This completes our discussion of the general model and two specific submodels. Before presenting additional submodels, we turn to the question of how ideological factors may influence, and be influenced by, conflict processes. After providing an ideological submodel toward the close of Chapter 7, we then turn to discussions of conflict groups and the mechanisms by which conflicts maintain themselves and ultimately are terminated.

Note

1. If three variables are predicted to have multiplicative joint effects on a dependent variable, this will imply a second-order statistical interaction among them.

Chapter 6

Ideological Supports for Conflict

Our concern is with a wide variety of conflict situations, ranging from those that involve micro parties, such as neighbors, coworkers, or spouses, to large nation-states as corporate actors. Obviously, ideological factors play very different kinds of roles depending on the nature of the conflict involved. Even though a conflict between two neighbors or coworkers may be of longstanding duration, and may have escalated in accord with a Richardson-Abelson type of dynamic process, the grievances, fatigue levels, and sensitivities involved may have little or nothing to do with what we ordinarily consider to be ideological factors. Instead, we may prefer to think of such conflicts as being influenced by a set of normative factors or rules that inhibit certain extreme forms of retaliation. In contrast, a conflict between two nation-states may very definitely involve a clash of ideological systems, each of which supports one or the other side of the dispute.

Even in the macro-level conflicts, it will rarely be the case that the parties concerned do not share certain beliefs or even a common ideology that, however, may be subject to differential interpretations or distortions in accord with the interests of the respective parties. This is not to say that leaders consciously manipulate ideologies in order to influence their followers, although this may sometimes be the case. As often as not, leaders may be rigid adherents to an ideological system, which they may subscribe to far more intensely than do other party members. Yet they may use or take advantage of such a belief system so as to improve both the degree and efficiency of the mobilization effort, as well as to consolidate their own power positions.

In this and the following chapter we shall be primarily concerned with macro-level conflict situations in which entire belief systems play a major role in shaping the nature of the conflict process itself. As Gurr (1970) has noted, most active participants may not be directly influenced by sophisticated ideological systems, but rather by a small number of slogans or simple rituals that have been linked to such more inclusive belief systems. "Making the World safe for Democracy," ridding it of "Communists and Atheists," or "Saving the Free World" are examples of such slogans, all of which represent shorthand, if not overly simplistic, representations of a very complex set of ideas Americans have inherited from Europe and then shaped in our own unique fashion. Lurking behind the slogans, then, is an ideological system that needs to be analyzed if one is to understand Americans' support of the several major and minor wars we have engaged in during the course of the twentieth century.

By our definition, conflict involves the exchange of negative sanctions and entails the inflicting of punishment and thus costs to both parties. Although there may also be the anticipation of future rewards, as well as whatever satisfactions direct aggression may bring, additional motivational incentives to individuals will generally be necessary if the conflict is to be sustained over any prolonged period. In any reasonably heterogeneous group some members may suffer more than others, and those who suffer the most may not be those who expect to benefit from the spoils of victory. Free riding can be expected, as we have noted, and most certainly will have demoralizing impacts on those members who have made the greatest sacrifices. Thus parties involved in conflicts will ordinarily be faced with serious problems of motivating their members to engage in these costly and often risky behaviors and of castigating those who do not. Belief systems or ideologies play a crucial role in this regard.

Many kinds of ideological devices are well-known. The opposing party or enemy is likely to be blamed for a large number of offenses, past and present, and to be depicted in an extremely unfavorable light: as immoral, dangerous, treacherous, inhumane, and generally deserving of even more punishment than is currently being meted out. Not only is extreme distrust of the opposing party reinforced by carefully contrived negative stereotypes, but by implication internal enemies are anticipated and deviants accused and punished as disloyal. Motives of those on both sides are oversimplified by seeing the opposing party as a "contrast conception" embodying the exact opposite of the "good" characteristics of the loyal in-group member (Copeland, 1939). Since the opponent cannot be trusted, one's own potentially illegitmate behaviors are seen as necessary defensive or preemptive measures.

Possible escapist reactions by one's own members are anticipated and discouraged by, for example, exaggerating the expected costs of defeat by a totally unscrupulous opponent. Cowardice or traitorous acts are punished by extreme sanctions applied not only to the individuals concerned but to members of their families or other reference groups, which can therefore be counted upon to apply effective informal controls on their members. And, of course, beliefs about the supernatural can practically always be modified so as to reinforce a highly compatible system of social controls and to alter subjective probabilities of success. Not only will God punish those who defect and reward those who make extreme sacrifices, but He will sustain us in our greatest need and ultimately assure our victory.

Belief systems cannot be created overnight, nor can they be altered in essential ways without introducing problems and increasing the risk of dissension. Therefore a certain groundwork needs to be laid prior to the outbreak of any given conflict so that existing principles may be readily invoked and applied to some specific target group. Furthermore, any ideological system will inevitably contain inconsistencies or will tend to favor one category of members over another, thereby possibly aggravating internal cleavages based on differing vested interests in either the conflict process itself or its expected outcome. Beliefs that are functional from the standpoint of inducing members to initiate a conflict with another party may be dysfunctional if it is necessary to attract coalition partners or if the conflict has become costly and is of far greater duration than was originally anticipated. And certain structural features of the situation, as well as characteristics of the conflicting parties, may make it much more difficult for some beliefs to be accepted than others.

In the remaining sections of the chapter we shall examine a number of complications involving the compatibility or incompatibility of various types of belief systems with a macro party's engagement in the conflict process. In doing so, we must keep in mind the heterogeneity of the party's membership, as well as the likelihood that any ideological system will almost necessarily have differing appeals to specific party segments and that most members will tend to select out only a very small subset of salient beliefs around which to justify or motivate their actions.

Setting the Stage

We recognize that some parties are much more belligerent than others. Structural factors can often be invoked to account for many such differences, as for example between nomadic and settled agricultural peoples or between geographically insulated societies and those that have long histories of warfare brought about by invading neighbors. Ideological factors also play an important role in many such instances, however, if only that of reminding members of their historical encounters with hostile groups. What kinds of ideological dimensions or features seem most conducive to belligerency, rapid and effective mobilization for conflict, or a paranoid orientation to the outside world?

Some ideological systems are much more simplistic than others are in the sense that they provide unambiguous (though possibly misleading) interpretations of others' actions, as well as guidelines for response. The "eye-for-an-eye" mentality of the Old Testament is a case in point, as is the contemporary revenge orientation that characterizes most of the Middle East, the Sicilian Mafia, and many smaller conflict groups such as the provisional wing of the IRA. It becomes a sacred duty to avenge each and every act of the opposing group, with no questions asked concerning the rightness or wrongness of one's own prior behaviors that may have provoked very similar behaviors by the other party.

In short, morality becomes nonreflective and requires immediate and clearly defined responses. Hamlets, pacifists, or others who may agonize over their alternative choices are defined as weaklings, as mentally deranged, or as serious internal threats to the ongoing system. Most members are then prepared to face any future acts of aggression with an almost predetermined and very limited set of alternative responses. Furthermore, their potential enemies are encouraged to anticipate such immediate and decisive responses. In effect, there is what Schelling (1966) refers to as a trip-wire mechanism in place. If the outsider crosses a well-defined boundary, the response is predetermined.

Simplistic trip-wire ideologies of this sort obviously have to be rigidly reinforced. A highly dogmatic religious system, such as that of the Shi'ite Muslims of contemporary Iran or certain Orthodox Jewish groups in Israel, is one highly effective mechanism for achieving this purpose. Where a population is reasonably well-educated and exposed to alternative belief systems that are far less simplistic, rigid, and demanding, however, it is likely that dogmatic religious orientations of this nature will generate an internal opposition that may have the opposite effect of splitting the larger group into opposing camps, such as presently exist in Israel. This is especially likely where the most dogmatic belief systems carry with them certain obvious disadvantages to important elements of the population, as for example traders or the business community, religious or ethnic minorities, women, or more highly educated persons.

Historically, there have been many instances where rigid belief systems have worked to the (objective) disadvantage of substantial elements of the population, especially where it has been simultaneously possible to withhold education from them while somehow convincing them of the inevitability or legitimacy of the current system. From a Western point of view, Muslim women have remained in such a disadvantaged position for centuries—partly because of physical controls and rigidly enforced rules of behavior but also because they have continued to accept their status as legitimated by a divinely inspired religious system.

Closely linked with ideological simplicity, yet analytically distinct from it, is the degree to which a belief system draws a rigid line between right and wrong, correct and incorrect ways of behaving, and the superiority of one's own group practices as compared with those of others. We commonly refer to the phenomenon of "ethnocentrism," admitting that it is a characteristic of nearly all groups but recognizing that ethnocentrism varies by degree. There are some societies or smaller groups that have constructed belief systems enabling members to consider themselves so superior to others that they believe that they will be doing them a favor by "civilizing" them by force and bringing them into the fold, thereby compensating them for whatever other losses they may have endured. If slavery results in the Christianizing of "savages," it is conveniently believed that the benefits so derived considerably outweigh their loss of freedom or the hardships of plantation life. A master race is almost obligated to rid the earth of inferior peoples, and of course to take control of their territory and possessions as well.

A "chosen people" or a secessionist ethnic group, when supported by highly ethnocentric belief systems, may maintain a conflict orientation for many years in spite of numerous failures. An ability to construct a history (whether accurate or not) that stresses a glorious past and a set of heroic figures and martyrs, villains and traitors, as well as a catalog of past injustices inflicted at the hands of unscrupulous enemies, undoubtedly helps preserve such an ethnocentric cultural emphasis, as does a distinct language and segregated educational system. Perhaps ironically, a long history of martyrdom and grievances against powerful enemy groups often serves to produce the very kind of ethnocentric belief system that perpetuates such conflicts into the present.

Given the information overload that potentially exists in all social systems, a certain amount of selectivity is inevitable. Belief systems often operate to disguise many features that serve to favor the interests of those who control or have the predominant say in creating and perpetuating the ideology. Successful ideological systems also involve mechanisms that assure that certain kinds of questions are *not* asked and that many kinds of possible goals are suppressed. Members are socialized to believe so strongly in certain "facts" or explanations that they remain basically unchallenged. Implicit assumptions are hidden from view, and those who question them are immediately defined as traitors, fools, or scoundrels.

Some of these unchallenged beliefs may have no immediate connection with conflict. For instance in American society it is taken for granted that free enterprise is superior to communism. Where these taken-for-granted beliefs are considered core elements of an ideological system, however, it becomes likely that many different kinds of conflict (e.g., racial conflict) will be *interpreted* or perceived as involving these core ideological elements by those who wish to rally group members behind them. In connection with the civil rights movement of the 1960s, black unrest was perceived as caused by outside agitators and communists who could be targeted as rejecting the "American way of life," rather than as stemming from genuine grievances of minority individuals who wanted to be treated as full-fledged members of the capitalistic system.[1]

When members of a group are socialized not to ask certain questions, they are also being instructed, by implication, to consider as outsiders or enemies those who *do* raise these questions. We then have another trip-wire mechanism, perhaps inadvertently designed to enable the group to organize for conflict and to draw the line between loyal and disloyal members. Obviously, however, the numbers and types of taboo questions vary across settings and depend on such things as literacy levels, the presence of competing ideologies available to the members, and the relevancy of the taboo questions to any given potential conflict. A society that has been historically oriented to conflict, and that currently faces hostile neighbors, is more likely than others to attempt to achieve tight control over its socialization system, not only in connection with formal education but within neighborhood and occupational settings as well. Socialization practices carried out in Nazi Germany, Maoist China, and certain of the Eastern European communist countries are cases in point, but similar controls are also operative in many smaller countries having right-wing dictatorships, to say nothing of the more subtle processes at work elsewhere.

Belief systems may also help set the stage for any particular conflict by placing a strong emphasis on a glorious past and—in the case of nation-states—territorial claims based upon this past. Given that many parcels of land have changed hands numerous times over the centuries, it becomes possible to select the most propitious time periods and to sanctify certain pieces of territory that "rightfully" belong to one's own nation but that have been illegitimately occupied by others. For Jews, the "promised land" of Israel was and is of crucial symbolic and practical importance, despite the fact that it had and has been occupied by Palestinian Arabs for a considerable period of time. The Palestinians, of course, have naturally selected a different period of time by means of which to lay legitimate claims to the same territory.

Supporting the claims of both parties to a dispute will be a number of beliefs about legendary heroes, sacred objects stolen by the other party, acts of treachery, barbarity and deceit, and subsequent attempts to regain the sacred objects or territory. An important objective in transmitting such beliefs, sometimes over long periods of time, is to extol the virtues of extreme sacrifice, militarism, and unquestioned loyalty in the event that in the future there should ever be opportunities to avenge these wrongs and regain the sacred objects or disputed territory. More generally, members of the group are encouraged to believe that bad things are always to be blamed on one's opponents, rather than on one's own group. They are thus made willing to fight "at the drop of a hat." Outsiders are not to be trusted, nor are those who come to their defense or who may suggest that blame for any given dispute may reasonably be allocated to both parties.

Ideological Strains and Inconsistencies

Any belief system of reasonable complexity will inevitably contain either outright inconsistencies or will in many concrete situations involve conflicting principles leading to dilemmas that can only be resolved by attaching differential weights to these principles. This, in turn, requires judgments concerning value priorities, opening up the possibility of major disagreements even among those who generally support the overall belief system.

Extremely simplistic ideological systems may resolve such inconsistencies by enunciating a single hierarchy of values or principles or a single authoritative mechanism for settling any possible disputes. Especially in instances where members are exposed to several competing ideological systems and rival authorities, however, we may expect major disagreements concerning the priorities given to one or another of these principles. In conflict situations, the efficiency as well as the degree of a party's mobilization efforts may be affected by such ideological strains and inconsistencies. Therefore it is important that interpretive mechanisms be established and consensus achieved before the period of conflict has begun or, at least, prior to the time that exhaustion or demoralization would otherwise tend to exacerbate any latent internal cleavages.

One of the most serious sources of strain that belief systems are "designed" to handle stems from the necessity of dealing with a diversity of individualistic needs and goals, many of which may have to be deferred or denied outright in order to achieve consensus and a high degree of mobilization. As already noted, selective incentives or some ideological substitutes are likely to be required to reduce free riding and to motivate reluctant members to make substantial personal sacrifices. To some extent this may be accomplished through tangible rewards such as increased salaries, promotions, medals of honor, or notoriety. Unfortunately, however, such rewards provided to some members may also alienate others. Less costly psychic rewards that do not create invidious distinctions will generally be necessary to induce more ordinary forms of cooperation. Members may be induced into believing that what would usually be considered personal sacrifices will ultimately be rewarded, perhaps in an afterlife or in the form of more concrete future benefits that will be bestowed once victory has been achieved. If so, of course, someone must be able to monitor such personal sacrifices and a supernatural being becomes an ideal candidate.

As a conflict continues, and as personal costs mount and unmet goals can no longer be easily deferred, beliefs may also be modified so as to adjust to changing circumstances. It may also become increasingly difficult to convince members of the benefits of active participation. Selective incentives become both more costly and more difficult to apply in an evenhanded fashion. Furthermore, the relative values attached to different kinds of behaviors may need to shift, with potentially serious implications for morale, leadership, and authority, and relative costs to different types of individuals.

To induce members to initiate or prepare for a conflict, it is helpful to convince them that potential costs will be small relative to anticipated benefits. The expectation is that the opponent can be defeated rather easily because of one's own superior courage, military organization, moral superiority, or supernatural support. As the conflict wears on and the opponent's strengths become sufficiently obvious, however, certain of these earlier beliefs may become discredited and may need to be supplemented by others that emphasize the negative consequences of defeat: the desperate and illegitimate nature of the opponent's behaviors, the extreme costs of surrender and the treacherous character of the opponent, the importance of sacrifices already made, and the belief that previous defeats can be blamed on a combination of bad luck and treasonous actions on the part of a few disloyal members. Minor victories must be made to seem major turning points of great symbolic importance. Those who speak in terms of compromise with the opponent or who attempt to place the blame for defeats on the group's own leaders must be discredited and silenced.

Needless to say, it will not always be possible to engineer major shifts in any reasonably complex belief system in a credible way unless the overwhelming majority of the group's membership have been "brainwashed" into accepting an extremely simplistic set of beliefs about their own superiority and the opponent's totally unscrupulous nature. Even the German faith in Nazi invulnerability began to crumble toward the end of World War II, as the devastating defeats on the Russian front and allied bombings began to signal the nature of the hopeless situation they were facing. Earlier beliefs about being a "master race" and the weakness and lack of resolve among their enemies may have, in fact, become dysfunctional toward the very end of the war.

As a conflict wears on, a party having any degree of complexity will undoubtedly develop leadership cleavages, with different leadership segments emphasizing different sets of beliefs or values. If initial victories cannot be maintained, say, because the opposition is hardening or because objectives become increasingly difficult to attain, rival cliques may struggle for control, developing new ideological features or emphasizing certain aspects while playing down others.

As the civil rights movement of the early 1960s achieved victories and turned to more difficult objectives, such as improving the economic status of Northern blacks, a series of defeats or at least nonvictories helped to encourage a more radicalized leadership element for whom nonviolence and religiously-inspired incentives were less important. The slogans "Black Power" and "Burn Baby Burn" displaced those of "Black and White Together." Even Martin Luther King, Jr. became a martyr whose death was interpreted to mean that whites respected and feared only those blacks who espoused a violent confrontation. A lack of success on the part of these black power extremists, in turn, led to a somewhat less confrontative stress on affirmative action programs and beliefs in the efficacy of political movements "within the system."

This tendency for ideological systems to bend but not break and to be modified in accord with shifts in leadership and trends in the conflict process might seem to suggest that beliefs are simply dependent variables that are easily adjusted according to the values of more important structural factors. One must keep in mind, however, that the delays involved may be long enough to continue to motivate actors to behave in ways that may have important impacts on the ultimate course of the conflict. Battles may be won or lost on the basis of very short-term considerations. Soldiers who believe ferverently in their religion or a charismatic leader may be induced to make extreme sacrifices. Beliefs that a conquering enemy will show no mercy may be sufficient to turn the tide. New recruits into an extremist social movement, especially when placed in small homogeneous cell groups, may be goaded to actions that enable them to "prove" their loyalty to the cause. Should they later waver or begin to question the ideology, they may then be replaced.

It is the flexibility of belief systems that permits their ready adaptation to the many objective changes that are likely to occur during the course of a conflict. The trick for the party in question is to introduce necessary specific modifications without undermining the belief sys-

tem as a totality. Ambiguities and apparent inconsistencies in an ideological system may, for this very reason, be entirely functional. One
can always "reinterpret" an ambiguous set of beliefs or emphasize or
deemphasize one or another of two apparently incompatible values.
A new leadership can point to "errors" made by its predecessors
without seeming to discredit the belief system as a whole. Thus a
belief system may evolve as an entity and yet continue to serve as a
powerful motivating force at any given moment in time.

THE DILEMMA OF TRUST

A very different type of strain in an ideological system may develop
as a result of the largely incompatible needs of motivating members
to initiate and engage in a conflict, on the one hand, and of preparing
for its termination, on the other. Of course if that termination ends in
a complete victory, there may be no incompatibility, at least over the
short run. But a compromise resolution to the conflict will depend,
very heavily, on mechanisms designed to build up trust between the
opposing parties. As is readily apparent in game-theory situations,
whenever two parties are in a partly cooperative, partly competitive
situation, the trust component becomes critical. The well-studied Prisoner's Dilemma Game is a case in point. In order to reach a mutually
satisfactory solution, rather than one that is disadvantageous to both
parties, each party may need to select that option that will work only
if the other party can be trusted to reciprocate with a similarly cooperative response.

In a conflict situation, ideological systems will generally tend to
depict the opponent as completely untrustworthy. Previous "treacherous" actions by that opponent will be highlighted, as will negative
stereotypes that reinforce a suspicious orientation toward any acts of
conciliation put forth by that party. Where rule violations have become common, where preemptive moves are believed advantageous,
and where group leaders have gained power as a result of the conflict
situation, the risks of a cooperative move on one's own part are likely
to be considered too great. Furthermore, it will be believed—
probably correctly—that such moves will be taken by the opponent as
a sign of weakness or fatigue.

Therefore the very beliefs that motivate members to support the
conflict will make it difficult for anyone—except possibly for a power-

ful and trusted third party—to take the initial steps toward reconciliation. Even were such steps taken, there would be no assurance that, having a similarly distrustful orientation, the opposing party would not take advantage of the temporarily vulnerable position of the first party. Thus a conflict once initiated becomes very difficult to terminate until both parties have become totally exhausted or unless one is the clear winner. Because of the support of intractable ideological props, a conflict that may have been initially perceived as rather minor and easily mediated is likely to have to run its course and to result in far more damage to both parties than was originally anticipated by either. We shall discuss this kind of question in considerably more detail in Chapters 9 and 10, here merely calling attention to the role that ideological systems may play in helping to sustain costly conflicts for very long periods of time.

Those who see through ideological strains or inconsistencies may attempt to point them out and argue for modifications. They may, for example, note favorable characteristics of the opponent or past injustices its members have experienced at the hands of one's own party. They may also try to enlist the help of neutral third parties, either to serve as mediators to the dispute, or to guarantee the safety of both parties during periods of vulnerability when trust is most essential. Unless and until the situation becomes perceived as nearly hopeless and the costs almost unbearable, however, it will be exceedingly difficult for those who espouse reconciliation to avoid being labeled either as traitors or cowards.

More than likely, the ideological system that has already been developed will contain built-in explanations designed to discredit such efforts as playing into the hands of the opponent. During the period of tension prior to actual initiation of hostilities, such discrediting devices will probably be developed and used against anyone who espouses moderate positions involving a degree of trust in the potential opponent. We have seen many such devices in place, for example, during the Cold War that has existed between the United States and the Soviet Union ever since the close of World War II. Those who seem to be too close to advocating reconciliation are, on both sides, discredited as naive, weak, or possibly even disloyal. As the Cold War subsides, these persons may return to favor, but any hostile act on the part of the opponent will, by the same token, weaken their position.[2]

JUSTIFYING A DUAL STANDARD OF MORALITY

Aggressive or punitive behavior directed toward members of the in-group is generally discouraged by an ethical system that stresses cooperative behavior, the positive characteristics of these others, and the need for loyalty and compassion. How, then, can one justify hostile behaviors toward members of other groups? How can the ethical system be compartmentalized so as to apply to some persons but not others? What kinds of distinctions can be made that are sufficiently flexible that they may be applied to a potentially wide variety of opposing groups? How can allies temporarily be counted "in", whereas shortly afterward it may become necessary to consider them as enemies? How, for example, was it possible for the American public to hate the Germans and Japanese during World War II and then to turn only a few years later against the Russians and Chinese, who had earlier been our allies? How is it possible to shift so rapidly from positive to negative stereotypes, or vice versa?

One mechanism, which is characteristic of both micro- and macro-level parties in conflict, is to consider all of one's own actions as "defensive" and those of the opponent as "offensive" or aggressive. We have a Defense Department, certainly not an Offense Department, or even any longer a War Department. "Our boys" (or men) are our defenders, rather than attackers or killers of innocent citizens. Regardless of changes in one's specific opponents, they may all be characterized as having the same base motives. Specific negative stereotypes may then be adapted to the circumstances and made credible, especially so in those instances where there has been very little prior close contact. Thus in World War II the "Jap" was considered treacherous and slippery, saying one thing and doing the very opposite. The German was depicted as haughty, ruthless, authoritarian, and immensely bigoted. Perhaps the same stereotypes could not have been so quickly shifted to either the Russian or Chinese Communists, but this did not matter as long as they could be considered dangerous to the "free world" and poised to attack or at least undermine capitalistic economies or weak but friendly (and of course democratic) third-world governments. One's own party is thus depicted as the high-minded protector against the would-be aggressor, no matter of what nature.

To lay the foundations for such a flexible belief system it is helpful, in the case of nation-states, to develop a mythology that stresses conflicts with a multiplicity of aggressors and to depict the lives of heroic defenders who, despite overwhelming odds, managed to save the day or at least inflict considerable damage on the invading enemy. It is not just Texans who have their Alamos. Such heroic figures are likely to be identified as having all of the positive characteristics of the in-group: being family men, churchgoers, simple farmers or peasants, and the like. The sharp contrast between their gentle and pacifistic behaviors toward their peers and their extremely aggressive (though of course defensive) behaviors toward the enemy help to justify similar responses toward potential future opponents. The locally popular images of Joan of Arc, George Washington, and Chairman Mao have much in common—despite the obvious differences in the ideological systems of their respective countries and times.

Another ideological device for reducing possible inconsistencies between a cooperative morality applied to the in-group and an aggressive one applied against a hostile opponent is to partition members of the other party into "good guys" and "bad guys" and to rationalize that one is attempting to save the former from the latter. Thus it was not the Vietnamese or Russian people who were our enemies, but their leaders and their system of government. Killing some of the good guys may be necessary in order to save them from themselves, so to speak. Better still, those members of the enemy whom we find it necessary to punish have become fanatics, and very devious and dangerous ones at that. Therefore they must be killed as a "defensive" measure.

It thereby becomes possible to believe that even though one's own party is fighting (but never aggressing against) an enemy, this is for the ultimate benefit of at least those of its members who have not become hopeless fanatics. In the end, they will appreciate our acts of heroism in saving them from themselves. If we can convert them to our own religion or provide them with a new government favorable to our own, they will be doubly grateful. With slight modifications in the specifics, say the nature of their leaders or religious system, this same form of reasoning can be applied to almost any would-be aggressor. A sense of one's own group's uniqueness and cultural, religious or ethical superiority, or ultimate destiny as a world leader, will reinforce such a basically "altruistic" orientation toward competing groups.

It may be necessary to appeal to third parties, however, in which case a somewhat different ideological orientation may be advisable. The "defensive" and heroic protector-of-mankind images may succeed in convincing members of the in-group but may strain the credulity of outsiders. Certainly, the image that the United States attempts to convey to Latin American countries—as that of the friendly protector against hostile European nations (and now communism in general)—is not accepted at face value by any of these nations. It therefore becomes desirable to split off the belief system that has been designed to appeal to members of the in-group from that which is intended to appeal to these third parties. Given the ubiquity of mass media and high levels of literacy among the elite of these countries, as well as the impossibility of insulating them from rival interpretations, this is no simple task. It is an additional source of strain in an ideological system designed to rationalize policies that are very likely to be interpreted by others as offensive and aggressive, rather than strictly defensive.

Ideological Supports for Dominance Without Conflict

When one party is clearly subordinate to another or is obviously receiving an unfair rate of exchange, one would ordinarily expect conflict to be endemic, or at least that the dominance patterns would require the repeated application of naked force. Yet we find that there are numerous instances where belief systems have been useful to the dominant party in inhibiting the subordinate party from rebelling. Sometimes there is merely the recognition that an unjust system cannot be changed because of the overwhelming superiority of the dominant party. In many other instances, however, the system is believed to be a just one, or one that has resulted from past sins that cannot be recalled, or that has been sanctioned by supernatural powers for inscrutable reasons. How can such belief systems be maintained, sometimes for centuries, without being seriously challenged? Why doesn't the subordinated party automatically develop its own counterideology to justify major changes in the status quo? Why is it that a group or category of persons may remain subordinated even where the dominant party is really not capable of applying sufficient force to oppose a serious uprising on the part of the subordinated party?

Philip Mason raises these and other questions in his book, *Patterns of Dominance* (1970). He notes that in Ruanda, before it was disturbed by Europeans, the Tutsi dominated the Hutu in spite of the facts that the latter were almost seven times as numerous and that the Tutsi possessed no superior weapons or other obvious physical advantages. They did so, of course, with the aid of a number of institutional mechanisms: economic, military, and social. Beliefs played a crucial supportive role, however. The Hutu considered the Tutsi to be their moral and intellectual superiors. Indeed, the contrasting stereotypes of the two groups had a very familiar ring. The Tutsi were believed to have the typical characteristics of a warrior class: to be intelligent, capable of command, refined, courageous, and cruel. The Hutu, in contrast, were thought of by both groups as having typical peasant characteristics: hardworking but not very clever, unmannerly but obedient, physically strong, extroverted, and irascible.

Such stereotypes were reinforced by segregation and by distinctly different socialization patterns. Structural arrangements basically involved a system of lords and vassals with reciprocal obligations remarkably similar to those characteristic of ideal-type feudalism, with Hutu individuals being tied by a series of obligations to a Tutsi lord on whom they could depend for protection. There were certain safety valves, as for example the possibility for a Hutu to select among alternative Tutsi overlords. Of great importance was the fact that the entire system, including the supporting ideology, virtually assured that each member of the subordinated group compared himself, not with the dominant Tutsi, but with other members of his own group.

From the standpoint of maintaining for centuries a system of domination without substantial conflict, perhaps the most successful belief system is that of the Hindu caste system of India. If one believes that one's place is a natural outcome of one's previous life, which cannot be recalled, and that one's fate in an indefinitely prolonged series of future lives is therefore dependent upon the faithful adherence to a rigid set of duties and rituals demanded in the present, one obviously will have to think twice about challenging an unfair system. Furthermore, since—for most individuals—there will be others belonging to still lower groupings and whose fate seems even less enviable than one's own, there is little incentive to form coalitions with them. For at least two millennia India institutionalized a hierarchically arranged system involving a confusing array of *jeti*, within which communal loyalties were strong but between which a whole series of religious taboos and rituals reinforced a psychological as well as a physical separation.

As Mason points out, one of the critical problems faced by a dominant group is to develop a system in which subordinate parties are placed in groupings that are large enough to permit ongoing primary ties that create a sufficient degree of loyalty that they may be counted on in times of outside crises, but yet not so large that there is any serious likelihood of their attempting to turn the tables or form effective coalitions. In India this was accomplished by means of a hierarchically arranged caste system supported by strong ideological and ritualistic underpinnings.

Dominant groups often require the assistance of some members of subordinate parties. Colonial powers, for example, needed local administrators, tax collectors, clerks, and other minor officials to serve as intermediaries with ordinary citizens. Overseers and foremen were employed to insure that productivity remained at a decent level. These colonial systems thus contained safety valves by permitting a degree of upward mobility, which also served to emphasize to others that those members of the subordinate group who were willing to play the game could gain for themselves and their families certain tangible advantages. Accompanying belief systems were also designed to exaggerate the probabilities of upward mobility for those who were willing to cooperate in this manner. Not surprisingly, "middlemen" placed in these roles—whether members of the subordinate group itself, mixed-blood offspring, or distinct third-party minorities—have often been the immediate targets of conflict groups such as the Mau Mau of Kenya or guerrilla cell groups in contemporary South Africa.[3]

If they are to be successful, ideological systems in such settings must somehow convince members of the subordinate group that they are so distinctly different from dominant-group members that they do not even think of comparing themselves with members of the elite. Physical segregation helps to reduce the opportunities for day-to-day contacts, but in situations in which physical separation would be too inconvenient, a series of rituals is likely to serve the same function. The idea of pollution was, and still is, critical in preserving caste distinctions in India.

A similar notion existed in the American South, where ritualistic modes of address regulated contacts between blacks and whites until rather recently (Dollard, 1937; Myrdal, 1944). These were also reinforced by an elaborate system of symbolic forms of segregation: separate rest rooms, drinking fountains, parks and playgrounds, movie theaters, hotels, and restaurants. The function of all these "Jim Crow" forms of segregation was basically that of reinforcing an ideological system that drew a hard-and-fast line between the two groups, so that blacks would hardly dare compare themselves with even the lowest-status whites (Vann Woodward, 1965). Beliefs concerning the "purity" of white women and the promiscuity of their black counter-parts further served to draw a sharp line between the two groups, as did the rigid bar on intermarriage. From the standpoint of the dominant white group, the function of the entire system was to keep blacks "in their place" by making it almost impossible for them to conceive of themselves as ever enjoying, or indeed as deserving of, the privileges of such a totally distinct dominant group. Thus the ideological system, together with rigidly enforced behavioral norms, served to draw a very sharp boundary between the two groups.

Whenever such rigid boundaries and the accompanying ideological support systems are challenged, however, as occurred in the American South during the 1950s and 1960s and as we witness today in South Africa, we often find that they take on a symbolic significance that may serve as a focal point of subordinate party mobilization. It was many of these symbolic forms of segregation and the "Jim Crow" legislation that accompanied them that became early targets of the civil rights movement—segregated buses and waiting rooms, restaurants and theaters, and the general patterns of "etiquette" that entailed extreme deference on the part of blacks. Once blacks began to see themselves as the social equals of whites, it then became much easier to compare themselves with whites on a number of other counts: educational attainment, occupational opportunities, and political power. Thus, the use of ideological props is sometimes a two-edged sword that remains effective only as long as the subordinate group accepts the basic premise of a sharp and inevitable distinction, rather than one involving differences and inequalities that vary only by degree. Today, the Tutsi and Hutu are engaged in bloody conflict.

Finally, as Mason also notes, a belief system that supports the domination of one party by another may be incompatible with beliefs that apply *within* the dominant group. For European democratic governments to justify a colonialist policy in Africa or Asia, it was convenient to rationalize authoritarian controls as somehow necessary, perhaps on a temporary basis because of the "backward" or "savage" nature of the indigenous population, or perhaps on religious grounds. How could suffrage be extended in the homeland and yet be restricted in the colonial territory unless the peoples in the latter lands were in need of "protection" or tutelage to overcome their "childlike" innocence? Potential ideological inconsistencies and strains were disguised by drawing a series of sharp distinctions between the governors and the governed. Thus paternalism and "indirect rule" became characteristic of British overseas policies, and the "White Man's Burden," the popular slogan. Spanish and Portuguese interests in the New World involved a combination of imperialism and the lust for precious metals, but these were always accompanied by the religious objective of gaining new converts to Catholicism. The interests of the Crown and the Church often clashed with those of settlers, however, and resulted in a series of ideological compromises that some scholars have argued helped to account for Central and Latin American racial patterns that have differed from those in the United States in their ultimate impacts on the way lines of cleavage were drawn. In Brazil, for example, sexual contacts between white masters and black slaves were not regarded as sinful and, indeed, seemed to reinforce the male "macho" self-image. Mixed-blood offspring were often placed in intermediate categories and did not find themselves in competition with a substantial number of working-class whites. The manumission of slaves was more extensive than it was in the American South, and slavery did not end as a result of a divisive civil war.

In our country, a mulatto child was automatically classified as "black." That is, he or she was placed into the lower group, thereby creating a setup resembling that of India's caste system. In contrast, in Spanish- and Portuguese-speaking countries the emphasis was placed on a color continuum, which sometimes, however, had equally harmful effects on darker-skinned individuals. Given that conflict lines are much more likely to be developed in settings where sharp distinctions (e.g. racial, lingusitic, religious) have been made between two groups, some of these initial cultural differences may have had considerable consequences for subsequent conflict patterns.

DOMINANCE IN TRADITIONAL AMERICAN FAMILIES

It is frequently noted that the ideal-type traditional American family system has been supported by many of the same kinds of ideological props as have existed in other types of dominance situations. In this system, the husband was placed in an authoritative decision-making role as head of household, and his wife and children were expected to obey orders and to serve in subordinate roles. In return, the husband and father was expected to serve as protector of his family and was held responsible for any deviant acts they may have perpetrated. For her part, the wife was placed somewhat on a pedestal and expected to remain sexually loyal, regardless of her husband's extramarital conduct. She was also expected to sacrifice her own interests to those of other members of her family and to serve as a model of moral integrity for them.

In parallel with the Tutsi-Hutu socialization patterns, as described by Mason, boys and girls were differentially socialized so as to encourage them to make comparisons only within their own gender. In particular, women were to aspire to become homemakers and never to expect to enter occupations "reserved" for men. Those "female" occupations suitable for unmarried women were extensions of the mother-homemaker role: nursing or teaching, or serving as seamstresses, maids, waitresses, or secretaries. The "world of women" was, in effect, segregated from that of men, and the "feminine mystique" (Friedan, 1963) was cultivated and passed along from one generation of women to the next.

It is to be presumed that a carefully cultivated and ideologically supported dominance system such as this also served to reduce conflict levels between the two sexes and *may* have reduced the extent to which physical abuse by dominating husbands was exercised. One may also surmise that such abuse took place relatively more frequently when transgressions or "insubordinate" behaviors occurred among wives. The problem is that accurate quantitative data on trends in wife-abuse are not available, so that today's apparently higher rate of such abuse may be more a reflection of more adequate data reports than anything else. Nevertheless, it remains that the "official" version of the traditional American family contained precisely the kinds of ideological supports that one would anticipate in those instances where domination is achieved with minimal overt conflict.

Notes

1. See Turner (1969) for a discussion of the conditions affecting whether collective acts of disruption and violence are perceived as legitimate social protest, individual criminal acts, or organized rebellion.

2. This weakening of the positions of those who support reconciliation in the face of hostile acts of the opponent is one of several mechanisms that may affect Richardson's (1960) sensitivity coefficient.

3. For discussions of "middleman minorities" and scapegoating see Blalock (1967), E. Bonacich (1973), and Gist and Dworkin (1972).

Chapter 7

Ideological Dimensions and a Theoretical Submodel

The social science literature on ideologies is often either highly general, as for example Mannheims's (1940) classic work on ideologies and utopias, or else overwhelmingly descriptive and consisting of extremely detailed discussions of the historical factors that gave rise to a particular ideological system, such as the Protestant ethic, the American frontier creed, or Nazi anti-semitism. Authors sometimes attempt to extract from their own descriptions a number of distinguishing features of a given belief system that they then highlight and use to account for specific behaviors of those who subscribed to the belief system in question. They may show little concern about problems of generalizability, however, or how ideologies operate to influence other kinds of behaviors in very different settings. This has meant that causal factors intimately bound to ideological dimensions are often neglected in systematic discussions of conflict processes in spite of the fact that nearly all authors admit to the importance of beliefs, misunderstandings, and "nonrational" factors involved in these conflict processes.

If one examines any reasonably complex historical process—as for example the rise of nationalism, imperialism or colonialism—the "mix" of ideological factors will also be sufficiently complex that the most relevant ideological dimensions or variables will usually be obscured. Similarly, a comparison of three or four distinct historical periods or settings will also yield far too many combinations of ideological features to enable one to do much more than speculate as to which of these factors were the most important.

Given the obvious difficulties encountered in obtaining documentary evidence regarding the degree to which relevant parties actually subscribed to and were influenced by specific beliefs, careful quantitative investigations of ideological systems have not been forthcoming. This does not mean, however, that merely because ideological variables have not been measured—and thus included in such empirical investigations—they are therefore unimportant. They may remain in the error terms of one's equations, but this, too, does not imply that such error terms are uncorrelated with whatever other independent variables have actually been included in one's theory. In short, the mere fact that ideological variables are difficult to measure does not imply that they can safely be ignored. To do so may result in highly misleading policy recommendations as well as a tendency to consider one's opponent's beliefs, assertions, or explanations as mere rationalizations, bluffs, or based on "mistaken" values.

Ideologies change, of course. Unless one is prepared to argue that historical shifts in belief systems are idiosyncratic or completely determined by "historical accident," it becomes important to try to specify how and why such changes occur by invoking some reasonably lawlike principles that are generally applicable regardless of historical time or place. This, in turn, requires one to pull belief systems apart in some way. The approach I shall use in the present chapter is to suggest a number of ideological dimensions that may be used to specify a set of variables and causal mechanisms linking not only these ideological dimensions to one another but also to other variables in the larger causal system represented by our general model for conflict processes. This set of ideological dimensions and previously discussed variables will then be combined into an ideological submodel, which will be presented in the closing section of the chapter.

When one examines a particular belief system, say the ingredients of Nazi anti-semitism, the temptation may be to perceive these dimensions or variables as being highly interrelated more generally. In short, the belief system in question may be seen as a tightly integrated whole. Whenever entire belief systems, such as particular religious doctrines, are diffused across political boundaries or transmitted across generations largely intact, this tendency to perceive them as tightly integrated packages may be reinforced. Yet a detailed historical analysis, such as Hannah Arendt's (1951) study of the rise of totalitarianism, will often indicate just how complex have been the historical strands leading to a particular ideological mix, thereby countering this temptation to see more integration and consistency than actually exists. The basic question posed by such detailed analyses of actual historical processes is whether or not one can pull the relevant ideological dimensions apart and then theorize as to how they are likely to be interrelated causally and what, if any, useful predictions can be made about similar processes that may occur in the future. I see no way of undertaking this task other than to attempt to specify a set of distinct, though often intercorrelated, ideological dimensions or variables.

How can "ideological variables" be causally interconnected, say in the same sense that a person's educational level may affect his or her later earnings, job satisfaction or voting behavior? When we say that education is a "direct" cause of income, we mean that, having specified a delimited set of other variables, a change of one unit in education will actually produce a change in the expected value of income, with controls on the remaining variables assumed to affect income level (Blalock, 1964). Operationally, this would imply that if we sent a large number of persons back to school for one additional year, their average incomes would actually be increased, holding constant the other explicitly delineated causes. Can we make similar arguments concerning ideological variables? I believe this is possible although we shall encounter considerably more difficult measurement problems, including ambiguities as to the choice of appropriate units of analysis, such as communities, nation-states, or "societies." Our concern in the present chapter is to delineate a set of fourteen ideological dimensions and to suggest some ways in which they are likely to be causally interrelated.

Before attempting to list these specific ideological dimensions, we may simply note some obvious points. Certain combinations of beliefs are more mutually compatible than are others. A very simple belief system, for example, permits one to place blame unambiguously on one's opponent, whereas a highly complex one that admits of multiple causation is more likely to lead to a much more ambiguous and evenhanded attribution of blame. A belief system that is highly fatalistic in nature is unlikely to induce adherents to immediate responses to outside threats. Placing the blame on others is highly compatible with a belief system that encourages, and justifies, extreme punitive actions and a willingness to break the rules of the game whenever it is believed that one's opponent has done so.

In many instances the causal relationships may be reciprocal, though with unequal coefficients. Ideological simplicity may reinforce beliefs that encourage vindictive actions, whereas the beliefs themselves may have a more minor impact on simplicity. As in the case where one is studying other types of nonrecursive models, lags of varying durations may be involved. Some ideological shifts may be discrete and readily identified with specific time periods, as for example the publication of an influential book or an announced policy change (e.g., Vatican II). Most ideological changes are likely to be continuous, however, if not with respect to the actual appearance of distinctly new ingredients then at least with regard to their acceptance or dispersion among a party's members. One may therefore expect to encounter many of the same kinds of methodological complications as have arisen in the study of other kinds of causal interdependencies.

As each dimension is introduced it will be briefly linked to those ideological dimensions that have already been discussed. Our general ideological submodel, which will be fairly complex, is deferred to the end of the chapter. It will be assumed that the argument applies to party X, with a similar one being appropriate for party Y. This separation of the two parties unfortunately does not permit the examination of the *relationship* between the two belief systems, as for example how ideological variables pertaining to X may influence and be affected by those appropriate to Y. It thus presumes that there are two parties being influenced by distinct ideological systems, rather than there being, say, a clearly dominant party that partly controls the belief system to which the subordinate party subscribes.

If one is dealing with a conflict between two "internal" parties, both of which are influenced by the same ideological system, the argument may need to be modified in certain ways. For example, a fatalistic orientation may favor party X over party Y in instances where the former is clearly dominant, and indeed X may attempt to manipulate the belief system so as to reduce conflict and maintain its dominant position. If it turns out that really major modifications are required of our ideological submodel to handle such situations, perhaps an additional set of variables may need to be introduced.

1. SIMPLICITY

The notion of ideological simplicity plays a key role in our subsequent discussion and in our ideological theoretical submodel. What do we mean by "simplicity" and is this notion itself multidimensional? Since party X's members may be highly heterogeneous with respect to utilities attached to a diversity of goals, and to expectancies as well, and since we have argued that such heterogeneity may play a crucial role in terms of both the degree and efficiency of the mobilization effort, it seems sensible to think of ideological simplicity in terms of goal hierarchies and the clarity with which choices among alternative means have been prescribed or proscribed. By a simplistic ideology we shall mean either one that stresses an extremely small number of goals to which members should attach very high utilities or one that specifies a clear-cut hierarchy of goals, as well as a set of conditions under which goals of lesser importance are to be sacrificed or deferred. Such a simplistic ideology will also specify an unambiguous set of means for attaining the most important goals.

Many highly simplistic ideological systems stress goals that are either irrelevant to any given conflict or that would be expected to inhibit members from taking part in conflicts except under unusual conditions. Thus, a belief system placing a major emphasis on attaining eternal salvation or release from earthly burdens by spinning prayer wheels might predispose members to engage in avoidance behaviors designed to minimize the risk of conflict. In contrast, a similarly simplistic religious ideology, also having as a goal eternal salvation, might call upon true believers to make extreme sacrifices in the form of suicidal aggressive acts against the infidel. The essential point is that the ideology prescribes a simple course of action to be followed under well-defined circumstances, with virtually no room for uncertainties or choices among a wide range of options.

Ideological simplicity of this sort makes coordination relatively unproblematic and a high degree of motivation virtually assured, as long as members wholeheartedly endorse the beliefs in question. Degree of mobilization—though not necessarily its efficiency—is thus likely to be much higher than in instances where the ideological system contains a large number of ambiguities that invite dissent or where it permits a wide range of combinations of goal hierarchies that encourage divergent vested interests in outcomes of different sorts. As already implied, however, certain simplistic belief systems may actually *lower* mobilization efforts if their primary emphasis is on goals that are irrelevant to the conflict (G_3 goals) or that are most readily achieved through cooperation with Y. Rather simple pacifistic or escapist and otherworldly belief systems of certain religious minorities are cases in point.

Some simplistic ideological systems may not specify means but may, instead, induce followers to accept whatever courses of action are prescribed by designated actors, whether they be priests, prophets or lay leaders. Provided that the belief system permits an unambiguous method of determination or recognition of such leaders, it may have the added advantage of permitting flexibility according to the nature of the circumstances or the opposing party. Thus, rather than specifying a rigid set of procedures or rituals to follow, the emphasis is placed on the blind acceptance of the "führer" principle, thereby facilitating coordination as well as mobilization. Where the belief system also guarantees rewards that cannot be empirically verified (as for example eternal salvation), we may have in place an ideology that is capable of inducing extreme sacrifices as well. The efficiency or effectiveness of the mobilization effort will also depend upon other factors, however, including the apparent effectiveness of the leader's plan of action and the responses of the other party.

An effective yet simplistic belief system will also provide credible explanations for failures or seeming discrepancies between what has been anticipated and what has actually occurred. The trick, here, is to maintain a high degree of acceptance of the ideology in spite of the circumstances. It will be helpful if the belief system makes disarmingly simple predictions that are sufficiently ambiguous that incorrect ones can be explained away, and if it promises rewards and punishments that are believed to be automatic but not yet easily verified. It would be reasonable to suppose that high levels of literacy and exposure to rival belief systems will tend to reduce the credibility of such simplistic but "slippery" belief systems, but recent history provides counterexamples that make one wonder about the gullibility of supposedly highly educated peoples in counteracting such simplistic belief systems when there are powerful vested interests involved. Again, the case of Nazi Germany comes to mind, as does the recent resurgence of fundamentalistic religious movements in our own country.

2. FATALISM

Fatalism usually refers to the belief that one's own actions cannot affect outcomes, either by increasing the probability that desired outcomes will occur or by reducing the likelihood of negative ones. In principle, the term might also be used to refer to an inability to make one's outcomes *worse*, but common usage stresses the more pessimistic orientation and we shall adopt this connotation of the term. A highly fatalistic ideology, then, is one that stresses resignation and passivity in connection with events that one might otherwise attempt to influence positively. The belief system may restrict such a passive orientation to a narrow sphere of potential events, or it may have a much more pervasive influence. For sake of definiteness, we shall confine our attention to those behaviors and events that have direct bearing on the conflict situation under consideration.

A fatalistic orientation of party X toward party Y implies that members of the former party will believe that there is little or nothing they can do to resist the actions of the other group, though other forces (beyond their control) may possibly intervene. Obviously, a totally fatalistic orientation suggests complete passivity or nonresistance and is thus virtually inconceivable in real-life encounters. But parties' adherence to fatalistic beliefs may vary by degree, as may the proportions of their members who take a fatalistic orientation toward any particular opponent. Generally, we would expect that fatalism will be highly correlated with, and produced by, low levels of power vis-à-vis that opponent and that it will in general be characteristic of weak nations or ethnic groups, lower castes and classes, unskilled laborers, or other underprivileged segments of some larger group.

Highly simplistic ideological systems may be fatalistic or the very opposite, but extremely fatalistic belief systems would seem to require a simplistic belief system of a peculiar type—one that postulates an extremely low level of "efficacy" in the case of virtually all actions party members may take. Thus the combination of low power and ideological simplicity would seem likely to produce a fatalistic orientation *unless* the ideology can specify some mechanism of escape that requires a distinct course of action: perhaps praying to a tribal deity or blindly following the dictates of a designated leader.

Some extremely weak or exploited parties may be characterized by a combination of a high degree of fatalistic passivity on the part of the overwhelming majority but extremist, almost desperate, actions by a very small minority. Sporadic uprisings among slaves or pariah castes, as well as violent acts by members of cell-like conflict groups, may be seen as efforts to shake the more general membership out of a fatalistic, passive mode of response. Perhaps paradoxically, then, a high degree of fatalism among a majority of a party's members does not necessarily imply a low level of conflict with a superordinate party. Sporadic conflicts of this nature are especially likely whenever the generally passive subordinate party is numerically large, so that its potential for gaining power is considerably greater than its present power.

3. ABILITY TO SHAPE EXPECTANCIES

Ideologies obviously impact on utilities by emphasizing the importance of some goals while downplaying others. They may also affect expectancies or subjective probabilities, which may depart considerably from what an outside observer might anticipate on the basis of relative frequencies or the experiences of the actors concerned. Just as fatalistically oriented ideologies may shift subjective probabilities of desired outcomes to near zero and of unwanted ones to near unity, so a more optimistically oriented belief system may shift them in precisely the opposite direction. Subjective conditional probabilities may be made to seem much higher (or lower) than unconditional ones, thereby encouraging or discouraging a given line of action.

Since many types of important events are replicated only a very few times, so-called objective probabilities may be very difficult to estimate, so that expectancies may need to be based on faith or untested (and usually oversimplified) working theories of causal processes (Blalock and Wilken, 1979). How likely is it that an enemy will attack? Will course of action A have a better chance of influencing one's opponent than action B? How long will the opponent's morale hold out given a certain level of inflicted punishment? How effective will one leader be as compared with another? What will motivate an army? How likely is it that God will intervene on our side? Belief systems may have a major role in enabling members to answer such questions, whether or not the answers provided eventually prove correct.

Belief systems may also vary in their effectiveness in persuading members to discount or explain away previous experiences as no longer being applicable. Another variable, here, is the ideology's ability to manipulate the expected benefits of victory or costs of defeat, perhaps by characterizing the opponent in a given manner, by exaggerating the value of land or natural resources that might be gained, or by linking the outcome of one particular conflict with those of others (e.g., the so-called "domino theory").

Certain types of highly simplistic ideologies may have distinct advantages over more complex ones in affecting such expectancies, especially when reality checks are difficult to conduct. To the degree that a substantial majority of a party's members endorse a single ideological system and are then in a position to impose their will upon the remaining members, this ability of belief systems to alter subjective probabilities may be considerable. One may take the position that to the degree that this occurs, the party's behaviors are "irrational," but this may presuppose a much higher correspondence between subjective and objective probabilities (or experience?) than seems realistic. Actors may indeed calculate their behaviors very carefully but base them on expectancies that have been heavily influenced by beliefs, many of which cannot be countered by reality checks.

Ideological systems that can rather easily manipulate expectancies will help to increase the degree of mobilization as well as to maintain it even after a series of defeats. For example, victory may be perceived as being "just around the corner." With a little more effort, perhaps an important third party can be induced to join the fray on one's side. God may be expected to reward heroic actions in some unspecified way. It does not follow, however, that the *efficiency* of the mobilization effort will be improved. Inaccurate expectations may encourage the use of inappropriate tactics or the failure to anticipate accurately the opponent's response. If prior experiences are downplayed sufficiently, or unrealistic expectations about one's own future performance maintained in spite of current cues to the contrary, this may obviously interfere with one's judgments as to optimal strategies. "Fanatics" often engage in suicidal behaviors that actually may do their cause more harm than good. Such actions may, for example, prove extremely divisive among the general membership of the larger party.

4. INSULATING FROM ALTERNATIVE BELIEF SYSTEMS

Simplistic ideologies usually require a high degree of insulation from competing belief systems. It is important at the outset to distinguish the notion of insulation—or protection against intruding forces—from mere isolation from them, which will also depend upon such factors as how many competing systems are present, the physical isolation of the party in question, and the degree to which other parties are interested in influencing the belief system in question. As we shall use the term, the idea of insulation refers to a property of the belief system itself to withstand competing systems regardless of whether or not they are actually present at the time as viable alternatives. A belief system that is merely isolated—perhaps because of spatial considerations—may break down very rapidly once a competing system becomes actively relevant. One that has its own built-in insulating mechanisms may resist outside modifications for very long periods of time, however.

In general, we would expect highly simplistic and dogmatic belief systems to be highly resistant to competing systems, provided that the former "fit" the interests of members and cannot easily be shown to have failed. Simplistic systems are also vulnerable, however, in instances where there are major segments of the membership that are disadvantaged by them and therefore tempted to search for alternatives. Therefore, membership homogeneity and successes in conflict outcomes may be preconditions for the ability of a simplistic system to withstand competitors. As long as Germany was successful in World War II, Nazism was not only highly popular but extremely resistant to allied propaganda. Once it became apparent that the war effort was hopeless, however, it crumbled very rapidly and, subsequent to the war, has been overwhelmingly rejected in Germany.

Ideological simplicity and rigid dogmatism, when reinforced with effective and often harsh controls over deviants, may thus effectively close out competing systems without incorporating any of their features. Another insulating mechanism—which, however, results in ideological modifications—is that of redefining or reinterpreting those features of the belief system that are most ambiguous. Catholicism has been remarkably successful in bending but not breaking, through devices such as permitting "deviant" social movements a degree of autonomy in reinterpreting, or emphasizing, certain aspects of what is admittedly an extremely complex theological system. From time to time, Papal decrees or gatherings of Cardinals may "clarify" or "redefine" certain principles to bring the belief system more into line with positions taken by the general membership or a highly vocal minority. Thus the "official" version of an ideology may change, sometimes almost imperceptibly, so as to maintain its most crucial features.

Competing belief systems will generally be sponsored by opposing parties, often with the aim of splitting off an important minority segment to whom the competing belief system has some potential appeal. Marxism, for example, was at one time thought to have appeal to blacks or other potentially disaffected Americans. One effective insulating mechanism is to combine overly simplistic and threatening interpretations of the competing ideology with a direct linkage with a hated enemy. Thus Marxism—a highly complex and diverse collection of political and social ideas—is virtually equated in America with Leninism and the USSR and is perceived as the polar opposite of both capitalism and democracy. Those who accept it, or who even accept the validity of some of its criticisms, are immediately labeled as traitors, fools, or knaves. In this instance, the "defense" against an intruding belief system consists of a highly simplistic "revision" of its contents, together with severe measures to assure that vulnerable members are not exposed to other versions that might be more favorably interpreted.

This suggests that a highly complex belief system, such as our own, can remain relatively insulated from an alternative system, so long as the latter is easily identified with a powerful opponent. Other sets of beliefs, as for example those emanating from major world religions such as Buddhism or Hinduism, may "sneak in" virtually unnoticed and gradually help modify a theological system that is not under direct frontal attack. Therefore, it is perhaps wise to distinguish between situations where a belief system resists a direct substitution effort and others where it resists more gradual modifications through what might be thought of as an ideological cooptation process.

5. CONSISTENCY WITH OBJECTIVE INTERESTS

Implied in our previous discussion is another dimension, namely the degree to which a belief system is actually compatible with the objective interests and socialization practices of party members. This will of course be a difficult matter to assess. Even though an outside observer might perceive that objective interests were being sacrificed by an adherence to the ideology in question, the members themselves may define their interests in terms of whatever utilities and subjective probabilities they attach to their goals, and these will at least in part be determined by the belief system to which they subscribe.

The human animal has certain obvious biological needs: to eat, procreate, and remain relatively invulnerable to outside attack or to environmental shifts that threaten survival. Few ideological systems will be so rigid as to deny these basic needs, but some may be more successful than others in enabling or motivating members to achieve and then maintain the behavior patterns necessary to assure survival at a higher than minimal level. Where there are competing ideologies, and where one is obviously more compatible with such interests than others, we would expect the former to have a distinct advantage. Therefore, whenever reality checks are possible we expect these to place limits on the nature of the belief system that will be accepted. If nothing else, the diffusion of a belief system across societal boundaries will depend not only on conquest and the relative statuses of the sending and receiving parties, but also on the content of the belief system itself.

One feature of a belief system that is relevant in this regard is its utility in helping members to explain away or rationalize whatever actions they deem necessary in combatting an opposing party. The belief that "savages" needed to be "saved" by Christianity or "civilized" by Western ideas was, for example, very convenient in squaring internal democratic practices with colonialism and imperialism on other continents. Racial beliefs in America have, for a long period of time, shifted conveniently according to the interests of the majority of white Americans and the changing nature of competition, as well as the needs for minority labor or loyalty during periods of stress. Stereotypes of peoples of other nationalities have shifted, almost overnight, depending on their status as allies or opponents in international crises.

In times of rapid change, simplistic belief systems that are also highly rigid are at a distinct disadvantage in accommodating to modifications in the objective environment. If it is to retain its appeal, a highly simplistic ideology must be sufficiently vague and permissive of authoritative reinterpretations. Therefore, a belief system that places the primary emphasis on obedience to a particular leader—regardless of the courses of action taken—may be far more effective in terms of its adaptability to changing circumstances than one that prescribes a fixed mode of response. Similarly, a belief system that depicts *all* outsiders or nonbelievers as suspect will be more flexible in this regard than one that specifies particular groups or competing belief systems as targets. Beliefs to the effect that our religion is *the* one "true" faith or that we are God's "chosen people" imply complete generality with respect to the opposing party or competing ideological system. A change in the nature of this opponent therefore does not require major adjustments in the belief system. Similarly, leaders who are given an ideological blank check with respect to means they may employ have a distinct advantage over those who must attempt to mold the ideology each time they wish to adapt their strategies to the situation at hand.

6. ETHNOCENTRISM

One of the accepted generalizations of social science is that nearly all groups are ethnocentric, in the sense of believing that their own group's ways are superior to those of others. Ethnocentrism obviously varies by degree, however, and we are certainly aware of many groups, as well as entire nations, that consider themselves inferior to others in selected ways. Extremely high levels of ethnocentrism, as for example a "chosen people" orientation, are likely to produce a reciprocated reaction on the part of nearly all actors with whom the party in question has contact, thereby increasing the probability of conflicts with them but also feeding back to reinforce any paranoid interpretations placed on their reactions. In particular, a high degree of ethnocentrism is highly compatible with a tendency to blame others for whatever occurs and to justify punitive acts toward them.

Minority groups or small societies with histories of prolonged conflicts with far more powerful neighbors may develop extreme degrees of ethnocentrism as a defense mechanism, as well as a general explanation for hardships of many types.[1] In comparison with those that adopt a more fatalistic or passive resignation orientation, such highly ethnocentric parties can often retain their identities over very long periods of time even where, as in the case of Jews, they have not been able to retain a territorial base. Where the territorial base also exists within some larger nation-state, the minority is likely to develop a separatist orientation rather than an assimilationist one. In recent years we have seen considerable evidence of the persistence of conflict groups within such enclaves: the Kurdish revolts in Iran, Iraq, and Turkey; the Basque terrorist movement in Northern Spain; the Tamils in Sri Lanka; the Sikhs in India; and the Provisional wing of the IRA in Northern Ireland. Chronic conflicts serve to reinforce highly ethnocentric belief systems, thus helping to insulate them from competing systems and perpetuating rigid boundaries between the party in question and its neighbors.

7. DEGREE TO WHICH BLAME IS PLACED ON OTHER PARTIES

A closely related though analytically distinct dimension is the degree to which a belief system places the blame for failures on other parties (though usually accepting credit for successes). A fatalistic system portrays problems and failures as being inevitable or at least beyond one's own control. In contrast, we are referring to the tendency to interpret these same events as the responsibility of other actors who, presumably, may be influenced to modify their behaviors. Both ideological devices may be seen as ways of reducing guilt or a sense of responsibility for what has taken place, and both are highly compatible with a simplistic orientation to social causation. If the (perceived as) guilty other party is clearly in a dominant position, fatalism becomes highly compatible with such a tendency to place blame on that dominant party. If, however, the guilty party's power is nearly equal to or less than that of the more paranoid one, such a tendency to blame others is likely to result in a highly combative, punitive orientation that frequently generates conflicts.

Paranoid ideological systems may be highly general in nature and directed toward almost any actors with which the party is in contact, or they may be directed toward particular enemies, usually traditional ones with long histories of combative interactions. Is the ideological system capable of shifting targets according to the circumstances? As noted, a "chosen people" orientation would appear readily adaptable to such shifts. Belief systems such as those that developed in Western European nations at the height of colonialism were capable of being applied to "savages" of many varieties, but because of the obvious dominance-subordination involved could not credibly be twisted so as to blame these "uncivilized" natives for most types of failures. Blame could be assessed in selected kinds of events, however, as for example so-called Indian "massacres" or slave uprisings. The guilt reduction mechanisms involved in such instances could be considerable, as there would be no need to look beyond the events in question to their more fundamental causes. A parallel ideological mechanism appears to be at work in contemporary interpretations of "cowardly" acts of terrorism directed against very strong parties by much weaker ones.

Similarly, the eye-for-an-eye revenge orientation characteristic of Middle Eastern value-systems places the blame for each immediate act on the other party, without considering the entire sequencing of reciprocated responses that maintains the conflict. Ideological simplicity clearly reinforces this mode of thinking, as does a high degree of ethnocentrism. It is also helpful if the party can construct a mythology (based on actual historical events, where possible) that traces out a long series of instances in which the party has been victimized by others, including traitorous acts by its own members. We also anticipate that all of these ideological features will increase the party's overall sensitivity to another party's responses, as for example a tendency to respond immediately and extensively to increases in armament levels.

8. ENCOURAGEMENT OF PUNITIVE RESPONSES

Blaming other parties is not quite the same thing as punishing them for their actions, though in the case of potential opponents having less or equal power than the party in question we would expect the two dimensions to be highly compatible. Especially in the case of subordinate groups, however, aggression may have to be inhibited or turned into sufficiently subtle directions that a more potent punitive response is not produced. Furthermore a punitive orientation may either be conditional on a particular behavior, as implied in the phrase "knocking a chip off the shoulder," or more or less automatic under highly general circumstances.

In the case of very weak parties confronted by much more powerful ones on whom blame has been placed, punitiveness toward certain internal scapegoats may be strongly encouraged. Thus, the blame for a party's own weaknesses or failures to achieve success may be placed on still weaker parties that can plausibly be linked with the more powerful opponent. Hitler blamed the Jews for Germany's prior defeat in World War I, and international Jewry—even Jewish bankers!—have been depicted as responsible for the rise of Communism. Japanese-Americans were immediately imprisoned after Pearl Harbor in spite of a total lack of evidence concerning their potential disloyalty. "Uncle Toms" among black leaders have been blamed, and sometimes punished, for perpetuating discriminatory practices. As we shall note in discussing conflict groups in the following chapter, those members of subordinate parties who serve as intermediaries or who otherwise cooperate with the dominant party are often the first targets of hostile actions by such conflict groups.

9. DICHOTOMIZATION AND DRAWING RIGID BOUNDARIES

Simplistic ideologies are also likely to encourage dichotomized, black-and-white thinking that draws or reinforces rigid boundaries around one's own party, as well as justifying aggression against outsiders. Dichotomized thinking is also characteristic of conflict groups that reject tendencies toward neutralism and that take the position that others must be either for or against them. Thus, dichotomization is highly compatible with a number of the dimensions we have already discussed and seems especially likely either immediately prior to the initiation of conflict or during the engagement itself.

Rigid dichotomization has certain disadvantages in conflict situations, however. If the opposing party is defined as totally "black," it becomes difficult to appeal simultaneously to diverse elements within that party or to encourage social movements within it that favor compromise or a cessation of hostilities. By failing to make distinctions between enemies and neutrals, such a set of beliefs also makes it difficult to appeal to third parties to play buffer roles or to facilitate negotiation processes. Therefore, any party that attempts to draw distinct lines between itself and others risks losing their support as potential coalition partners or as actors who will be motivated to restrain a victorious opponent from engaging in vindictive punitive actions. Almost by definition, the drawing of rigid boundaries and overly sharp distinctions, though it may motivate one's own members to drastic actions, also tends to alienate those who have been placed on the other side.

10. EXTENT OF AMBIGUITIES

Nearly all belief systems contain ambiguities concerning the conditions under which given lines of action should be taken, how conflicting principles should be handled, and the ways in which positive and negative sanctions can be expected to result from specific behaviors. Some systems are less ambiguous than others, however. Again we would expect that highly simplistic belief systems will, in general, be less ambiguous than more complex ones. One function of dichotomization and the drawing of distinct boundaries is, of course, to reduce such ambiguities and to permit prompt and decisive responses. Certain kinds of ambiguities may be almost deliberate, however, even in the case of highly simplistic and otherwise rigid belief systems. Ambiguities permit flexibility of interpretation on the part of decision-makers, from whose point of view the ideal belief system may be one that espouses a blind faith in their leadership regardless of the specific courses of action taken. Given an unstable environment and an inability to predict an opponent's responses, any belief system that rigidly prescribed some courses of action while prohibiting others would obviously be dysfunctional.

Ambiguities with respect to the nature and timing of sanctions may also be useful in controlling potential deviance, provided that the prescribed and proscribed behaviors have been well-defined. The postulated existence of an all-seeing supernatural power with inscrutable sanctioning powers can provide a very useful and generalized mechanism for assuring loyalty, especially in instances where thoughts and behaviors cannot easily be monitored by other human actors.

Where scepticism concerning such supernatural powers already exists, however, these very same ambiguities may be far less effective than a detailed list of do's and don'ts together with an accompanying set of expected, though partly nonverifiable, sanctions. The Ten Commandments is one such list that has withstood the test of time. Given the tendency for situations to change and for such specific lists to generate ethical dilemmas, there will also typically be a need for ideologically supported "interpreters" to help resolve such ambiguities and to rationalize actions that, on the face of it, would seem to be incompatible with such directives. The commandment, "Thou shalt not kill" has seldom been interpreted as applying to one's immediate enemies, though it may vaguely be applied to enemies in general.

Ideological ambiguities seem especially likely if there is a need to appeal to a highly heterogeneous membership having diverse interests that cannot be permitted to lower the degree or the efficiency of mobilization. The appeal to platitudes while playing down specifics is one such device. Making the world safe for Democracy or supporting the "Free World" sounds very nice, as long as one does not become too specific as to how such democracies are defined or precisely why a particular government's policies justify its being included as a member of the "Free World." Political slogans are often left unexamined, as a way of assuring loyalty in an otherwise ambiguous and potentially divisive situation. It is as though nearly everyone recognizes that there are underlying ambiguities that should not be discussed. Those who insist on doing so run the risk of being labeled disloyal or as troublemakers who do not really understand what others take for granted. Precisely why God should be on the side of one's own party rather than on that of the opposition is the kind of issue that does not get debated. Dichotomized thinking, a tendency always to blame the other party, and an extrapunitive orientation all generally reinforce such a tendency to leave many potentially embarrassing questions unasked.

Therefore many kinds of ambiguities will remain, even in the most simplistic of belief systems. Where there are rather distinct cleavages involving membership groupings having very different goal hierarchies or divergent interests, such ambiguities provide leverage for rival leaders to emphasize one set of values at the expense of another or to select features of the total belief system that support their own positions. The greater the number of ambiguities, the easier it is for opposing factions to claim legitimacy on some basis. If the party in question is obviously winning the conflict such rival leaders' appeals may be ineffective, but if defeats or nonsuccesses predominate, this ability to capitalize on underemphasized aspects of the belief system may bolster their appeal. This is especially likely whenever goals that are highly important to a major population segment have had to be deferred or where the segment currently in power appears to have differentially benefited from the conflict.

11. FLEXIBILITY

As already noted, some belief systems have the characteristic of bending without breaking and of incorporating elements of other belief systems without destroying their own major tenets. They may also afford realistic interpretations for defeats or setbacks, failed policies, or leadership changes without losing their overall credibility. How can this be accomplished? A belief system that is sufficiently complex will usually contain a large number of "loopholes" as well as outright ambiguities and inconsistencies, so that certain features may be played down or emphasized as the occasion demands. As long as members are willing to accept the interpretations provided by legitimated authorities such as members of the priesthood, or by charismatic leaders whose policies remain unquestioned, a belief system may remain basically intact despite numerous setbacks.

Ideological flexibility of this sort will generally assist a group in achieving consensus in spite of heterogeneity of interests, as long as there is the impression given that nearly everyone will benefit. The trick is to offer a little something to everyone, even where in many instances rewards may be unverifiable. Especially useful in this connection are emphases on otherwordly objectives, backed by reasonably definite assurances that compliance will facilitate their attainment.

As noted, a postulated all-seeing being may help out whenever the monitoring of individual members' behaviors is difficult or costly and whenever sanctions are expected to be imposed in the distant future. A priesthood capable of taking advantage of ideological flexibility and changing circumstances can also assist in directing members' actions against specific targets such as infidels or communistic atheists. In some instances, as in the case of the Salem witchhunts, they may also link such targeted individuals to postulated enemies (e.g., the Devil) of those supernatural forces presumed to be siding with the in-group. The unverifiable nature of such linkages may go unnoticed or be disclaimed if challenged. Ideological flexibility may thus be combined with a high degree of specificity as to courses of action to be taken and parties to be targeted.

12. LOYALTY TO CENTRALIZED LEADERSHIP

We have implied that belief systems may also vary according to the degree to which group members are expected to demonstrate loyalty to a centralized leadership, including the unquestioned acceptance of commands to take specified courses of action. Such loyalty may be highly conditional, as for example when such commands are clearly compatible with well-specified regulations or codes of conduct. We are especially referring, however, to belief systems that encourage members to develop unconditional loyalties involving the acceptance of commands without questioning them. The ideal-type code of conduct endorsed by military organizations represents a point close to this extreme of the loyalty continuum. Closer still, perhaps, is the kind of loyalty attached to a charismatic leader such as Adolf Hitler.

Extreme loyalty of this nature obviously makes possible a very high degree of mobilization—which may remain substantial in spite of many apparent failures as long as the leader in question remains in command. In some respects as well efficiency will be improved in that immediate actions are facilitated. To the degree that the actions taken are foolhardy or easily countered by the opponent, however, efficiency may be diminished. In retrospect, the nearly blind acceptance of Hitler's decision to invade Russia led to early successes but then ultimate failure because of the Führer's rigidity and underestimation of Russian will. In this instance an extremely high level of unquestioned loyalty to the party's leader made it difficult to adapt to the changing circumstances of the war and made negotiation next to impossible. Of course, a more "rational" leader might have been able to maximize degree and efficiency of mobilization simultaneously.

Ideologies may also differ with respect to the degree to which loyalty is supposed to be attached to particular individuals, as persons, or to those who occupy specific positions. In the former instance problems of succession will arise, as has been frequently noted by historians. In the latter, however, there will be the question of who decides on the rules of transition and how to regain the loyalty of those members who favored the losing candidates. It seems rather difficult to develop belief systems that successfully induce unquestioned loyalty to such leaders in instances where there has been substantial disagreement as to the rules of succession. Once more, if unseen supernatural powers can be invoked to justify the results of the selection process, so much the better. Kings and emperors have often attempted to invoke divine sanctions to assure such loyalties, some having been more successful than others (Bendix, 1978).

13. EMPHASIS PLACED ON COLLECTIVIST GOALS

Given that human beings are powerfully motivated to survive as individuals and to pursue what are defined culturally as "selfish" goals, belief systems must cope with the problem of motivating members to make personal sacrifices for the good of the group. Some ideological systems, including our own, place very heavy emphases on the importance of individualistic goals or on loyalties to much smaller units such as families or local communities. In such instances the call for sacrifices for the benefit of the larger group are likely to be highly conditional on the existence of an obvious threat. The problem then becomes that of developing belief systems that are capable of identifying such threats before they have become overwhelming, while at the same time discouraging or sanctioning individualistic desires or "selfish" behaviors in the presence of such threats.

It therefore becomes highly important to identify concrete opponents with obviously hostile intent and the power potential to threaten the party's very survival. Thus the need to sharpen distinctions between good guys and bad guys and to specify trip-wire mechanisms that will immediately alert dormant individuals. Certain leadership elements or population segments may consistently serve the function of playing such alarm-sounding roles, or the roles may shift according to the nature of the threats being posed. A generalized tendency to blame other parties for past conflicts, a mythology that lionizes past heroic leaders, and an emphasis on simplistic explanations also facilitate the mobilization process.

Unless the belief system places a very heavy stress on the importance of collectivistic behaviors and the paramount importance of group as compared with individualistic goals, it may be difficult to sustain such a self-sacrificing orientation over prolonged periods of time. Especially as new generations—who have not experienced the previous crisis—begin to take over leadership roles and engage in day-to-day behaviors unrelated to potential outside threats, it may be difficult to regain the momentum produced by a prior crisis situation unless a collectivist orientation has been fostered.

A generalized paranoic set of beliefs to the effect that individuals must constantly be on guard against imagined enemies may be useful in this connection, especially if it contains unverifiable elements. Conspiracy theories are a case in point, provided that those who reject them can convincingly be made a part of the conspiracy, thereby effectively quieting the internal opposition. We would therefore expect collectivistic belief systems to stress the necessity of guarding against outside threats, real or imagined. They are also likely to encourage severe sanctions against dissenters and to attempt to link them, via conspiratorial theories, to these outside threats. An intense loyalty to a centralized authority will also reinforce these processes.

14. EXPANSIVENESS

Finally, belief systems may vary considerably in terms of the degree to which emphasis is placed on converting nonmembers, whether by persuasion or force. A chosen people may wish to remain exclusive, perhaps hoping that at some future time the tables will be turned in their favor. Certain religious sects, especially those that emphasize a highly strict code of moral behavior, may also prefer to remain exclusive. Others strive for new converts, however, perhaps as a power grab or as an assurance that other religious groups will not predominate. Similarly, ideological systems may be used by nation-states with expansionist ambitions, as is often claimed to be true in the case of the two superpowers.

In general we would expect expansionist belief systems to be highly compatible with conflict orientations. Often there is a strong impetus to engage in punitive behaviors directed against nonbelievers combined with a willingness to forgive and accept converts who disclaim their prior loyalties. Thus expansionist orientations may involve dichotomized thinking (e.g., the "saved" versus the "damned") but are probably incompatible with the drawing of too-rigid boundaries. They also seem compatible with a high degree of ethnocentrism, with emphases on the need to make personal sacrifices on behalf of the collectivity of true believers, and with the encouragement of loyalty to those leaders willing to engage the group in expansionist activities. Highly simplistic and dogmatic creeds may under some circumstances attract disaffected members of other groups but may also serve to crystallize and alarm the opposition, as well as making it difficult to appeal to those who have been socialized to accept a very different set of beliefs.

Here, and elsewhere, many of the intuitively "obvious" interrelationships among our list of dimensions are likely to be highly conditional on structural factors as well as the remaining ideological dimensions we have attempted to specify. Furthermore, as our wording has implied, many of the causal connections among these dimensions are likely to be reciprocal. If a high degree of ethnocentrism or a tendency to blame outsiders is already "in place," this may make it easier (or more difficult) to adopt certain new elements without producing strains or inconsistencies in the ideological system. The temporal sequences involved, however, are likely to be somewhat idiosyncratic to the situation or for other reasons may be difficult to specify.

A Submodel for Ideological Factors

The submodel provided in this section will be needed only in those instances where ideological factors must be treated as endogenous and, therefore, subject to modification as a conflict process unfolds. Ideological variables may be treated as exogenous or as givens in many kinds of simple situations where conflicts are of relatively brief duration or involve micro-level parties such as marital dyads or other kinds of small groups. Whenever the parties concerned are major corporate actors such as nation-states or quasi-groups that undergo transformations during the period in question, however, the belief systems to which they subscribe may also undergo modification. Such changes in belief systems may, in turn, feed back to influence some of the other variables that appear in our general model. If so, an ideological submodel may prove useful to help account for these changes.

As we have just noted, it will usually be difficult to pin down causal sequences as one attempts to interrelate ideological dimensions. Furthermore, the sequencing that occurs in any given instance may be primarily due to historical accidents, as for instance the borrowing of one or another element from another ideological system subscribed to by a neighboring party. Political conquest, as for example that of Central American Indians by the Spanish in the 16th century, may be responsible for the forced introduction of a foreign ideology, such as Catholicism. Over time, however, only certain features of the new belief system may be accepted, while still others may undergo modification so as to make them more compatible with important elements of the original belief system. In the resulting "acculturation" process some of the strains discussed in Chapter 6 will undoubtedly be accentuated, with the mutual compatibility of two or more dimensions influencing the ways in which the belief system in question is ultimately modified.

Our causal diagrams cannot really represent such processes without becoming overly complicated. In the extreme we might connect every pair of dimensions by double arrows, indicating a two-way flow of influence. This would make the model completely untestable, however, unless there were a substantial number of predetermined or exogenous variables included in the system or unless temporal sequences could be specified and data collected at the appropriate intervals.[2] Instead, we have opted to restrict the model by including only those arrows that imply the most important flows of influence. Given the paucity of data and prior theoretical formulations of this type, the model should be regarded as highly tentative and subject to major reservations if applied without modification to specific instances.

In the model of Figure 7.1 the fourteen ideological dimensions are located toward the center of the diagram. Around the fringes of the figure have been placed selected variables of importance in our general model of Figure 5.2. Also in these locations are variables pertaining to X's relationship to Y: such factors as X's dependence on Y, X's vulnerability and sensitivity to Y, X's level of trust and expectations

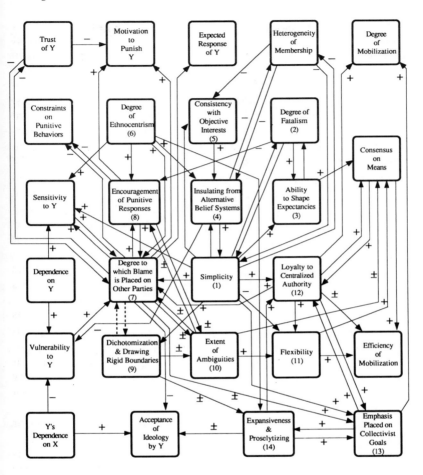

Figure 7.1 Ideological submodel

as to Y's responses, X's motivation to punish Y, Y's dependence on X, and Y's acceptance of the ideology in question.

At the extreme right of the diagram have been placed certain outcome variables: the degree and efficiency of X's mobilization and the degree of consensus among X's members. These variables, in turn, can be expected to impact on other variables in the system according to the mechanisms specified in our other models. Since the "dependent" variables appearing at the extreme right may impact on subsequent values of the variables that appear to the left of them in our diagram, there will then be indirect feedbacks of ideological factors on themselves. In most but not all conflict situations, we may anticipate that such feedback processes will be relatively slow as compared with changes in other variables. If so, they may be ignored in all but the most long-term analyses.

SIMPLICITY, FATALISM, SHAPING OF EXPECTANCIES,
INSULATION, AND INTERESTS

The first dimension we discussed, ideological simplicity, has been placed at the center of the diagram since a very large number of arrows connect it to other variables in the system. Numbers corresponding to the section numbers used in our discussion of the ideological dimensions have been inserted in the .ower center portions of the boxes of each of our ideological dimensions, so as to make it easier to follow the argument and to link it with the previous discussion. In this section we are concerned with the first five dimensions only.

Ideological simplicity, dimension 1, is shown as reciprocally linked with fatalism and the ability of the ideology to remain insulated from competing belief systems. These connections are by no means simple ones, however, as noted in our earlier discussion. The general observation is that ideological simplicity reinforces insulating mechanisms, and vice versa, and that fatalism ordinarily requires a simplistic belief system as a necessary condition for its widespread acceptance. As we noted, however, many kinds of simplistic systems are not fatalistic and, indeed, imply the very opposite: an activist orientation to the outside world, including potential opponents.

The ability of a belief system to shape expectancies, our dimension 3, is taken as reciprocally linked to fatalism in a rather obvious way. It is also taken as heavily influenced by the ideology's simplicity, which permits actors to modify their subjective probabilities toward either extreme of zero or unity. Arrows have not been drawn from dimension 3 to simplicity, however, since we are assuming this particular feedback mechanism to be relatively weak in most instances. Similarly, there are no arrows linking dimensions 3 and 4, the shaping of expectancies and the ability of an ideology to provide insulating mechanisms. Dimension 5, the consistency of the belief system with the party's objective interests, is taken as a function of simplicity and as having a positive impact on the ideology's insulating capacity.

This set of five ideological dimensions is directly linked to "outside" factors only through the heterogeneity of the members' goals, which has been placed at the top of the diagram. Heterogeneity is taken as reciprocally linked to both ideological simplicity and the capacity of the ideology to remain effectively insulated from competing belief systems. It is also taken as a cause of the ideology's consistency with objective interests, if only in the negative sense that an extremely heterogeneous party will also have a diversity of interests that cannot all be satisfied by any ideological system, particularly a simplistic one. The nonideological variables appearing to the left in Figure 7.1 are not directly linked to any of these five ideological dimensions, except for the arrows from insulating capacity to X's vulnerability to Y, and from simplicity to sensitivity to Y.

ETHNOCENTRISM, BLAME PLACEMENT, PUNITIVENESS, AND DICHOTOMIZATION

Ideological dimensions 6–9 have been placed toward the left of the diagram since three of them are taken as being directly linked to several of the nonideological variables located on the extreme left. Degree of ethnocentrism is taken as having positive effects on both the placement of blame on other parties and the encouragement of punitive responses, as well as the fourth dimension, the belief system's insulation capacity. It is also assumed to have positive effects on the ideology's expansiveness and the tendency to proselytize (dimension 14).

The placement of blame on other parties plays a key role in the model, being positively and reciprocally linked to the encouragement of punitive responses and X's sensitivity to Y, and negatively linked reciprocally to X's trust of Y. It is also assumed to be positively affected by simplicity and vulnerability to Y as well as by the degree to which there is loyalty to a central authority (dimension 12). Blaming the other party is taken as a factor that weakens constraints on punitive behavior toward Y but that strengthens the emphasis on collectivist goals (dimension 13). It is also assumed to have a negative impact on Y's acceptance of the ideology in question and to have a possible direct and reciprocal connection with the tendency to dichotomize and draw distinct boundaries. The tentativeness of this last prediction is indicated by the dashed lines connecting this particular pair of dimensions.

A reciprocal causal link is postulated between blame placement and the extent of ambiguities in the ideology (dimension 10), with the indeterminacy of the sign being indicated by the "±" symbol in the figure. An arrow has also been drawn from blame placement to the expected response by Y, which has been placed at the top of the figure. The sign of this particular relationship is not predicted as Y's responses will undoubtedly be multidimensional.

Dimension 8, the encouragement of punitive responses, is connected with several previously discussed dimensions, as we have already noted. In particular, it is assumed to weaken any constraints placed on actual punitive behavior that might result from guilt mechanisms. An arrow with a negative sign has been drawn from fatalism to punitiveness suggesting that a highly fatalistic belief system seems incompatible with any kind of response at all, especially a punitive one. For much the same reason as indicated in connection with blame placement, the sign of the reciprocal linkage between punitiveness and ideological ambiguities is taken as indeterminate.

Finally, the ninth dimension, the tendency to dictotomize or to draw rigid boundaries, is assumed to be reinforced by ideological simplicity and to have direct but indeterminate effects on ideological ambiguities and the ideology's expansiveness (dimension 14). In particular, we have already noted that the drawing of rigid "in-versus-out" boundaries may inhibit expansiveness or proselytizing tendencies, whereas a dichotomizing tendency in general may encourage them by motivating members to "rescue" the other party's damned by making them members of the in-group.

AMBIGUITIES, FLEXIBILITY, LOYALTY, COLLECTIVISM, AND EXPANSIVENESS

The remaining five ideological dimensions have been placed toward the bottom right portion of the diagram and are assumed to be linked more closely than the previously discussed ideological dimensions to the nonideological outcome variables that appear to the extreme right. We have already commented on linkages of other dimensions to the extent to which the ideology contains ambiguities, but this tenth dimension is also assumed to be a positive contributor to the ideology's flexibility and to have an impact on the degree of internal consensus among a party's members. The sign of this latter relationship may depend, however, on whether or not the ambiguities are "functional," in the sense of glossing over potentially troublesome issues, or whether they encourage schisms over alternative interpretations of the ambiguous features of the ideology.

Dimension 11, the ideology's flexibility to bend but not break, is assumed to be negatively impacted by its simplicity but positively affected by loyalty to a centralized leadership (dimension 12). The latter linkage is based on the assumption that such a leadership will be in a position to gain ready acceptance for "official" modifications of troublesome portions of the ideology. Ideological flexibility is then assumed to have positive effects on two important nonideological variables, the degree of consensus among party members and the efficiency of the mobilization effort. Of course this assumes that most members are willing to gloss over any incompatibilities in the belief system that may remain in spite of this ability of the belief system to accommodate new ingredients. This suggests the possibility of a statistical interaction between flexibility and loyalty to a centralized authority, a feature that has not been incorporated into the diagram.

Loyalty to a centralized authority, as noted, is assumed to have a positive effect on the degree to which blame is placed on other parties and to be reinforced by ideological simplicity. The model also implies positive linkages with degree of mobilization and with consensus, with the latter variable also feeding back to influence loyalty positively. Whether or not such loyalty also improves the *efficiency* of the mobilization effort, however, will depend upon decisions made by this leadership. Therefore the sign of this direct linkage is taken as indeterminate.

Dimension 13, the emphasis placed on collectivist as contrasted with individualistic goals, is assumed positively affected not only by simplicity and the degree to which blame is placed on other parties, but it is also assumed to have reciprocal and positive linkages with loyalty to a centralized authority and expansiveness. Collectivism is postulated to have a positive impact on degree of mobilization but no direct linkage with efficiency. Finally, ideological expansiveness is expected to reinforce loyalty to a centralized leadership, as for example a religious prophet or charismatic political figure. It is also predicted that expansiveness will have a direct impact on the acceptance of the ideology by Y, but with the sign of this relationship being indeterminate and conditional on such factors as Y's dependence on X and the methods used in the proselytizing effort.

This concludes our rather tentative discussion of ideological dimensions and the corresponding ideological submodel. Ideological variables will play a critical role in our subsequent discussions in Chapters 9 and 10, of conflict-sustaining and conflict-terminating processes. Before turning to these processes, however, we need to discuss another set of critical factors that impact upon them, namely how the heterogeneity of one party may affect the responses of the other, and how conflict groups impact upon these processes.

Notes

1. At the individual level, analogous processes may produce paranoia or a high degree of suspiciousness, resulting in an inability to trust others.

2. In a simultaneous-equation model involving k mutually interdependent endogenous variables, there must be a sufficient number of predetermined variables (either exogenous or lagged endogenous variables) to permit one to *leave out* at least k-1 variables from each equation.

Chapter **8**

Responses to Heterogeneous Parties and Conflict Groups

Thus far we have allowed for certain implications of a party's heterogeneity, such as its consequences for degree and efficiency of mobilization, free riding, and surveillance capabilities. Our heterogeneity submodel, presented in Chapter 5, incorporated these and other factors. We have also allowed for dissimilar thresholds among rioters or agents of control, but we have otherwise not directly addressed the problem of how the diversity of interests among a party's members may affect the conflict process itself.

In the present chapter we shall focus more specifically on the question of how the other party's reactions may be affected by such heterogeneity. As an important special case, we shall also discuss conflict groups and how a party's heterogeneity impacts on, and is affected by, the presence of one or more conflict groups. Problems of control over conflict groups are also relevant to how the other party reacts and, in particular to the ways in which the overall conflict process becomes self-sustaining and is eventually terminated—subjects that will be the focus of our attention in Chapters 9 and 10. Before addressing these latter matters, however, we shall present our conflict-group submodel at the close of the present chapter.

Whenever a party, say X, contains members with truly divergent orientations, this fact may have a bearing on the other party's responses as well as on the strategy that the former party employs. If X consists of a set of very loosely related subparties such as coalitions among city-states or territories controlled by rival chieftans or warlords, it may become possible for Y to play one off against the other or to make an example of one or two so as to influence the others. For instance, a number of major empires have been created through a process of savagely destroying a few defeated enemies and their villages or cities while conveying the message to others that if they surrender peacefully, their own lives and properties will be spared. By a process of divide and conquer, the other party is able to take advantage of the diversity of interests within the party of concern.

There may be certain advantages of diversity and a rather loose control system, however, especially when the more moderate members of the party of concern, here X, can make a convincing argument that they have little or no control over their own extremist members. The potential actions of such extremists can, for example, be used as a bargaining weapon akin to Schelling's (1956, 1966) notion of commitment. If X's leaders can convince Y that, if Y were to sustain its present policies or modify them in the wrong direction, then extremist elements among X's members could no longer be controlled, then X is in effect telling Y that the onus of the risk-taking is on Y, not X. At the same time, because of their perceived or actual weakness in controlling their own extremists, moderate leaders of X are communicating to Y that they, themselves, cannot be held accountable for the actions of their own deviant members.

In the second portion of the chapter we shall discuss conflict groups which may, indeed, act as out-of-control extremists of this type. Here we may focus on the nature of party Y's response to such a potential threat. If party Y is willing to hold all members of X responsible for extremist actions, and if the extremists are unable to protect party X's "innocent" members from punitive actions by Y, then there may be a dampening of the extremist actions. During World War II there were occasions where Nazi occupation troops used chance mechanisms to punish entire villages for the actions of members of the so-called "underground" resistance movement. For instance villagers might be lined up and every 20th person shot.

Such arbitrary punitive actions may, of course, further arouse and solidify the opposition or, if publicized, bring third parties into the conflict on the side of the victimized party. Knowing this, terrorists within party X may deliberately attempt to goad the other party into drastic punitive acts of this nature. Even if they succeed in doing so, however, it does not necessarily follow that the counterreaction will also develop or that important third parties will actually be drawn into the conflict. The only result may be further harm to innocent members of their own party.

In such instances we are dealing with actions and reactions that cannot unambiguously be attributed to an entire party. Therefore they afford that party the opportunity of deniability. It is not Catholics in Northern Ireland who attack Protestants, it is the Provisional wing of the Irish Republican Army. It is not the U.S. Government that is invading Nicaragua, it is the Contras. If a party cannot, in fact, control its own agents in such instances—and this is often actually the case—these agents are in an excellent position to influence the level of conflict between the two major parties. Whenever tensions are being reduced extremists may create another "incident," leaving the impression that their actions have the tacit approval of the larger party's membership. Since this may actually be the case, the opposing party must then decide on an appropriate response and whether that response should be targeted on the extremist elements alone or the entire membership.

One such response may be to turn its own extremist elements loose, while looking the other way. We may then witness a situation in which extremist agents on both sides engage in overt conflict, with the supposedly more moderate elements being vicarious witnesses to the fray. Still other persons will be genuinely innocent victims. The nearly anomic situation that has characterized Lebanon during the decade of the 1980s has many of these features. Needless to say, once this type of "informal" conflict has gotten underway it may be very difficult to control, as extremist elements on both sides gain increasing autonomy from their respective party's formal leadership.

In situations in which one party, say Y, is considerably stronger than the other, there may be a loss-of-face phenomenon at stake for the dominant party. In such instances the weaker party may be using the fact that it cannot control its own extremists to help create a response dilemma for the stronger party. An overresponse, unless justified, can also produce a loss of face for the stronger party, since it will be presumed that it has lost control of the situation and has had to resort to bullying as a desperate response. Therefore, the stronger party is likely to make every effort to pin responsibility onto the entire membership of the weaker party or even to assume direct control of the situation. The British government has found it desirable, if not necessary, to introduce army troops into Northern Ireland with the hope of controlling its extremists without at the same time having to take more drastic steps. Israel invaded Lebanon in 1982 for much the same ostensible reason. As we can see in both of these instances, such a step is fraught with risk if the control effort is unsuccessful. Extremist elements are likely to gain increasing sympathy and internal support, and the more powerful party may be unable to punish them without at the same time undergoing huge expenses and internal dissension concerning its "bullying" role.

We have in this instance a special case of the general point that principals and their agents may have only partly overlapping interests and that agents may sometimes have an important independent influence on the course of a conflict. Since the control over a party's agents is a matter of degree and may be difficult for either party to predict, a party's extent of organization and its heterogeneity may be important factors that need to be considered in any analysis of a conflict situation. The degree to which the actions of the agent are visible to all concerned and are not conducted in secrecy, the extent to which agents themselves control conflict resources, the availability of alternative agents who can serve as replacements, and the internal power of such agents vis-à-vis the general party membership will all be important factors.

Whenever the party of concern is extremely polarized, one may expect that such agents will tend to fall toward one extreme pole or the other, and this will perhaps drive them into close cooperation with others who share their own positions and into a secretive, clandestine role vis-à-vis those at the opposite pole. America has of course witnessed a number of such instances where clandestine operations—conducted by extremists but with the secret blessing and material support of high governmental officials—were carried out without the knowledge of other governmental officials or the general public. The more general point is that conflict processes can be affected as much by processes that are internal to one or both parties as by those that involve the responses and counterresponses of one entire party to the other.

We next turn our attention to a very important type of subparty, the conflict group that is likely to be specifically organized to engage in protracted conflicts, with or without the blessing of the general membership of the larger party. We shall then construct a submodel that indicates how such conflict groups may affect and be influenced by some of the other variables contained in our more general model of conflict processes.

Conflict Groups

Whenever a larger party finds it either impossible or highly costly to carry out a campaign involving extreme conflict, small cell-like conflict groups may emerge to engage in these processes. Although Dahrendorf (1959) referred to conflict groups in more general terms as interest groups that engage in a wider variety of forms of conflict, I am using the term in approximately the same sense as do Simmel (1955) and Coser (1956) to refer to smaller, tightly controlled groups specifically organized to engage in more extreme types of conflict.[1]

Such groups are usually characterized by exceedingly strong, almost total commitments on the part of their members, self-imposed segregation from the larger population, secrecy and rigid internal controls over deviants, simplistic ideological systems, and highly exclusive recruitment processes. Examples of such conflict groups are the Mau Mau of Kenya, the Provisional wing of the IRA, Communist revolutionary cell groups, the Mafia, the Weathermen of the late 1960s, and the Ku Klux Klan during the Reconstruction era.

Conflict groups of this nature are often associated with weak, exploited parties, such as colonial peoples or minorities having prolonged histories of being in subordinate roles. We also find them in rural settings in countries with authoritarian governments and among separatist-oriented ethnic groups that are often located near the boundaries of a nation-state's territory. Where the subordinate group in question has on numerous occasions failed to achieve success by a variety of alternative means, certain extremist elements of that party may resort, in desperation, to violent means that depend for success on their being dissociated from the larger population as a whole, while nevertheless receiving the tacit approval and assistance of the larger membership.

Sometimes conflict groups may be created or, if already in existence, be secretly encouraged to do the "dirty work" of dominant parties that desire to maintain control by using extreme violence on selected targets but that also need to place the blame for such acts on third parties. The Ku Klux Klan played an important role in intimidating blacks, Catholics, Jews, and their sympathizers by using means that were foreclosed to legitimate authorities. Similarly, secret "death squads" have recently been employed in several Latin and Central-American countries to intimidate those who were suspected of joining or sympathizing with incipient resistance movements. In Lebanon, certain terrorist groups were purported to be working informally with the governments of Iran, Libya, and Syria to embarrass or intimidate the U.S. and other Western powers. Rival conflict groups, as for example "gangland" secret societies, sometimes struggle with one another in settings where none is sufficiently powerful to come out into the open where it would be far more vulnerable to legal forces controlled by the government.

As implied in our previous discussion, whenever a subordinated party can be characterized by a combination of very high utilities but low subjective probabilities of achieving independence or revenge, we may anticipate a high degree of volatility with respect to choices among means. If any given line of action appears to achieve even momentary success, thus raising subjective probabilities above their current levels, we would expect a rapid switch to this means on the part of a substantial proportion of the membership. Disillusionment may be equally abrupt, however, as the efficacy of the means in question becomes dubious. Given the high utilities attached to the objectives, we may therefore expect marked swings in strategies, as well as considerable debate as to their relative merits.

Under such circumstances one would also predict a splintering of the party into to rival factions espousing widely differing strategies. If no concerted course of action appears to offer any real hope of success, the situation is ripe for the emergence of extremist groups oriented either to going it alone, or to forcing other elements of the population into cooperation or at least nonresistance to their mode of operation. If more moderate leaders have recently failed to achieve successes, the easier it will be for such conflict groups to discredit previously used tactics and to gain acceptance of their own tactics. This in turn will help them obtain the protection they require to maintain their anonymity, to prevent informers from cooperating with the enemy, and to expand to a larger social movement oriented to more open guerrilla warfare.

From the micro perspective, such conflict groups are likely to attract as members those individuals who subscribe to simplistic belief systems that stress the need for personal sacrifice, the total immersion of the self in some larger cause involving extreme loyalty to the in-group, and an intolerance of those who oppose it. Such individuals, often young male adults or adolescents, are then socialized to disciplined forms of violence through a combination of symbolic rituals of membership and an exposure to extremely strict disciplinary measures designed to weed out opportunists. New recruits usually find it necessary to prove themselves during an early phase of their socialization and are totally immersed in a tight social network and provided with a rigid and dogmatic ideological system that stresses the need for extreme actions in order to accomplish some ultimate goal. The terrorism being espoused thus offers an opportunity for extreme forms of aggression rationalized in idealistic terms.

In this manner, extremist behaviors are often accompanied by a form of idealism that seems puzzling and hypocritical to outsiders but that is highly functional for members who might not otherwise be capable of such violent forms of behavior. Promises of ultimate rewards for total commitments are often combined with equally strong threats of punishments for desertion that are reinforced by periodic ritual murders of those whose loyalty has come under question. Given the necessity of maintaining the total commitment of conflict-group members, it is also usually demanded that normal ties with family and previous friends be either cut off entirely or be weakened so as to preserve a willingness to take extreme actions that might even endanger them. The essential point is that conflict-group members must remain willing to take major risks on command and to engage in highly disciplined forms of behavior that are not inhibited by attachments to outsiders.

For conflict groups to be successful over a prolonged period of time, there must be a substantial proportion of the larger group who gain vicarious satisfaction from acts of aggression against the opponent and who provide tangible support in the form of refuge, provisions, and a normative system that serves as an incentive for potential future recruits. Martyred members of conflict groups often become folk heroes to be emulated by the young. Those who have sheltered them at considerable personal risk are also likely to receive recognition, whereas those who have opposed them—or, worse still, have turned them over to opposition authorities—will be maligned or censured in more extreme ways.

If the conflict group's strategies appear successful, and particularly if the responses of the opposing group suggest signs of weakness or lack of resolve, extremist thinking often begins to take over more generally. It may then become incorporated into the ideology of the larger party in question, making the task of recruitment into the conflict group that much easier and the opposition of moderates far less effective. Processes such as these seem to have characterized both the Palestinian support for the Palestinian Liberation Organization (PLO) and the Irish Catholic support for the Provisional wing of the Irish Republican Army (IRA) in Northern Ireland. Likewise, historical accounts suggest similar processes were at work for several decades during Reconstruction in many Deep South communities, where it became exceedingly difficult for moderate whites openly to combat the terrorist programs of the Ku Klux Klan.

CONDITIONS FAVORING CONFLICT GROUPS

The radical black psychoanalyst Frantz Fanon, in his classic work, *The Wretched of the Earth* (1963), dealt with conflict-group formation, though he did not use that particular term. Illustrating his argument in terms of the Algerian struggle against French colonialism, Fanon pointed out that colonial territories are often characterized by a native elite that is oriented toward the colonial power and that performs an intermediary function in maintaining control over a passive majority. Such an elite, which is usually urban, collaborates with the colonial power and in turn receives tangible rewards in the form of middle-rung positions in authority structures and a certain amount of derived prestige. Although possibly ambivalent toward the colonial rule, such an elite also often attempts to emulate members of the alien society and accepts many features of its culture. The French emphasis on the assimilation of a very small number of such local elites served to reinforce this tendency to undermine the native cultural system, as well as to provide a safety-valve mechanism permitting upward mobility for those members of the subordinate group willing to play the game.

Fanon stressed the harmful effects on the psyche of the exploited subordinate group of this kind of divided loyalty and cultural split-personality. He went much beyond this, however, to the advocacy of conflict groups devoted to overthrowing and undermining such local elites who had succumbed to a colonialist mentality that was serving to prevent mobilization of an effective resistance movement. Terrorism directed largely against such internal elites was seen as a necessary mechanism for the ultimate overthrow of the colonialist power, in this instance France. As we know, the prolonged resistance movement in Algeria not only proved successful, but—with the assistance of Fanon's and other similarly radical ideological literary works—also served as a model for subsequent uprisings elsewhere in Africa and other third-world areas.

It is no surprise, then, that conflict groups often direct their attacks on relatively unprotected members of the in-group, especially those who are rather obviously allied with the dominant power. In South Africa we are witnessing a similar phenomenon with the assassination—by forming necklaces of burning tires—of minor black officials and police officers who have cooperated with the dominant white regime. Similar assassinations of black loyalists were perpetrated by secret Mau Mau cell groups active in the liberation movement against the British in Kenya. Where the dominant colonial power has opted to rely heavily on such local elites as intermediaries in the control process and has also begun to weaken its direct ties to the colonial territory, such local elites are much safer targets of aggression than are members of the colonial power itself. As in the case of Algerian terrorists, however, a conflict group may also attempt to bring the conflict closer to home by infiltrating the territory of the colonial power itself and assassinating some of its leaders.

Since the actual damage inflicted by a small number of such acts is likely to be minor and more of symbolic than of strategic importance, conflict groups must be both willing and able to conduct very protracted conflicts with their adversaries. In effect, reliance is placed on wearing down the opposition without engendering extreme forms of suppression or punishment of the entire group, of which the conflict group is but a small part. This often depends on self-imposed inhibitions within the dominant party, which are then interpreted as signs of weakness.

If there is a high degree of mutual dependence so that the stakes are high for *both* parties, however, these inhibitions against suppressive retaliation are likely to be weakened, and the entire subordinate party membership may be held responsible for extremist forms of violence. As we have already noted, terrorist acts against Nazi occupation forces in World War II were sometimes met by far more extreme forms of repression such as the arbitrary decimation of the local population. In these instances we may certainly infer very high utilities on the part of German officials to suppress incipient forms of resistance. Because of their own acceptance of Nazi ideology, such retaliatory acts could be rationalized by these officials with low "moral cost" to themselves. Innocent villagers were punished so as to make them more willing to deny members of the resistance movements their needed population-base of support. Such tactics, combined with methods of inducing informants to come forward, effectively reduced the impact of underground conflict groups until such a time when the power of the German occupying forces was considerably weakened toward the close of the war.

The successes of many third-world conflict groups seem to have depended on a combination of economic and political factors, most of which reduced the tangible benefits of colonialism for popularly elected European governments in England, France, Belgium, and the Netherlands. European political parties and important segments of the citizenry who opposed colonialist rule were reinforced by a growing recognition that the continued occupancy of distant territories involved a major drain on depleted economic and military resources. In those instances where there were miniscule numbers of white settlers, as in most of central Africa, the mere anticipation of protracted conflicts and open guerrilla warfare apparently was sufficient to motivate a peaceful withdrawal process. Where settlers were more numerous, as in Algeria and Kenya, it required actual terrorist acts to motivate the withdrawal, but the essential ingredient was the raising of the costs of occupation and control to levels that were prohibitively high relative to the costs of withdrawal.

As this suggests, conflict groups may ultimately succeed but with extremely high costs to the larger population from which they were recruited and sustained. Even where the dominant party may eschew extreme repressive measures, an underground opposing conflict group may emerge in instances where the official policy of the controlling party is more benign. In Northern Ireland, for example, Protestant extremists have employed violent tactics similar to those used by the IRA. Until both sides have become sufficiently exhausted to encourage their members to withdraw their tacit support for the violence, an escalating Richardson-type process may develop and maintain itself for a very long period of time. Once such a process has gone sufficiently far, it may require unusual acts of heroism to expose those members of one's own party who have perpetrated violence on the other group, if only because effective social control mechanisms have broken down. Beyond a certain point, the actions of moderates become interpreted as traitorous or cowardly and are therefore increasingly subject to extreme sanctions. It may require a powerful, neutral third party to dampen the process, and few such parties may be willing to undergo the considerable costs of playing such a role.

Another likely outcome of a protracted struggle is that if a conflict group should gain the leadership after the opposing party's defeat, it may retain many of its features and continue to terrorize targeted members of the in-group. In Africa, where conflict groups have been formed along tribal lines—as for example the Mau Mau movement among the Kikuyu—hostilities may be directed toward rival tribes with which there have been traditional hostilities. The result may be a pattern of domination that differs little from the previous one except for a change of guard. Where counterconflict groups emerge, there may be no outside party willing to pay the costs of intervention. More moderate internal leaders may have become totally discredited as a result of their identification with the previous colonial power. Civil wars resulting from processes such as these have become endemic to post-colonial Africa.

By their very nature, conflict groups require patterns of behavior that are not easily changed once the conflict has subsided. Members are socialized to distrust outsiders, to guard against infiltration, and to expect a total commitment from their comrades. The belief systems developed under such circumstances must not only be highly simplistic, but they must also serve to justify extreme behaviors as being necessary to achieve the ultimate objective. Some all-embracing ideology, such as Marxism or a dogmatic set of religious beliefs, may serve as a disguise for more selfish motives that, if unmasked, could not possibly sustain the degree of motivation needed to engage in highly risky forms of behavior. Furthermore, those who espouse the same general purposes but are willing to employ only more moderate means must be discredited, since a failure to do so would undercut recruitment efforts and also possibly raise doubts among current members concerning the necessity of their own extremist tactics. A basic distrust and suspiciousness of nearly everyone may be cultivated as a protective device. The "enemy" is defined in very broad terms to include a substantial proportion of the larger party on whose behalf the conflict is being waged.

Conflict groups are also likely to focus on long-term and sometimes nebulously idealistic objectives, since they may need to sustain numerous setbacks as well as alienated reactions from those they are purporting to help. From here it is but a simple step to defining all nonmembers as disloyal to the ultimate cause or as basically selfish individuals unwilling to make the necessary sacrifices. Self-selection has probably been at work during the recruitment process, so that initially hostile and amorally aggressive individuals are overrepresented among the membership. Providing such individuals with a belief system designed to disguise such aggressive motivation in terms of self-sacrifice and idealism may then serve to unite otherwise disparate individuals into a tightly-knit unit having a devotion to duty that seems highly "irrational" or fanatical to outside observers.

Goals of conflict groups may also become displaced, so that the people they are initially attempting to help become merely instrumental to them in accomplishing their remote objectives. A guerrilla army may terrorize and exploit local peasants in the name of liberating them from a colonial power. Efforts by local peasant leaders to resist the guerrillas may be met with torture and assassination, all in the name of the ultimate cause. If the war is protracted, as is often the case, unwilling members of the local population may be forced to serve as recruits, or their villages may be destroyed or exploited. In such a manner, a conflict group may actually become an unwelcomed third party to the more general conflict—one that serves to perpetuate hostilities long beyond the point where they are desired by the larger group that is supposedly being served. Conflict may become an end in itself, rather than merely a means.

The voluntary psychological and sometimes physical isolation of a conflict group from those it is claiming to assist is likely to increase the difficulty of bringing the conflict group under control once it is obvious that its behavior has become dysfunctional. Unless the conflict group is heavily dependent on the logistical support of the larger community, it can rather easily go underground and recruit future members by appealing primarily to the most aggressive elements of the population. Though the number of terroristic acts directed at the opposing party may diminish, this may merely reduce any inhibitions about killing innocent bystanders or extending the bounds of "legitimate" targets. Whatever paranoid tendencies may have previously existed may only be intensified, as members see themselves being set upon by those they have been attempting to help. Meanwhile, the opposing party may seize upon the occasion to discredit those who are attempting, unsuccessfully, to bring the conflict group under control.

Thus there may be a considerable delay in reducing the overall level of conflict, largely because there are so few social control mechanisms available to moderates. Given the probable reactions of ambivalence and fear among the general population, it may also prove difficult to sustain a program designed to discredit the conflict group, since there will almost inevitably be a series of ambiguous events and minor crises that may also play into its hands. Hostilities may simmer for a decade or more.

As the fatigue factor begins to predominate, however, conflict groups may find it increasingly difficult to recruit new members or to induce the larger population to supply logistic support and protection from the other party. If some conflict-group members or potential recruits can be provided with satisfactory alternatives, internal cleavages may develop with the result that the conflict ideology begins to soften. For example, there may develop a secondary set of justifications that stress that conflict strategies are only necessary as defensive measures. Intrapunitive tactics, such as the self-imposed hunger strikes that occurred among imprisoned IRA members, may become necessary to reinforce their martyr image among the general populace.

Failures almost inevitably lead to cleavages and disagreements as to the extent of conflict needed for ultimate victory. Once such cleavages develop, it is then much more difficult to maintain secrecy and internal discipline, with a resulting increase in the level of distrust among members. Such a fractionating process need not lead immediately to a reduction in total conflict, however, as evidenced by examples of the split in the Black Muslim movement in the 1950s and 1960s, the somewhat later fractionating of the Black Power movement, and the many cleavages that exist among PLO factions in Israel, Lebanon, and other Middle Eastern countries. Attempted negotiations with moderating factions may merely serve to renew the efforts of more extremist elements, leading to the formation of additional conflict groups with slightly different ideological supports. An opposing party that fails to recognize such cleavages may not realize that the leaders with which it is attempting to negotiate are not in a position to make binding agreements.

THE GENERAL ROLE OF CONFLICT GROUPS

Although conflict groups obviously serve to induce and perpetuate conflicts that sometimes work to the disadvantage of the larger groups they are purportedly aiming to serve, one must not overlook the positive consequences, particularly in those instances where a subordinate party has undergone a prolonged period of subjection

without any real hopes of change for the better. Not only do the
actions of conflict groups provide vicarious satisfactions to the populace at large, but they also help to raise subjective probabilities of
wearing down the dominant party and of achieving ultimate victory.
As we have noted, this possibility becomes a realistic one whenever
the opponent is constrained in the punishment it metes out to the
general membership while it is also unable to locate and punish the
actual perpetrators of violence. If the benefits of continued dominance and control are rapidly diminishing, fatigue may mount more
rapidly in the dominant group than in the subordinate party. Therefore, a low degree of dependence on the subordinate party by the
dominant one will generally improve the conflict group's likelihood of
success.

Equally important over the long run, the emergence of conflict
groups may serve as a catalyst to encourage other leaders to play
more active roles and to awaken the general membership from its
passive acceptance of its subordinate role. Where conflict groups
have expanded into guerilla movements that have successfully challenged the dominating party, some of their leaders may "mellow" and
become folk heroes with sufficient popularity to lead new governments. The success of such leaders will depend, of course, on the
degree to which their earlier tactics have received the active support
of the "liberated" masses, rather than having terrorized and alienated
them. Chairman Mao's tremendous popularity, for example, was obviously attributable to the fact that his Communist revolutionary army
gained a highly favorable image with the Chinese peasantry during
the period of Japanese occupation and the war of liberation against
General Chiang. Unfortunately, however, Mao did not mellow sufficiently to work out accomodation mechanisms with more moderate
leaders. His conflict-oriented philosophy was never really adapted to
the necessity of relying on a more technically trained and bureaucrati-
cally oriented leadership once the need for a conflict strategy had
diminished.

We have also suggested that conflict groups operating on one side,
say a subordinate party, may generate countermovements among the
opposition. These countermovements may be especially effective
whenever legitimacy is at stake, and where the dominating party can
either excuse or disclaim responsibility for terrorist acts by these
countergroups, while at the same time surreptitiously supporting
them. Arbitrary and brutal acts on the part of police or army person-

nel may be discounted as necessary in the line of duty, for example. The result may be an escalating series of violent acts on both sides, without any important modifications in the distribution of power. Moreover, moderating forces are likely to be weakened under such circumstances, thereby making it all the more difficult to reach an accomodation.

In any given instance it may be difficult to predict in advance whether or not the long-run consequences of conflict-group formation will be beneficial or harmful to the party in question. If other approaches have failed in the past, and if conditions have become intolerable for members of one of the parties, we may be almost assured that conflict groups will emerge and begin to set a process in motion that may be difficult to control. In effect, they are playing the "threat game" discussed in the game theory literature (Kelley and Thibaut, 1978). If one party controls the allocation process, the only tactic that may be available to the other party may be that of threatening to make matters worse for *both* contestants unless a more equitable allocation is forthcoming.

In the next chapter we shall consider in some detail a number of mechanisms that sustain conflicts for long periods of time in spite of considerable costs, which are often much greater than either party had anticipated at the outset. Dynamics that are internal to one or both parties often inhibit the operation of conflict-reduction processes. As has been suggested in the present section, conflict groups may play very important roles in this respect. Before considering this matter, however, we turn to our summary submodel for conflict groups.

A Submodel for Conflict Groups

The submodel to be discussed in this section will obviously only be relevant when there are conflict groups that operate somewhat autonomously of the larger parties themselves and that therefore may engage in behaviors that are distinct from those of other members. As we have already noted, conflict groups sometimes are hostile to more moderate elements of their own parties and will be subject to varying degrees of control by them. They also may be perceived as distinct by the opponent, here party Y, and may be censured in very different ways from other party X members. Conflict groups also vary with respect to the degree to which they are protected from Y's sanctions, as well as the support they receive from other party X members. For all of these reasons, it may therefore be advisable to develop special models that allow for such complexities. Our submodel linking conflict groups to these and other factors is provided in Figure 8.1.

Four kinds of exogenous variables appear in the left and top portions of the figure. The duration of the conflict is taken as a direct cause of three kinds of variables: the goals and utilities of party X members, their motivation to punish Y, and their unresolved persistent grievances. The block of ideological factors is assumed to influence goals and utilities and the motivation to punish Y. Two additional predetermined variables are the past successes of the conflict group(s) in question and the past successes of rival groups, which we presume to be those with more moderate orientations.

Both of these variables are assumed to affect the heterogeneity of the goals and expectancies of the general party membership, though the signs of these linkages are taken as indeterminate. The idea here is that if conflict groups have enjoyed considerable previous successes as compared with those of their rivals, then they are likely to produce a reasonably homogeneous set of utilities and subjective probabilities among the larger party membership. The same, of course, applies to more moderate rivals. In contrast, if both types of groups have a mixed history of successes and failures, this is likely to result in a much more heterogeneous set of opinions among the general membership. These same two predetermined variables are also assumed to have direct impacts, though with opposite signs, on the degree to which there is internal support for the conflict group.

The power of rival groups, which appears at the bottom left in the diagram, is taken as an important factor not only in connection with the degree of support for the conflict group, but also with its ability to recruit new members and to intimidate the general membership of the party. The model postulates a positive feedback loop (with both arrows having negative signs) between the power of rival groups and the conflict group's ability to intimidate. Intimidation may weaken these other groups, but their power in turn may inhibit punitive behaviors directed toward these other members.

Unresolved persistent grievances are expected to have reciprocal effects with the goals and utilities block as well as direct effects on motivation to punish Y, party heterogeneity, and internal support for

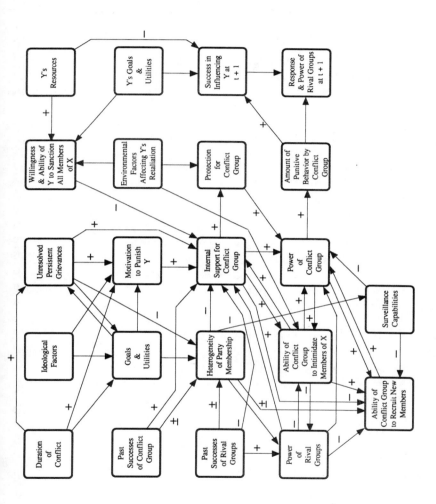

Figure 8.1 Conflict-group submodel

Source: Adapted from Blalock (1987, p. 34).

the conflict group. The general idea that we elaborated on in our prior discussion is that past grievances, especially when experienced by a relatively weak party, are likely to result in strong utilities to punish Y but not necessarily in such punitive actions themselves. If a conflict group exists that is actually in a position to inflict negative sanctions on Y in spite of considerable risks, it is then likely to receive internal support, thus increasing both its autonomy and actual power. Positive feedback loops have also been drawn linking the power of the conflict group with both its ability to recruit new members and its ability to intimidate other members of party X.

The surveillance capabilities of party X may also be critical in this connection. It is assumed that party heterogeneity will have a negative impact on surveillance capabilities, if only because a very heterogeneous party is likely to contain members who can successfully protect the anonymity of conflict-group personnel. If the larger party is able to keep the conflict group under close surveillance, this is expected to inhibit the group's recruitment efforts and its general level of autonomy and power. Not represented in the model, however, is the possibility that the larger party's surveillance capabilities are likely to interact with the degree of internal support for the conflict group. A conflict group that enjoys considerable internal support seems unlikely to experience close surveillance, whereas one that is perceived as a serious risk is much more apt to undergo such surveillance in those instances where the capacity for doing so is sufficient.

Party Y's ability and willingness to retaliate, both against the conflict group members themselves and the general party membership, is also likely to affect the internal support the conflict group receives. As we have previously noted, if Y is willing to apply extreme measures not only to the conflict group itself but to innocent members of X as well, we expect this to reduce the degree of internal support the conflict group receives and thus its power. Another kind of exogenous factor in the model consists of the block of variables lumped together under the label of "Environmental Factors Affecting Y's Retaliation." These variables are assumed to affect three kinds of factors: Y's willingness and ability to censure all members of X, the protection the conflict group receives, and the ability of the conflict group to intimidate other members of X. Two other variables treated as predetermined in the model are Y's resources and Y's goals and utilities, both of which are taken as direct causes of Y's willingness to censure and the success of the conflict group in influencing Y at the later time t+1. These variables pertaining to Y are located toward the top-right corner in the diagram of Figure 8.1.

Finally, the autonomy and power of the conflict group is taken as a cause of the amount of punitive behavior it actually employs against Y, with this latter variable in turn affecting both the success in influencing Y at t+1 as well as the responses and power of rival groups at t+1. Since these latter variables will, in turn, affect the relative power of future levels of many of the variables in the model, the processes are assumed to have a dynamic quality.

We have not attempted to specify any variables that affect lag periods or possible impacts on the variables that have been treated as exogenous in the model, however. Over the long haul, such factors as ideological variables and X's and Y's relative resources will undoubtedly be affected. As we shall note in the next chapter, the duration of the conflict may also be lengthened to the degree that conflict groups on both sides remain in a position to engage in punitive exchanges in spite of high fatigue levels on the part of the general memberships of the two larger parties. Thus the relative power positions of conflict groups and their more moderate rivals may also be critical. These will undoubtedly vary during the course of the conflict itself, adding a further complication to our already highly complex theoretical model.

Note

1. Dahrendorf (1959) uses the term "conflict groups" to refer much more broadly to parties engaged in class conflicts. I am referring, instead, to tightly controlled groups specifically organized to conduct continuous, acute conflict as their primary function. Coser (1956, pp. 99–103), citing Simmel (1955), refers to such groups as "struggle groups."

Chapter 9

Sustaining Conflicts

By definition any conflict will entail costs and punishments for both sides, and these costs may accelerate as the conflict wears on. Therefore, it is important to understand the factors that affect a party's ability and willingness to maintain or possibly even accelerate the level of conflict at any given time during the process. One or both parties may have initially underestimated these costs, as well as the determination of the other party to continue absorbing punishment over a prolonged period of time. Therefore, continued reassessments may be necessary so as to predict subsequent responses, including possible peace overtures.

Not only are total costs and the duration of conflict likely to be underestimated initially, but such costs will almost inevitably be unevenly distributed among each party's members. Some, particularly those in leadership positions, may continue to enjoy net benefits or at least be in the position that, for them, the expected costs of peace or conflict reduction may continue to outweigh those of continued conflict. Other members, however, may be experiencing far greater costs than were originally anticipated. Not only will there be differential exposure to risk, as in battle situations, but a number of goals that are irrelevant to the conflict itself may have had to be deferred. Utilities for these unmet goals can be expected to increase, perhaps at an accelerating rate, whereas utilities favoring the conflict itself may be approaching satiation. Thus the "mix" of utilities may differ both across individual members and over time.

A critical factor in virtually all conflict situations will be actors' expectations regarding the consequences of either escalating or deescalating the conflict. Many members may not be aware of costs being borne by others on both sides. To the degree that a centralized leadership is able to hide losses from view or successfully understate their extent, it may become possible to mislead members into underestimating such costs or to convince them that victory is just around the corner. Myths concerning the party's own invincibility, a history of miraculous victories, or courageous acts of heroism may also distort subjective probabilities of victories. Other myths or even an accurate historical record may also convince members that the costs of suffering a defeat at the hands of an unscrupulous opponent would be considerably greater than the costs of maintaining conflict. All of this is to say that deception may be practiced not only toward the opposing party but toward one's own members as well.

The success of myths, secrecy and deception will obviously depend on a number of factors, including the party's homogeneity with respect to both goal hierarchies and also the experienced costs and benefits of the unfolding conflict. An extremely heterogeneous party may undergo more internal strains as the conflict's beneficiaries attempt to convince those who have borne the greatest costs that the conflict must be continued.

The initial causes of and support for the conflict may be important in this connection. Where there was initial disagreement as to whether or not to engage in conflict, and where internal opposition groups have not been totally discredited or silenced, increasing costs may lead to renewed cleavages and even open rebellion. It may also be more difficult to hide costs from view and to maintain credence in an overly simplistic ideological system. Where the conflict was initially used by a party's leaders to discredit rivals or to distract members' attention from internal problems or shortcomings, such opposition leaders may regain the initiative whenever the conflict situation begins to create extreme hardships or uneven burdens on members, or whenever defeat seems almost inevitable to substantial segments of the total membership.

Considerations such as these obviously bear on the fatigue factor and on the degree to which the party of concern is dependent upon the opposition party. Although it seems unwise to attempt to delineate general stages through which all conflict situations pass, it is important to recognize that dynamic processes will be at work and that, as a conflict wears on, there will be modifications in each party's internal structure that may influence a number of variables in our general model. Such changes may be examined from the standpoint of the micro level, where individual actors' goals, expectations, and behaviors may be modified. They may also be analyzed from the standpoint of resource depletion and replenishment, leadership struggles and internal cleavages, and ideological support systems. These, in turn, will be influenced by the actual and expected behaviors of the opponent, as well as by the perceived costs and benefits of continued conflict to the other party.

The basic question with which we will be dealing in this and the following chapter is that of how and why conflicts are sustained in spite of the obvious costs to both parties. Related to this is a second critical question to be discussed in the next chapter. What factors affect each party's expectations as to the costs of *concluding* the conflict, short of a decisive victory? How are conflicts ultimately brought under control in situations where fatigue factors begin to dominate but where distrust and fear of the opponent remain strong? What role, if any, can third parties play in the conflict resolution process?

Impacts of Initial Causes

The actual or perceived causes of a conflict obviously may impact upon its subsequent course, though undoubtedly in complex ways. If the onset of the conflict has been abrupt and is perceived to have been brought about by a specific and dramatic event, such as the bombing of Pearl Harbor or the invasion of one country by another, there may be a much greater consensus on the need to sustain the conflict than in instances where initial causes were far more diffuse and subject to dispute. Rarely, of course, do we expect members of even an aggressive party to blame themselves for initiating a conflict. Instead, they are likely to cite "historic" grievances such as the occupancy of territory rightfully belonging to their own peoples or, perhaps, continued exploitation by the other party. Even so, the initiation or onset of conflict may be much more crisp in some situations than in others, making it more plausible to place the blame squarely on the shoulders of the opposing party.

An important factor in this connection is the extent to which there was initially a high or low degree of consensus concerning the need to engage in conflict with the other party. Except in situations involving highly coordinated corporate actors, we may anticipate initial disagreements as leaders evaluate the pros and cons of entering into a conflict situation. Those who favor conflict may attempt to portray their opposition as weak, naive, overly trustful, or selfish. Once the conflict has begun, such an opposition may subside, especially during periods of initial enthusiasm or early victories. The internal opposition may not have been totally discredited or removed from positions of power, however, and this may affect their future roles once the costs of conflict have begun to mount and it has become apparent that costs and benefits are not being shared equally among all group members.

In the case of relatively weak or subordinate parties such as racial or ethnic minorities, there may be a high degree of consensus on the nature and extent of grievances, but considerable disagreement over alternative means. We have already commented on the dilemmas faced by parties with high utilities for conflict and the resolution of grievances, but with low subjective probabilities of achieving satisfactory results by any particular means. In such instances militant leaders may insist that conflict strategies are the only remaining recourse, whereas moderates may stress the expected costs of engaging in conflict and risking the vengeance of a powerful dominant group. Past practices of such a group may be invoked, either to convince reluctant members that the risks are worth taking or that the punitive response will be too extreme. As long as the conflict is going well and concessions appear to be resulting, moderates will be discredited. As costs begin to mount more rapidly than gains, however, internal cleavages may reemerge.

A critical factor in these instances is the degree to which opposition leadership has been totally displaced or disgraced, with its support groups disbanded or discredited during earlier phases of the conflict process. Where such a moderating leadership group has simply removed itself temporarily from the scene rather than being forcefully imprisoned or assassinated, we would expect that as the tide begins to turn such an opposition will be in a better position to undermine the conflict effort.

Another possibility, of course, is that a totally distinct opposition leadership will emerge and be supported by that segment of the population that has the most to lose by a continuation of the conflict. A case in point may be the student-inspired opposition to American participation in the Vietnamese war, a war that was proving far more costly than had been initially anticipated and that was of direct concern to draft-age males on college campuses.

Whenever those initially opposed to the conflict have successfully been portrayed as cowards or villains, or as too sympathetic with the enemy, it may be virtually impossible for them to live down such unfavorable images. A highly simplistic ideological system that places primary blame for unfavorable events on the opponent is also likely to lead to a dichotomized image of leaders as being, on the one hand, either saints or heroes or, on the other, traitors or villains. If so, then if there is to be a subsequent internal opposition group formed it may be necessary for this to be led by members of the heroic element. Given the benefits accruing to this group, however, this is unlikely to occur unless costs become extreme and defeat seems almost inevitable. The German General Staff did not begin to question Hitler seriously until defeats began to occur and his rigidities were obviously becoming dysfunctional.

Yet if costs become readily obvious to nearly all and if opposition leadership among the hero group actually does emerge, collapse may occur much more suddenly than would otherwise be anticipated. Indeed, an internal revolution may take place. Where the external opponent is either unable or unwilling to impose its own leadership after the collapse, such a revolutionary movement may come to power. Opposition groups may even gain growing support, being perceived as undergroud movements oriented to freeing the group's membership from a misguided or ruthless tyrannical leadership. The inability of Germany to take advantage of the collapse of the tsarist regime in Russia, of course, made it possible for the Bolshevicks to gain power very soon afterward. Similarly, Marshal Tito emerged as a folk hero and dictator in Yugoslavia, in part because the defeated German and Italian opponents were not in a position to dominate that country, nor was Russia sufficiently interested or inclined to make the considerable effort to put a puppet leader in his place.

As briefly noted in the introduction to this chapter, a long history of grievances against an opponent is likely to make an initial consensus on conflict more likely and to reinforce those ideological features that simplistically tend to place the blame for nearly all unfavorable events on the opposing party. This will of course undermine efforts by moderates to discourage the engagement in conflict and will also make it far more difficult to terminate the conflict once costs have begun to mount.

Trust of the opponent is a critical variable in this connection. A party that is perceived to have caused a long list of prior grievances can hardly be expected to behave favorably in the future, regardless of any promises it may have made. Indeed, a period of prolonged prior conflict may induce both sides into a "do or die" frame of mind in which the total destruction of the opponent may appear to be the only realistic alternative. After a series of long and nearly disastrous wars with Carthage, Cato and other Roman leaders of like mind decided to destroy the city once and for all, and succeeded in doing so in 146 B.C. American history is also replete with instances in which troublesome Indian tribes have been virtually wiped out in revenge for so-called "massacres" of white settlers.

A prolonged history of continuous or episodic conflicts, either with the present opponent or others that have been lumped into the same category, will have produced an extensive list of culture heroes and martyrs, as well as an ideology that explains these prior conflicts in a favorable light. There is likely to be a strain toward ideological simplicity, at least with respect to interpretations for past conflicts and prescriptions for dealing with future potential opponents. Russia's history of enduring major invasions, particularly from Western Europe, undoubtedly reinforces any paranoid tendencies directed toward the inheritor of Western European power, the United States. Separate incidents, such as the invasions by Napoleon and Hitler, may be seen as linked components of a single longer and more basic struggle.

Thus, the time perspectives of peoples who have been placed over and over again in the paths of more powerful opponents may be much longer than of those having more fortunate histories, and their forgiveness coefficients correspondingly much smaller. Defeats and invasions, with accompanying atrocities, are more likely to remain vivid in the minds of losers than are one's own victories over weaker opponents. The American Civil War, and even a glorification of its most horrifying moments, has been a much greater part of the tradition of the South than it has elsewhere in the United States. Few Americans pay any attention to the Mexican-American or Spanish-American wars.

Sensitivity coefficients are therefore likely to depend on the outcomes of prior encounters. Extremists are also more apt to have greater appeal than moderates whenever vivid accounts of past encounters can be kept alive. By the same token, extremist leaders will be tempted to use these histories to their own advantage and to rely heavily on oversimplified versions of those aspects of an ideological system that relate to conflict processes. The initial "causes" of past wars are especially likely to be presented in simplistic terms and blamed on the other side. Group members are thus conditioned to expect that future conflicts will be initiated by the opponent, and any paranoid tendencies will be reinforced by these oversimplified versions of past events. A positive feedback loop often exists between interpretations given to prior and to current events.

Goals, Beliefs, and Costs

At the micro level, one must always anticipate a multiplicity of individual goals, differing preference hierarchies, and divergent interests. To the degree that a party is heterogeneous with respect to these goal hierarchies and only loosely organized, the relative mixes of such goals among leaders and followers, or advantaged and disadvantaged members, will also be important. Furthermore, such mixes are likely to alter as a conflict wears on and as differential costs and benefits become apparent. Any account of the dynamics of conflict processes must therefore deal with such changing preferences, as well as the satiation of certain goals and the forced delayed gratification of others.

In very general terms, we have already noted that goals may be categorized in terms of the roles they play in a conflict process. In particular, certain goals of party X's members will be shared with those of party Y's members. We have referred to these as G_1 goals, which have the property that the satisfaction of such goals by members of party X implies an increased probability that party Y's members will also have them satisfied. Bringing the conflict to an end, for example, will obviously benefit both sides in many ways, if only through the cessation of the mutually punishing behaviors. Preventing the use of extremely lethal weapons such as poison gases or nuclear bombs will also be to the interest of both sides, as may the preservation of the neutrality of certain parties that may later serve in the role of intermediaries.

Although we shall not emphasize them, there may be other goals that are highly compatible with such G_1 goals and that, for present purposes, we may subsume under the same general heading. These include the goals of gaining favor with the other party, reducing the risk of personal injury, and achieving greater control over other threatening features of one's environment that have no direct bearing on the conflict, per se, but that require the use of scarce resources that may have been needed to sustain the conflict. There may be an agreement, for example, not to tamper with a common water supply or to damage medical facilities or sacred religious shrines.

Other goals, which we have referred to as G_2 goals, are such that their attainment by one party reduces the probability of their being achieved by the other. These include any goals over which the two parties are in competition—scarce land, resources, power, wealth, prestige, and the like. Such goals are often major causes of conflicts and commonly receive primary attention in most discussions of conflict processes. Indeed, we have already noted that they are sometimes built into definitions of conflict in such a way as to merge competition and conflict processes in a confusing way.

There are certain kinds of G_2 goals that do not involve "competition" in the usual sense of that term, however. Suppose members of party X desire to injure or aggress against party Y, perhaps to gain revenge or simply for sadistic reasons. Clearly, the attainment of such objectives will imply the failure of party Y members' survival goals or at least their wishes to avoid or reduce injury. Therefore, we may wish to include under the heading of G_2 goals a number of objectives that some writers might refer to as "irrational" or "fanatical." Similarly, if members of party X wish to dominate or control party Y we might not refer to such objectives as "competitive," except in the sense of "competing for control." The goal category under consideration is thus somewhat more general than what is implied by the notion of competition for scarce resources.

Finally, we have also made use of a third, almost, residual, category of G_3 goals to refer to goals that are basically irrelevant to the conflict itself but that may have to be deferred or are only partly satisfied because of the conflict. In wartime these might include all sorts of personal plans, career opportunities, schooling, postponed marriages or childbearing, and the sacrifice of both time and material possessions. This residual category of goals becomes especially important as a conflict wears on and as delayed gratifications increase the utilities attached to these G_3 goals, relative to those more directly relevant to the conflict itself. In general, they will contribute to the fatigue of both parties in an accelerating manner as the gap between goal aspirations and goal attainment widens.

As a conflict commences, we may anticipate that G_2 goals will begin to dominate, though the pace with which this will occur can be expected to depend upon a number of factors. Where the causes for the conflict remain under dispute among a party's members, with a significant segment blaming those in control, G_1 goals may even temporarily increase in importance among this segment, serving as rallying points for those who favor an immediate termination of hostilities or the granting of concessions to what may be perceived as legitimate grievances by the other party. Thus in the civil rights conflict of the late 1950s and 1960s, there were many white Southerners who pointed to common interests between blacks and whites. Indeed, many white leaders of the Southern labor movement, which was at the time beginning to make important gains in the textile industry, often sided with blacks in their struggles for better jobs and working conditions.

As the conflict continues and mutual hostilities result in injuries to both sides, however, those who were initially attempting to moderate the damage are likely to lose ground if they continue calling for compromise resolutions and emphasizing common goals. Control is likely to pass to more extremist leaders, as G_1 goals become less salient in the general membership or are even renounced in favor of revenge, hardened bargaining stances, and the modification of belief systems in the direction of simplicity. Where the other side can rather easily be blamed for some dramatic event that is believed to have caused the conflict, the position of such moderates and the utilities attached to G_1 goals will both be weakened. Where the general membership can be made to believe that a single cause has been totally responsible for the conflict, such a moderate leadership may have been silenced from the outset. Indeed, it will be to the interest of the conflict's proponents to develop such an extremely simple explanatory model, placing the blame squarely on the other party and thereby virtually assuring that internal opposition will be totally discredited.

As suggested earlier, whether or not G_1 goals will regain their importance toward the end of a conflict will partly depend on whether or not internal opposition leaders have been discredited or disgraced during the early period when these G_1 goals were submerged. These goals' later reemergence will also depend upon the intensity of the conflict during the intervening period, on the hatred that develops between the two parties, and on whether or not the entire opposition membership or just its leadership has been blamed for the confrontation.

Symbolism may play an important role in this definitional process. In the minds of most Americans, was it German and Japanese people who were responsible for World War II, or was it Hitler and a small group of Nazi extremists and Hirohito and the military elite in Japan? To what extent did Americans retain sympathy for the average German or Japanese citizen during the course of a very brutal war which, however, was still relatively remote from middle America? If blame is placed primarily on the leadership, then it becomes possible to invoke important G_1 goals, provided only that the originally guilty parties have been replaced. In retrospect, the very rapid decay in Americans' hostilities toward both Germans and Japanese that occurred almost immediately after World War II may be partly explained by overly simplistic theories that placed the major blame on a few leaders rather than on the populace at large.

The importance of common goals may also be a function of the mutual dependence of each party on the other. If X is the sole supplier of important goals of Y's members, and vice versa, then there will obviously be a common interest in renewing the exchange of positively valued goods and services, even while negative sanctions are being exchanged as well. The more intense the conflict, however, the more critical it will become to each party to locate alternative exchange partners or to reduce the importance attached to goals that can be satisfied only by the other party. Therefore, we would ordinarily expect that mutual dependencies (for positively valued goods) will be reduced as the conflict intensifies, thereby diminishing the importance of the common interests of the two parties. This may be somewhat mitigated, however, by strategies to cut off alternative sources of supply so as to coerce the other party into submission. Whether or not this succeeds will depend on the power and interests of third-party suppliers. If these suppliers are successful, post-conflict dependencies between the contending parties may be reduced.

As a conflict endures, certain kinds of G_2 goals may satiate, whereas others may begin to predominate. Excitement in winning battles and the motive of gaining revenge will almost certainly encourage the continuation of a conflict, especially if costs are minimal or can be hidden from view or explained away as being due to early mistakes or traitorous acts of members who can rather easily be scapegoated. We predict that such goals will satiate except among extremist elements or among those who gain unusual satisfaction in inflicting damage on others. Absorbed punishments and the continued threat of harm posed by the opponent will, in contrast, also tend to increase aggressive impulses, the desire for revenge, and calls for an all-out commitment to the conflict. Overall, then, we would expect G_2 goals to remain strong during the entire course of the conflict, so that its resolution must depend on increases in the importance attached to unsatisfied G_3 goals and possibly reemerging common interests between the two parties.

At the individual level, where sacrifices of G_3 goals have been endured and where doubts as to the merits of the conflict may always have existed, any potential opposition to the conflict may have to be suppressed. A kind of "collective ignorance" phenomenon may then emerge, as doubts and perceived costs increase but are not communicated to other members. Enthusiasm for the conflict may wane and result in increasing levels of free riding and secretive efforts to satisfy G_3 goals that have had to be deferred. There may, for example, be extensive cheating in order to bypass food and gasoline rationing, as occurred as the costs of World War II began to be shared by the average American citizen. This, in turn, may require a diversion of resources to control minor acts of deviance, many of which may have become so extensive that they must be virtually ignored. As previously noted, the success of these control efforts will be a function of the party's surveillance capacity and total available resources.

Ideological props may be increasingly needed to support a given level of mobilization as the appeal for "self sacrifice" begins to wear thin, as exhaustion sets in, and as an "every-man-for-himself" orientation begins to predominate. Presumably, if privatized beliefs about the conflict become extensive enough, there will be an increasing and perhaps accelerating awareness of a common opposition to the conflict. Under certain circumstances, such as a dramatic victory by enemy forces, there may then be an otherwise inexplicable sudden collapse of the conflict effort. If the phenomenon exists to a high degree within both parties, the conditions may be ripe for a successful conflict resolution effort.

In an authoritarian atmosphere—or one that is controlled by the actions of extremist conflict groups that successfully terrorize more moderate elements—this kind of privatized collective ignorance may persist for a very long period of time. Where moderate elements are absorbing the major costs of the conflict but are inhibited from open rebellion for fear of punitive measures on the part of conflict supporters, there may arise a kind of analogue to the "prisoner syndrome" used to analyze responses of hostages to their captors. Such hostages may come to identify with their captors through a psychic response to an extremely terrifying situation. To do otherwise would be to endure not only very high risks of alienating one's captors, but of losing control over one's own impulses.

As a result, the captive comes to take over the beliefs and objectives of the captor. In much the same way those members of a party in conflict who feel powerless to rebel, and who would risk extreme sanctions if they did so, may come to endorse the conflict primarily as a protective or defensive mechanism. Their overt behaviors may be indistinguishable from acts of those who wholeheartedly favor continuation of the conflict, making it all the more difficult for a viable opposition group to emerge.

Conflicts that have impacts that are close to home differ in important ways from those with impacts that are more remote. Contrast, for example, a war of expansion being fought on foreign soil and using an army primarily composed of mercenaries, with a setting in which battles are being fought in the immediate vicinity with casualties among civilians being an almost daily occurrence. Guerrilla warfare or acts of terrorism may take place primarily in remote mountainous terrain or in highly populated urban areas, as for example in Northern Ireland or Lebanon. Costs will be almost impossible to hide from view in these latter instances, whereas in the case of more remote conflicts the costs to the populace may be far more indirect: such things as food shortages or increased taxes or authoritarian controls.

When the implications of a conflict are immediate, direct and obvious, the privatization of doubts will be much less frequent, since suffering is more likely to be spread more evenly among the local population and losses will be more visible and readily associated with the conflict itself. This does not mean that resistance to continuation will be any greater, however, as there may also be a much greater hatred of the opponent and readiness to engage in direct aggression against any members of the party or its sympathizers. It will be considerably easier to assess the relative costs that different members have undergone, however, with there also tending to be greater salience of such costs in the everyday lives of the party's members. Those who have suffered the most may resent others who have not, but again this does not necessarily imply that the former will be more opposed to continuation than the latter, as there may be a tendency to believe that those who have suffered the most must not be allowed to have suffered in vain. Heroes and martyrs are also more likely to appear as real persons with whom one can easily identify and their acts perceived as much more critical for the welfare of the membership.

One of the most important differences between conflict situations that are close at hand and those that are remote, then, may be in the relative volatility or sensitivity to *changes* in the situation. Close-at-hand conflict situations may involve a far greater intensity of effort, tighter disciplinary controls on potential deviants, and far more negative beliefs and emotions toward the opposing party. But they may also entail a greater awareness of the costs, far more fatigue, and perhaps a greater willingness to settle for compromise once losses begin to occur and it becomes apparent that victory either cannot be achieved at all or can occur only at considerable additional cost.

Virtually all interpersonal or micro-level conflicts are by definition "close to home," so that costs should be obvious, sensitivity coefficients high, and volatility pronounced. Even at this level, however, there may be certain processes analogous to the privatization or collective ignorance phenomenon, if one considers psychodynamic processes such as repression or suppression as having some of the same consequences. Individuals may effectively deny the reality or severity of costs they are experiencing, or (perhaps more likely) the costs being borne by the party with whom they have been in prolonged conflict. If the conflict endures more or less unwitnessed by outside parties, all sorts of distortions may never be countered by "reality checks." Fortunately, in the case of individuals in dyadic conflict situations, there are likely to be multiple third parties, at least some of which may have strong interests in providing such reality checks and in persuading one or both parties either to withdraw from the conflict situation or to recognize that, at some point, the costs of continued conflict will begin to outweigh the benefits.

CHANGES IN BELIEFS AND SUBJECTIVE PROBABILITIES

Whatever belief systems that existed at the time the conflict was initiated may undergo modification as the conflict wears on and as costs begin to mount. As was previously noted, there will very commonly have been an underestimation of the total costs as well as of the duration and intensity of the conflict, in part because of a tendency to inflate one's estimate of one's own resources and staying power and to deflate those of the opposition. This tendency will be especially likely whenever a party's members have been enticed into the conflict by leadership elements in need of a high level of total commitment at the outset. A faith that the war will be short and the enemy's resistance easily overcome is frequently encountered within highly ethnocentric societies, which is to say a very high percentage of the world's most active aggressors. A belief in a glorious history of past victories will similarly work to reinforce the conflict effort.

In the case of conflicts involving corporate groups, there will also often be an accompanying faith that tribal deities or other magical helpers are squarely in favor of engaging in any conflict involving a righteous cause. Indeed, deities may be perceived as offering challenges or hurdles that can only be overcome through extreme sacrifices. Since their ways may be taken as inscrutable by mere human beings, a blind faith in their powers and wisdom may be used to undermine more "rational" efforts to reassess the costs and expected benefits of the current conflict. Beliefs about magical helpers may also reinforce a longer time perspective among those whose immediate suffering has become extreme. Of course deities' preferences typically can only be interpreted properly by a priesthood whose support for the ongoing conflict is often assured through co-optation by the controlling elites.

How are unanticipated costs, major defeats, desertions of allies, and an opponent's stubbornness to be explained away, and how can the belief system be altered rapidly enough to adjust to unforeseen consequences? What new beliefs can replace earlier more optimistic ones? These are critical issues that may need to be resolved if momentum is to be sustained. Needed adaptations may not be made in time to prevent collapse of the mobilization effort if costs can no longer be hidden from view or explained away.

To the degree that information can be controlled through secrecy or because the conflict is occurring in remote areas, costs may be disguised as "challenges" or as mere temporary setbacks, or they may be explained away as having occurred only in the past and thus as unlikely to continue. It will also be helpful to have in place a series of beliefs concerning the motives of those who serve as messengers conveying any bad news. Such persons may be depicted as agents of the opponent whose purpose is to alarm or demoralize. Their information may also be discredited as dated, inaccurate, or "planted," whereas that provided by authorities is to be treated as totally accurate. Where reports refer to the past, as will necessarily be the case, it may be claimed that subsequent events have now made them irrelevant. Furthermore, disturbing messages may be required to pass through a series of filters, such as official press releases or commentaries by trusted authorities. Blaming the messenger or skeptic not only produces additional internal scapegoats as targets for pent-up aggression, but it also tends to drive doubts underground, thereby reinforcing privatization and collective ignorance of the extent of the potential opposition to the conflict.

Stereotypes of the opponent may need to be modified. Threatening beliefs about rebellious minorities or "outside" labor agitators may be invoked. Enemy soldiers who blindly follow orders may become fanatics, deviousness becomes treachery, or footsoldiers become "hordes." Enemy victories become "massacres" of innocents, whereas the same behaviors by members of one's own group are described as "battles." The enemy in victory may be depicted as totally ruthless and exploitative, with histories of past encounters undoubtedly having been interpreted so as to reinforce such beliefs and expectations about the consequences of a possible defeat.

In general, it may become necessary to amplify those negative stereotypes that depict the opposition as threatening, totally unprincipled and without compassion, and capable of acting in complete disregard for the rules of the game. The costs of a defeat are thereby made much more salient as compared with the initially expected benefits of an early and easy victory. The fear of failure may begin to predominate over the expectation of success. Correspondingly, those members whose commitment to the conflict is less than wholehearted are likely to be seen as even greater threats to the party's survival, thereby further reinforcing the privatization of doubts.

Defeats and costs may nevertheless be difficult to hide and must therefore be explained away. Internal scapegoats, strategic but rather excusable "errors," or unforeseen natural events may be invoked by those who control the information flow, but to the degree that members actually experience costs or witness the conflict first hand, even such tactics may fail to prevent members from merely displaying the outward appearance of endorsement. Whether or not doubts remain privatized or become public may then depend on the power of internal opposition leaders who have begun to perceive that expected costs outweigh potential gains. Where it has become obvious that costs are being differentially borne, interest groups favoring termination of the conflict may emerge, first as quasi-groups but perhaps later as opposition conflict groups or at least as a more highly organized legitimate leadership.

Throughout the above discussion it has been implied that leaders often "manipulate" other members' goals through a variety of devices. This may indeed be the case. It should also be kept in mind, however, that leaders *themselves* may change during the course of a conflict, as unexpected events occur, as costs mount, and as their own goals either satiate or have to be deferred. They may, perhaps, mellow over time. In general, however, we would anticipate that leaders will rather more often retain a vested interest in seeing the conflict through to a satisfactory conclusion, and this is likely to mean that their G_2 goals will continue to predominate and that they will rationalize the need to manipulate other members in whatever ways they can.

Structural Factors Sustaining Conflict

Structural factors that operate during the course of a conflict to influence both parties' behaviors will, of course, be highly specific to the nature of the conflict being analyzed. At the very micro level, where one is examining conflicts among individual persons, such structural factors will for the most part be exogenous in the sense that they cannot be easily influenced by the parties themselves. Also, if such conflicts are relatively brief, these exogenous factors will usually remain constant over the duration of the conflict. At the macro level, however, structural factors are more likely to be endogenous and therefore influenced by the unfolding course of that conflict. If so, it becomes especially important to bring these variables explicitly into one's models. Our discussion will therefore focus primarily on such macro conflict-situations, although we shall make a few remarks concerning micro conflict-situations as well.

DISTRIBUTION OF COSTS AND BENEFITS

Given that both costs and benefits of a conflict will almost inevitably vary across different segments of a population, we would anticipate that the conflict will be most likely to continue whenever the greatest costs and smallest benefits are experienced by the least powerful members. It is frequently pointed out that wars are made by old men but fought by the young. Kings, nobles, and military elites have often precipitated major wars, the costs of which have then been borne by peasants and ordinary soldiers. In the United States, blacks are currently represented in disproportionate numbers in the armed services, and this was reflected in higher casualty rates in the Vietnamese War. Where shortages exist because of continued conflict, elites are often in better positions to "pull strings" or to afford black market prices.

As implied in our previous discussion, however, it is the *perceived* costs and benefits that are critical, as well as the perceived *differentials* across the relevant categories of group members. An ideology that successfully conveys the belief that "we are all in this together, suffering alike" may therefore serve to counter more objective evidence of differential gains and losses. To the extent that it is believed that those who are gaining the most are also suffering the greatest costs, certain vested interests in maintaining or intensifying conflict levels may be less obvious. Where the conflict is close at hand, and thus the costs and benefits made more readily visible, it may become much more difficult to maintain the credibility of such "egalitarian" belief systems. If so, cynicism and distrust may increase and pass beyond the threshold of collective ignorance.

The percentage of the total membership that is actively involved in the conflict also affects the resource depletion rate and levels of personal fatigue, as well as the satiation of those goals that reinforce the conflict—the desire for excitement, direct involvement in a "cause," and the satisfaction in seeing the opponent punished. Where there are sufficient numbers so that members can be rotated in and out of front-line combat, other irrelevent G_3 goals can be partially satisfied. In the aggregate, high levels of continued involvement by a high percentage of the total membership almost necessarily contribute to overall personal fatigue levels. At the opposite pole, where the active combatants are easily replaceable individuals with temporarily high dedication levels, the fatigue factor may be minimal. In such situations, the costs to the general membership will be relatively low and the psychic (and possibly material) benefits of the active combatants will be sufficiently high to compensate for their high expected costs.

The depletion rate of needed material resources will of course depend on many factors and is undoubtedly most reasonably compared with the existing stock levels and expected future replenishment rate. An important factor in this regard is the availability of substitutes and the elasticity of demand produced by G_3 goals. Where gratification can be delayed for very long periods, there are considerably more degrees of freedom available to those in a position to allocate additional resources to the conflict effort. Where substitute resources cannot be found, nonlinearities produced by satiation and widening gaps between expectation and attainment levels can become critical. The simple rule that good things satiate, bad things accelerate may not always hold.[1] In general, however, such nonlinearities may function to bring support for a costly conflict to an accelerating rate of decline unless ways can be found to satisfy intensifying, unmet G_3 goals. The greater the relative power of those experiencing such unmet needs, the more leverage that may be placed in support of conflict resolution measures. Egalitarian systems that have substantial numbers of members with inflexible G_3 goals and that are also undergoing high levels of resource depletion are likely to be especially prone to high fatigue levels.

Where a large proportion of the total membership experiences average costs that are relatively minor, the degree of mobilization may actually increase and be easily sustained for a prolonged period of time. This is because there will almost inevitably be compensating gains in the form of vicariously experienced revenge against the opponent, a degree of excitement and commitment to a common cause, and increased opportunities for participation and recognition. As was discovered in World War II and again in the Vietnamese War, the modest levels of destruction produced by bombing attacks may have actually increased levels of enemy resistance, presumably because the costs were insufficient to outweigh these other factors. The far more destructive atomic bombs dropped on Hiroshima and Nagasaki, however, resulted in an immediate Japanese surrender.

MOBILITY OPPORTUNITIES

Conflicts produce channels of upward mobility for some members, not only through combat roles, but also because of displacements in the economy, opportunities for different kinds of leadership roles, and various kinds of new services for which the demand has been much lower in times of reduced tension. Blacks in the U.S. gained economically during both world wars, and in subsequent years the armed services have served as a relatively open avenue for upward occupational mobility for blacks, other minorities, and women (Jaynes and Williams, 1989). During the civil rights era, young black militants emerged, at least temporarily, as newsworthy spokesmen for black nationalism. College youth in many countries have used protest movements not only to demand political and social rights but also as pathways to leadership positions. Leaders of conflict groups, if successful, have emerged as national leaders in a number of developing countries. As a general rule, then, we would expect that the greater the number of members who experience benefits from the conflict in the form of upward economic or political mobility, the easier it will be to sustain or even increase the mobilization effort. The more powerful these individuals become and the greater their opportunities to reward others for similar behaviors, the easier it will be to sustain the momentum.

One must recognize that there are definite limits to such mobility processes, however, as well as a corresponding downward mobility of other segments of the population. Once in positions of power, those who have benefited from the early stages of the conflict may become reluctant to permit others to do so, thereby possibly producing resentment and a splintering of previously homogeneous followers into rival opposition groups, some of which may prefer more extremist tactics and others more moderate ones. As a general rule, the longer the duration of the conflict and the fewer the obvious benefits, the greater the tendency for conflict-related mobility to slacken and for splintering to take place.

RELATIONSHIPS WITH COALITION PARTNERS

Another structural variable is the degree to which third parties have been drawn into the conflict and the extent to which these parties have interests in common with the major party of concern. Presumably, such third parties will augment the resource base and perhaps help to replenish resources at a rate that is comparable to the resource depletion rate. If so, this may hold fatigue levels down to the point where the conflict can be sustained for a much longer period. As costs begin to mount, however, or as the conflict alters in such a way as to create opposition groups within these third parties, the efficiency of the mobilization effort may be adversely affected. The range of feasible alternative actions may be reduced in order to retain the third party's cooperation, with the result that there may be increasing *dissensus* among members as to whether or not the coalition partner is to be retained.

The relatively high degree of cooperation between a nonviolently-oriented Southern black leadership and white liberals that existed during the earlier stages of the civil rights movement persisted as long as continual gains were being made. As the nonviolent movement began to founder and as younger black militants emerged in more powerful roles, there were increasing demands that whites be displaced from leadership roles in CORE and other militant groups and that they be made to play only very secondary roles in the movement. Toward the end of the 1960s a very definite anti-white orientation among younger black separatists drove many white liberals out of the overall movement and forced others into far more passive or defensive roles as mere background supporters. As a result, the coalition was considerably weakened. Many of the psychic benefits experienced by white liberals during the early stages of the civil rights struggle began to be outweighed by the perceived and actual rejection they began to experience as black leadership began to change and extremist tactics became more prevalent.

Coalition partners also undergo costs that, in some instances, may make them unwilling or reluctant supporters of one or the other of the two parties, and that may drastically limit the forms that the conflict may take. As a case in point, consider an interpersonal conflict between a husband and wife in which one or perhaps both of the parties attempt to involve the children in such a way as to bolster their own positions. Such children may serve as a "shield" to help block the punitive actions of the stronger party or to inhibit extreme forms of violence on both sides. Where positive bonds exist between the children and both parties, this may indeed serve as an important conflict-reduction mechanism.

If, however, such a coalition tends to give the clear advantage to the otherwise weaker party, say the wife, the stronger one may consider the coalition to be an instance of rule violation. The result may be an escalating set of countermoves that leaves the relatively innocent third party in an intolerable position and may even subject it to additional physical harm. Although extreme violence in the form of wife and child murders is indeed rare, we suspect that, when it does occur, it may be at least partly a result of mother-child coalitions of this type. Fortunately, it is undoubtedly more frequently the case that the introduction of children as third parties serves to inhibit rather than increase conflict intensity. Solid empirical studies tracing out the dynamics of intrafamilial conflicts of this nature are very much needed.

SPATIAL SEGREGATION FROM OPPONENTS

The degree to which the parties in conflict are spatially segregated is another structural factor that is likely to affect the nature and possibly the duration of the conflict process. It is frequently pointed out that segregation, say of two ethnic groups such as blacks and whites, serves to reduce many kinds of day-to-day frictions that would occur in normal contact situations. Where contacts between members of very different groups are functionally necessary, as in market situations, these may be regulated by a system of etiquette that preserves the dominance of the one group over the other by emphasizing status differences or confining the contact to ritually prescribed interaction patterns (Dollard, 1937; Doyle, 1937).

Both physical separation and highly regulated contacts tend to reduce the strength of common G_1 goals by a number of mechanisms that we shall not attempt to model in the present work.[2] These include a reduced number of commonly held beliefs and values as well as fewer opportunities for highly personal contacts to develop. Thus, there is a conflict-inhibiting function of spatial segregation, accompanied by another set of features that may aggravate a given conflict once it has been initiated for whatever reason. There are likely to be fewer common interests between the ordinary members of both parties, as well as a bifurcated leadership structure that may actually have vested interests in furthering or intensifying the conflict in order to solidify its position and maintain the segregation. It is not only minorities or subordinate groups that encourage such conflict-oriented leaders to take advantage of the situation for their own benefit. During the civil rights era a number of white "Law and Order" politicians rose to positions of considerable influence by deliberately raising the general level of tension and then exploiting racial hatreds.

The greater the spatial segregation of the combatants, the less likely that nearly all members of both groups will directly experience the conflict or bear its major costs. Indirect costs may be less obvious to those far removed from the conflict scene, who may enjoy a vicarious sense of excitement to the degree that events are vividly described in the mass media, as were the summer ghetto riots of the 1960s. Reduced prior contacts favor the development of unfavorable stereotypes and simplified belief systems that reinforce the notion that the conflicting parties are "opposites" or contrasts to one another (Allport, 1954; Blalock, 1967; Copeland, 1939). Without an extensive period of prior friendly, nonregulated contacts, such unfavorable images of the other group can take hold rather rapidly once the conflict begins.

Segregation also increases the importance of the notion of a power gradient and the advantages of the home base. For instance, the high degree of residential segregation of American blacks in large urban ghettos provided a power base for black militants and an obvious advantage over police or National Guard members brought in to control urban riots. Finding themselves in hostile territory and in settings where even very slight offensive moves were likely to produce an immediate and very hostile crowd, urban police forces often found it necessary to retreat or merely observe events until reinforcements arrived. Since the particular locations of riot sites were almost impossible to predict in advance, police were thus kept on the defensive during critical periods of the rioting process. As outsiders they were defined as the enemy, even in those instances where their supposed mission was to prevent injury and damage to the property of black as well as white citizens. By the same token, most of the suffering and indirect costs of conflict were borne by the local black residents, whereas the larger white population merely vicariously witnessed the unfolding events on their television sets.

In the case of most kinds of interpersonal conflicts, spatial separation can be relatively easily accomplished, provided that the more vulnerable or losing party does not have considerable "sunk" costs that inhibit spatial movements. Not only does spatial distance make it more difficult to perpetrate frequent acts of aggression, but in many instances it will serve both to facilitate a "cooling off" period and a weakening of mutual dependency between the two parties. Where one party is more mobile than the other, as for example a father who may simply "move out" of an apartment and be relatively less concerned about his children's daily lives, this gives a decided advantage to that party. In effect, the mobile party's alternative sources of rewards or $CL_{alt:}$ make him less dependent on a particular spatial location and permit him to find ways of punishing the partner that are unavailable to her.

Recognizing this, of course, relevant third parties (e.g., the judicial system and state legislatures) may alter the rules so as to favor the relatively less mobile party. Where interpersonal conflicts become patterned, as for example marital conflicts involving children, institutionalized control mechanisms may be set up to protect the disadvantaged party. Unfortunately, however, such mechanisms may have unanticipated or indirect impacts that have precisely the opposite consequences from those that were originally intended. So-called "no fault" divorce procedures, for example, may have lessened the intensity of many marital conflicts, but to the financial disadvantage of the more dependent spouse, usually the wife (Weitzman, 1985).

QUASI-GROUPS AND CORPORATE ACTORS

All of this suggests that the nature of the opposing parties may make a considerable difference in connection with the dynamics of the conflict process. One very important difference between relatively more loosely organized quasi-groups and corporate actors is relevant in the present context. This has to do with the implications of varying degrees of organizational structure for the manner in which a conflict may build up or wind down and eventually terminate.

In the case of a quasi-group with a very loosely coordinated decision process, a conflict can simply be allowed to die out or accelerate without there being any formal action taken. Treaties would be difficult to enforce, given the lack of authority to agree to specific terms on behalf of the total membership. Formal negotiations and third-party interventions also are likely to be less definitive, as it is difficult to hold specific members accountable for agreements made. Since the leadership structure is likely to be diffuse, open-ended, and nonhierarchical, those who disagree with formal agreements that have been made by one set of leaders may readily disown them and very deliberately violate them so as to sustain the conflict. The extreme volatility of the multiple-party conflict situation in present-day Lebanon is a case in point. There is simply no set of leaders capable of controlling the actions of independent militias that consistently violate temporary truce arrangements or that escalate hostilities at the very times that others are attempting serious negotiations.

By the same token, leaders in quasi-groups can simply withdraw from a conflict and can more easily save "face" than their counterparts in corporate groups, who must be more accountable for their actions. In struggles between two very loosely organized quasi-groups, a conflict may simply end without any formal action being taken, as fatigue levels in both groups result in a gradual reduction of tensions or a mutual retreat to strictly defensive strategies. Both leaders and followers may drop out or reemerge according to whether or not they perceive their needs as being satisfied. In such instances neutral third parties may take advantage of the situation by using informal inducements to cool off the disputants without having to negotiate any formal terms of agreement. Indeed, it would be exceedingly difficult to lock such terms into place until the memory decay factor could become significant and common G_1 goals had regained their importance relative to G_2 goals.

In the case of quasi-groups it may not be necessary to overthrow or totally replace a given leadership structure in order to alter the course of the conflict. Instead, there may be a gradual replacement of one set of elites by another. Any particular leader would also be in a somewhat easier position to alter an earlier stance, given the diffuseness of the group structure and the lesser accountability expectations. Drifting into and out of conflicts can be expected to be more common in the case of quasi-groups than it is with more formally organized parties.

In dealing with such a loose-knit opponent, a corporate actor may indeed find this frustrating. Hall (1989), for example, points out that during the 18th century the so-called Apache, Comanche, and Navajo Indian "nations" were really a bunch of loosely organized bands with ill-defined boundaries. Raids perpetrated by any one such band were attributed to entire "nations," however, and therefore retaliations by the Spanish were often misdirected to relatively innocent elements of the population, thereby insuring further vengeance raids. Likewise, treaties made between the U.S. Government and very small Indian tribal bands in the Pacific Northwest had a fictitious quality to them in that governmental authorities were never quite sure with whom they were dealing. Sometimes they even "created" tribal chiefs in order to have a formal opposition they could hold accountable in case of violation. Needless to say, very powerful corporate actors have also violated such agreements, sometimes by formal action but also by failing to censure the actions of internal quasi-groups, such as white settlers, who simply bypassed them.

In this particular example we see that it is sometimes functional for a tightly organized corporate group to maintain loose ties with internal quasi-groups or smaller conflict groups that can perpetrate hostile acts or "test the waters" in such a manner that the corporate group can disclaim responsibility for their actions. Many terrorist groups in the Middle East, for example, appear to be cooperating with, if not actually taking orders from, the governments of Libya, Syria, and Iran. Other governments cannot hold their counterpart governments responsible for their actions without drastically escalating tensions. Furthermore, terrorist actions can be secretly called off or held in check without any loss of face on the part of the formal leadership with which they are cooperating. In such a manner, formally sanctioned actions can be avoided and the level of conflict either gradually accelerated or reduced without there appearing to be any single leadership element responsible for such shifts.

RELATIONSHIPS TO EXTREMIST ELEMENTS

As was previously stressed, there will invariably be differential costs and benefits of any conflict to various members of both parties. Those who are benefiting the most will therefore tend to favor its continuation and may engage in extremist tactics to assure that it does not end prematurely. Controlling such extremist behaviors will generally require coordination and a reasonably high degree of centralized leadership that is more characteristic of corporate groups than of loosely organized quasi-groups. There are therefore definite risks associated with turning power over to conflict groups or other extremists, whose strategy is to burn bridges behind them so as to make it difficult to terminate a conflict short of outright victory.

As a conflict wears on and fatigue begins to take over, it indeed may be only the extremists who wish to continue the struggle. Furthermore, there will probably be a tendency for each party to perceive extremists from the opposing camp as being readily controllable by its other members, so that each party will be held responsible by the other for keeping such elements in line. In contrast, extremists may look upon more moderate members as disloyal, weak, or naive and may seize the opportunity to undermine the efforts of those rival leaders more willing to compromise with the opponent. They may also turn in frustration against innocent members of their own party, especially in those instances where they have cut off close emotional ties with them. This may then further increase the overall level of fatigue.

It will be difficult to predict how these processes will unfold in any given instance. Indeed, to the degree that extremist elements enjoy a high degree of autonomy of action, it may prove nearly impossible to bring the conflict to an abrupt and conclusive ending. In such a case, much may depend on the extent to which extremists genuinely identify with the interests of the population at large and are willing to operate consistently with these interests in mind. To the degree that a tightly organized conflict group has been successful in isolating its members from contacts with more moderate members, in developing a simplistic and rigid ideology of conflict, and in solving problems of recruitment and retention of a sufficient number of willing adherents, it may successfully sustain a high level of conflict regardless of the wishes of the general membership.

As we suggested earlier, if the opposing party is sufficiently ruthless to punish "innocent" sympathizers of the conflict group, it may place the conflict group in a dilemma. Such a dilemma may be softened to the degree that conflict group members have cut off psychic ties with family or former friends, however, so that they in effect become indifferent to their fate. When this occurs the conflict has essentially become one involving three distinct parties: the two original opponents and the extremist group. It can probably be brought to a conclusion only when the conflict group has either totally accomplished its purpose or been annihilated. Mediators who attempt to enter the scene will merely be lumped with the opponent by conflict group extremists.

In the long run, the success of extremist groups is likely to depend on the resources they possess and the damage they can inflict on the opponent, and these will in turn depend upon that opponent's remoteness and the power gradient. Whereas it may be very difficult for a terrorist group to invade an enemy's territory, it may be much easier to wear down an opponent that is close at hand or residentially interspersed with one's own group. It would have been rather difficult in the late 1960s, for example, for militant black youth to inflict much damage on the larger white population as long as their actions were confined to inner-city neighborhoods. Instead, they selected as targets members of the urban police force whom they defined as invading and alien forces in the black ghetto. Similarly, Islamic extremists have had a greater impact in the environs of Beirut or even selected large European cities than they have in the United States. Where the power gradient is steep, such conflict groups are at a distinct disadvantage in carrying the conflict to the doorsteps of the opponent.

Extremist groups may have a considerable impact on the critical factor of trust, however. After a prolonged conflict, genuine peace is likely to require a rather lengthy period of calm, perhaps facilitated by marked reductions in contact or the presence of a well-policed neutral zone located along disputed boundaries. Since conflict groups are often used in the role of precipitants, irritants, and probers of the opponent's determination, any acts of aggression they perpetrate are likely to be attributed to the party at large. Official leaders may speak in conciliatory terms and yet support such provocative behaviors as long as they can be disclaimed. Knowing this, members of the other side are likely to be suspicious whenever hostile actions are taken by supposedly isolated extremist elements.

The basic trust needed to create a more cooperative environment may never emerge, so that the peace is at best a very tentative one and, at worst, a brief interval between periods of overt conflict. From this perspective, it may be unwise for any opponent to trust a party that cannot bring its own extremist elements under tight control. This will pose a strategy dilemma for such an opponent, a topic to which we shall turn in the following chapter before presenting our final causal model dealing with conflict-sustaining and conflict-terminating processes.

Notes

1. I owe this observation to a set of remarks made by the late Clyde H. Coombs.
2. For a more extended discussion see Blalock and Wilken (1979), Chapters 13 and 14.

Chapter 10

Terminating Conflicts: A Final Model

As a conflict wears on, unless victory is obviously close at hand it will become necessary to make some difficult choices and to convince others to accept the implications of these decisions. At any point there will be the problem of reducing one's own vulnerabilities and costs while still inflicting maximum damage on the opponent, but as resources are depleted and personal fatigue levels become intolerable there may be fewer realistic alternative ways of simultaneously achieving these joint objectives. To the degree that a party's membership is either heterogeneous or was ambivalent about the conflict to begin with, it will also be advantageous to disguise or play down the true costs being borne, while still responding so as to reduce further harm. It will also usually be advisable to try to convince the opponent that damage inflicted has been minimal, so as not to provide the incentive to continue. And how can one signal a willingness to negotiate without at the same time displaying signs of weakness and lack of resolve?

There will often be a set of basic problems centered around the question of how a conciliatory or moderating course of action will be interpreted, both internally and by the opponent. Is it a sign of defeat or the result of cowardly or traitorous decisions? Or is it simply a recognition that a stalemate exists and that this is the best the party can get under the circumstances? Where the initial goals leading to the conflict have been unclear, it may sometimes be possible to convince a party's members that a "moral victory" has been won or that objectives have been accomplished. Where there have been rather obvious major losses, however, such as that of an important piece of territory or the weakening of control over a rebellious minority, such a position may not be believable and may play into the hands of extremists who may prefer to continue the conflict at all costs. In this sense, objectives that have been vaguely defined at the outset may afford greater flexibility in selecting a conflict-concluding strategy at almost any later opportune time. We have already noted that a quasi-group may be able to terminate a conflict without any formal action being taken at all.

In the case of reasonably complex parties, we have argued that there is likely to be a rivalry for leadership, as well as internal cleavages brought about by differentials in costs and benefits of the conflict. One of the central problems for such parties is that of winding down the levels of exchange of negative sanctions without, at the same time, losing power to extremist elements or those currently experiencing net gains from the conflict. To the degree that a leadership has had to rely on supplying major rewards to those most actively engaged in the conflict—rewards that are likely to include recognition for heroism, the control over resources related to the conduct of the conflict, and greater autonomy of strategic decision-making—there is likely to be a corresponding loss of power to such individuals.

Therefore, a strategy designed to maximize participation during early phases of the conflict may prove dysfunctional at a later stage when there is an apparent stalemate and when personal fatigue levels become pronounced. Any move toward early conciliation is likely to be defined as premature, disloyal, and even cowardly by those who have been most actively involved and who may have endured the greatest costs as well as benefits. On top of everything else, then, those in leadership positions who are prepared to conciliate may find themselves in vulnerable positions in relation to their more combative rivals. Furthermore, should such a rivalry become overt, there might be an impairment of the mobilization effort as well as a diversion of needed resources in order to help reduce the internal cleavage.

To the degree that the conflict has been experienced close at home so that costs have become readily apparent, there is likely to be among the general membership an increased hostility toward the opponent, as well as stronger utilities for aggressive revenge. This combination of motives, coupled with a strong desire to reduce their own costs and suffering, is likely to produce considerable ambivalence, in contrast to mere indifference. This is apt to lead to a highly volatile situation, as both costs and benefits of continued conflict begin to mount. Slight changes in subjective probabilities may then throw the balance in either direction. In such instances, ideological factors are likely to play critical roles in affecting beliefs and expectations, as are those actors who are in a position to manipulate them. Extremist challengers to more moderate leaders may be able to take advantage of such a situation by exploiting this ambivalence and promising a quick and dramatic resolution to the dilemma via a leadership change and an all-out effort to achieve total victory.

Assuming that both sides are experiencing fatigue, the opposing side may also be faced with comparable cleavages and dilemmas. Let us assume that party Y is willing to suggest accommodative mechanisms, as for example a tentative cease fire or some informal negotiations at a neutral location. Since one of the mechanisms used to motivate members of each party is to cultivate a high degree of distrust of the opponent, any such conciliatory move is likely to be discredited by the other side as involving possible treachery or as merely providing an opportunity to recuperate or to replenish depleted resources.

To the degree that extremist elements in party X have either gained control or are in a position to challenge those of its leaders who also prefer a conciliatory response, party X is very likely to reject the initial moderating effort, thereby providing ammunition to extremists in party Y. If party Y's extremists force a withdrawal of the proposal or a very sharp increase in the conflict effort by Y, then this will also reinforce extremists in X, and the conflict cycle may begin to reescalate in spite of high fatigue levels on both sides. Past losses and accumulated costs will be too substantial to permit the risk of negotiating with an untrustworthy opponent. Many possible options will simply be cut off from consideration. The resulting dynamics may appear to have stemmed from "irrational" behaviors on both sides, but given the beliefs and subjective probabilities that have been generated by the conflict process itself, the actors may simply be applying a maximizing strategy consistent with rational-actor theories.

As fatigue begins to set in and costs begin to mount, it may become necessary to motivate members by increasingly stressing the costs of defeat in contrast to the benefits of victory. Such a "strategy" may serve to reinforce the pattern we have just been describing: increasing distrust of the opponent, power gains for extremist elements, and greater resistances to moderating efforts. Recognizing that the opponent is likely to seek revenge to the degree that it has also been the target of punitive actions, there may be fear of a bloodbath or highly exploitative arrangement should that opponent prove victorious. Schelling (1966) indeed notes that historically it has often been the case that the most extreme acts of barbarism have occurred not during the course of battle but only *after* a conflict has ended, with victorious soldiers being allowed to act out their aggression on defenseless citizens once they could do so with impunity. A fear that this might occur at the hands of a treacherous opponent would, of course, serve as a powerful incentive to continue the conflict in spite of high current costs. A move toward conciliation would indeed be risky in the view of those who believe such an outcome likely.

To counter such a belief system, the opponent may attempt to convey the position that only the guilty will be punished and that the conflict has not been with the membership at large but with specific rulers or leaders. To the extent that the opponent is aware of differential costs being borne by members of the other party, it may also attempt to point this out and to appeal to the primary "losers" on the grounds that their interests will be protected should they pursue a more moderate course of action. The problem, however, is to get such a message across in a *believable* manner (Schelling, 1956). Third party mediators may play a critical role in this regard.

A very different strategy is that of attempting to reduce the psychic costs of the ongoing conflict by inducing members to alter their goals so that they place lower utility values on objectives that can easily be controlled by the opposing party, thereby reducing the dependency on that party. Goals that do not require the consumption of competing resources can be stressed: such things as ascetic religious fulfillments, sexual or hedonistic pleasures, satisfactions derived from ritualistic practices, or an emphasis on symbolic awards such as citations for heroism or meritorious service.

There may also be a deliberate attempt to increase the time perspective of members, so that current sacrifices seem of lesser importance. A retreat into a more glorious past may serve not only as a vicarious escape to a more pleasant period of history but also as a reminder that greater efforts may be needed to achieve a similar state in the future. Another safe alternative is to locate internal targets of aggression so as to provide a degree of revenge against the opponent. A racial or ethnic minority that can readily be associated with such an opponent may be especially vulnerable and may serve as a safety valve inhibiting other forms of internal cleavage or dissension.

The dilemma or risk involved in emphasizing these kinds of escapist reactions is that, in stressing G_3 goals that are basically irrelevant to the conflict itself, attention may be deflected from the mobilization of resources needed to defeat the opposition. It may indeed be difficult to retain a high level of commitment among party members without at the same time deflecting energies in nonproductive directions. A form of free riding may therefore inadvertently be encouraged, as members begin to devote their attention more and more to such escapist activities, leaving the major risks to others. A preexisting ideological system that contains built-in escapist mechanisms permitted under carefully controlled circumstances may serve to strike a reasonable balance, as may periodic ritualistic observances that also constrain such safety-valve mechanisms. Adolf Hitler was purportedly a master in achieving such a balance among average German citizens, and the scapegoating of Jews and other "undesirable" categories was undoubtedly a consciously devised part of the total motivating package.

Finally, either party to a conflict may consider rule violations as a strategic alternative, thereby running the risk of an accelerating pace of rule violations on both sides or the intervention of powerful third parties on the side of the opposition. Rules defining the legitimacy of a given set of means will generally tend to favor one side more than the other and may be especially critical during later stages of a conflict, when one side may be running low on resources or viable legitimate courses of action. Frequently, such rules are designed to prohibit or make very costly the use of extreme offensive strategies such as the introduction of chemical, biological, or nuclear weapons. They may also serve to limit attacks on innocent citizens or those who for one reason or another have been removed from combat (e.g., prisoners or the wounded). In limiting the total damage to both sides, however, they may also serve to reduce fatigue, and possibly unequally so to the advantage of one party over the other.

Each side will in general attempt to manipulate the situation so that such rules will be defined in its own favor. Any ambiguities in the rules themselves or any barriers to the observation or detection of rule violations are likely to be exploited, with the result that the lines between legitimate and illegitimate behaviors become blurred. One thing that may be critical in this respect is the novelty of the situation. Where conflicts have taken much the same form over a long period of time, rules are much more likely to be explicit, clearly defined, and inclusive, as compared with instances where there is no tradition and experience involving prior similar conflicts. Also, a tradition of such conflicts is likely to have resulted in a relatively explicit set of procedures for conflict resolution. Among other things, the institutionalization of conflict resolution procedures helps assure each party that agreements will be binding, thereby increasing trust levels on both sides.

Much obviously depends on the anticipated roles to be played by powerful third parties and the degree to which such parties are strongly motivated to maintain the regulatory system of norms that define the rules of the game. Where one or both of the contesting parties believe that such third parties do not exist, are too weak to exercise a stabilizing influence, or will not be motivated to do so, there will be pressures on the side of selective rule violation whenever legitimated means appear unworkable or too costly. We have here an instance of Merton's (1949) well-known theory of deviance. The more important the goals, the greater will be the tendency to use whatever means appear most efficient in achieving those ends.

In the case of micro-level conflicts at the interpersonal level or even labor-management conflicts, the problem is not so much one of a lack of potential intervening third parties as it is of enabling and motivating them to monitor ongoing interaction patterns, including rule violations. If such third parties intervene only at a point at which the conflict has become severe, as for example when an actual physical assault has been reported or when both parties have reached a total impasse, then many of the potential advantages of intervention will be irrelevant.

Also, if the parties in conflict are only of minor importance to the potential intervener, what will be the incentives for intervening? Even in the case of parties that are mandated by law to intervene—as for example the police or social agencies in cases of spouse or child abuse—evidence is likely to be sufficiently ambiguous to permit them to avoid interference until, in many instances, it is too late. Here the problem of control is a combination of the sheer numbers of minor conflicts, only a few of which can be monitored, and of the lack of incentives to third parties for playing what usually amounts to a thankless role.

If the kind of "close-in" monitoring characterizing, say, extended families is unavailable or ineffective, the overwhelming majority of small-scale conflicts may have to be resolved by the parties themselves. Where considerable inequalities exist with respect to the resources available to one or the other of these parties, such internally-policed conflict processes may result in stabilization at the cost of exploitation and dominance of the one party by the other. The only effective generic type of control mechanism may be one that serves to reduce the total power or degree of mutual dependency between the two parties so that escape from the situation becomes a viable alternative for both.

Perceiving a Stalemate

When a stalemate exists, the costs of continuing the conflict are likely to greatly exceed the benefits. Rational actors should begin to take steps to end the conflict on as favorable terms as possible. Stalemate situations are not always obvious, however. Opposing troops may be "dug in" to fixed positions, but one never knows for certain how close the other party is to exhaustion or what unforeseen events may occur giving final victory to one party over the other. In more diffuse conflicts, as for example those that involve loosely organized quasi-groups, neither the objectives nor the degree of progress in achieving them may be at all clear. Once more, it is the *perception* of a stalemate that is the critical factor. As long as one or both sides believe that further gains can be made without undue costs, they are likely to continue the struggle.

Secrecy and deception may play important roles in this connection. Even when one party recognizes that further gains can come only at the expense of far greater costs, it may be disadvantageous to admit this openly to the opponent for fear that this will encourage a sudden spurt of energy by the other party. Bluffing may become especially pronounced as both sides begin to wear down, and this implies that signals may be difficult to interpret. Where there exists considerable dissension among a party's members and an open debate as to whether or not a stalemate in fact exists, it may be difficult to hide such a dispute from the opponent, thus giving it an advantage. Therefore, at the critical point where actual losses are beginning to outweigh expected gains and where there is a realization that further gains can come only at the expense of even greater costs, there may be a corresponding pressure to cut off such debate and to resort increasingly to secrecy, the distortion of unpleasant facts, and the suppression of organized opposition. None of these tactics may succeed, however, if the processes producing disillusionment and exhaustion have gone too far. Thus the situation is likely to be delicate and highly unstable.

Where there is a rather obvious and steep loss-of-power gradient, as for example in a war between two nation-states, the nature of the stalemate may be much more clear-cut and obvious. This is especially likely in instances where the opponent must cross a major barrier, such as a mountain range or large body of water, and where defensive resources are substantial. An invading and more powerful army may reach a point where its resources are stretched too thinly and where it seems advisable to dig in, build fortifications, and hold the line at some natural boundary. Guerrilla bands may be forced to withdraw to mountainous terrain where they remain safe but yet can do little damage to more populated areas.

In instances such as these there may continue to be small-scale forays by each side into the territory of the other, but the larger conflict may for all practical purposes come to an informal or formal conclusion. We must recognize, however, that even rather steep loss-of-power gradients may be difficult to measure in precise terms and may be altered by modifications in weapons systems, unforeseen natural events, or ingenious strategic maneuvers. So uncertainty will remain a factor in assessing whether or not a genuine stalemate exists or will remain in place.

Another type of gradient may also be relevant, though our argument in this connection is not well-formulated. Whenever the mutual dependency between two parties is high, *both* the positive and negative features of a given outcome are likely to be of considerable importance to each party. Each can inflict substantial costs on the other, and the benefits of renewed cooperation will also be more substantial than they are in low dependency situations. The cost-benefit ratio (or difference) may be the same in both low and high dependency situations, but *changes* in these ratios (or differences) will generally follow a steeper gradient in the high dependency than in the low dependency situation. Put in another way, an exogenous shift in any factor favoring the one party over the other will be more critical in high dependency situations, resulting in a greater shift in, say, the cost-benefit ratio of continued conflict.

This consideration is somewhat similar to the previously noted distinction between absolute and relative power made by Bacharach and Lawler (1981). In high dependency situations the absolute power levels of both parties will by definition be high, regardless of whether or not their relative powers are approximately equal. This means that either may do considerable damage to the other, and it may be the *absolute* cost factor—rather than the difference between costs and benefits—that is critical in determining fatigue levels and possibly also the perceptions of stalemate situations. In other words, perceptions of stalemates may be affected by the degree to which the mutual dependency level is high or low. High mutual dependency implies that there is more at stake for both parties.

Third parties may play critical roles in such high dependency and high fatigue situations. First, they may serve as intermediaries in the communication process as each attempts to feel out the other without overcommitting itself. Neutral third parties, even if not especially powerful, may enable each party to perceive the nature of the stalemate more clearly and to assure each that the other is willing to enter a bargaining process. In this connection they may help to clear up misconceptions and misperceptions and to interpret each party's principal concerns to the other.

Second, more powerful third parties may help to enforce treaty agreements or effectively assure each contending party that the other can be trusted to abide by decisions that have been mutually agreed upon. They may even serve in organized police-keeping roles, as for example as occupants of demilitarized zones between disputed borders. Finally, they may facilitate more long-term negotiations designed to increase the level of mutual trust and to address those fundamental issues that may have caused the initial conflict, as well as to reorient both parties toward objectives of mutual interest (Young, 1967).

That such happy resolutions of macro-level conflicts often do not occur in the real world indicates that ideal third parties of this nature are indeed rare and that, where they do exist, neither party may be sufficiently inclined to take advantage of their assistance. Such conflicts often have a way of dragging on long after the point where they are to the advantage of either party. Stopping conflicts, once they have begun, is generally far more difficult than their initiators could possibly have anticipated, given their usually overly simplistic perspectives.

On this very sobering note, we conclude our verbal analysis of conflict processes and turn to our summary model of conflict-sustaining and conflict-terminating mechanisms. We shall then move, finally, to a very brief discussion of how this and the previous models may be used to assist those who wish to extract policy implications in the case of highly specific types of conflict situations.

A Submodel of Conflict-Sustaining and Terminating Processes

Our final submodel dealing with the sustaining and termination of conflict processes is highly complex and is presented in Figure 10.1. As usual, we shall attempt to link this submodel with variables previously discussed, most of which are inserted toward the fringes of the model of Figure 10.1. For present purposes it is advisable to split apart certain of the previously used boxes so as to distinguish, for example, among types of goals and specific ideological dimensions. Once more, the reference will be to party X unless otherwise specified, with party Y variables appearing toward the right of the diagram. We shall in general proceed from left to right and top to bottom in discussing the diagram.

No specific statistical interactions or nonlinearities are predicted in this particular model, though in many instances they may be anticipated. In particular, the greater the duration and intensity of the conflict, the stronger many of the other relationships may become. Nonlinearities due to satiation or threshold effects may also be more pronounced in these instances. Although duration is taken as exogenous in the model, it should also be recognized that a conflict's duration obviously will depend on the success or failure of negotiation efforts, as well as prior levels of a number of the other variables in the model. Its role in the model is to serve as a relatively simple indicator of the cumulative impact of prior stages of the conflict.

As always, additional variables may need to be inserted to cover special cases or further complexities and elaborations. Where the parties in conflict are single individuals, a number of the variables included in the general submodel may be irrelevant and their coefficients set equal to zero.

1. IDEOLOGIES, PRIOR GRIEVANCES, GOALS, AND CONSENSUS

Toward the top left-hand portion of the figure are a number of variables involving subjective factors relating to perceptions of initial causes, ideological supports, the clarity of objectives, grievances, the relative importance of goals, and degree of consensus. Ideological simplicity is assumed to increase the ideological support for the conflict, clarity of objectives and perceived initial causes of the conflict, and the amount and nature of the support expected from deities or other types of magical helpers. There is also a positive, reinforcive feedback loop predicted between perceived clarity of causes and ideological support for the conflict, as well as a similar positive feedback loop between ideological support and prior grievance levels and the utilities attached to G_2 (competitive) goals, with both of these latter variables positively affecting the degree of consensus on means. Support expected from deities is assumed to be positively affected by grievance levels and to reinforce the level of ideological support for the conflict.

Ideological simplicity is also assumed to affect positively the strength of belief in myths of invincibility, which in turn reinforce the ideological support for the conflict. Ideological support and the extent of prior grievance levels are also predicted to reduce the importance of G_3 (irrelevant) goals, including those that, especially in later stages of the conflict, may actually be encouraged as compensatory or escapist goals. Also, a high level of prior grievance levels is expected to reduce the original heterogeneity of goal hierarchies, thereby increasing the degree of consensus on means relating to the conflict effort.

Basically, in this set of subjective variables we see a number of reinforcing mechanisms at work, all of which operate to increase or sustain the degree of support for the conflict effort. As implied in the previous discussion, this support system may begin to break down during the later stages of the conflict as costs and fatigue levels become excessive. Such a longer-term feedback mechanism has not been explicitly built into the model of Figure 10.1

2. DURATION AND INTENSITY, COSTS, PUNISHMENTS, AND GRIEVANCES

The duration of the conflict is taken as an exogenous cause of the amount of prior punishment that has been absorbed, the excess of actual over expected costs, and the amount of resource depletion. Actual costs are likely to exceed expected costs to the extent that the duration and intensity levels of the conflict were underestimated. The average intensity of the conflict is also taken as a cause of prior punishment absorbed and resource depletion, and is also assumed to be involved in a reciprocal relationship with the degree to which there has been rule violation by both X and Y (though violations by Y have not been included in the diagram).

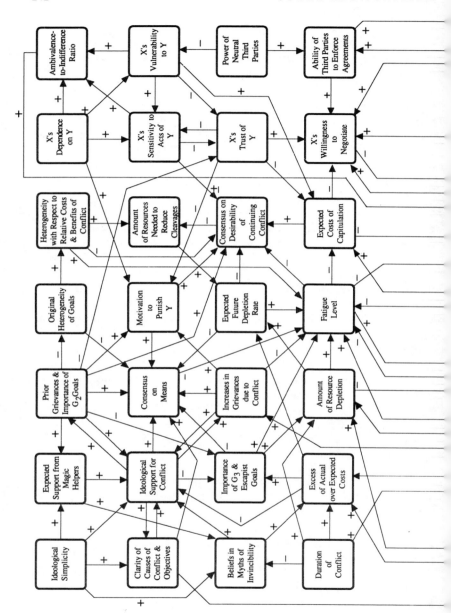

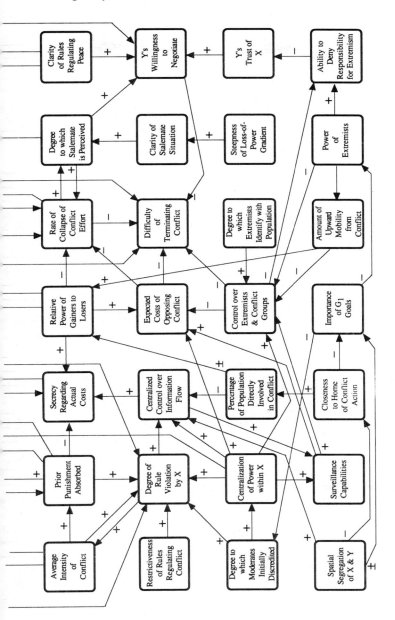

Figure 10.1 Maintaining and terminating conflict submodel.

The assumption here is that the rules most likely to be violated are those that regulate conflict by outlawing extremely punitive courses of action, and that a high intensity level will encourage both sides to violate such regulations. Rule violations, in turn, can be expected to intensify the level of conflict, though not necessarily its duration. It is then likely that the level of prior punishment that has been absorbed will further increase grievance levels, over and beyond those that existed at the outset of the conflict. These increased grievance levels will also create a positive feedback loop with ideological support and will positively affect the motivation to inflict further punishments on Y.

3. RULES, CENTRALIZATION OF POWER, SECRECY, AND EXTREMISTS

The restrictiveness of the rules that regulate the conflict is taken as an exogenous cause of rule violation. Not depicted in the model, in this connection, is the influence of powerful third parties that may have been responsible for the rules in the first place and that may or may not be willing to enforce them during any given stage of the conflict. The degree to which moderates have been discredited during earlier stages of the conflict is assumed to have been influenced by prior levels of G_1 (cooperative) goals and to affect positively both the degree of rule violation and also the current centralization of power. Power centralization, in turn, is presumed to have important effects on the control over information flow (and thus the ability to hide costs), degree of rule violation, amount of resource depletion, expected costs of opposing the conflict effort, and the degree of control over conflict groups and other extremist elements. Not shown in the figure are degree and efficiency of mobilization, which may also be taken as functions of centralization or concentration of power.

Extremist elements may or may not belong to or be controlled by a centralized authority. Where they constitute a distinct set of actors, our analysis of conflict groups is likely to be relevant. In this particular submodel, the power of extremists is taken to be nearly exogenous, except for being negatively influenced by the average strength of G_1 goals that favor cooperation with party Y. The degree to which the central authority is able to control such extremists will depend on the concentration of power within it and the degree of general support for extremist courses of action (not included in Figure 10.1).

Surveillance capabilities are taken as influenced by the centralization of power and the centralization of control over information flow, with surveillance capabilities in turn increasing both the party's control over its own extremists and also the expected costs of opposing the conflict effort.

Another variable treated as exogenous is the degree to which extremists identify with the interests of the general population, with this variable helping to modify or limit extremist actions. Expected punitive responses from Y, also not included in this particular model, were previously argued to affect the power of extremist conflict groups, relative to other more moderate elements of the population. A high degree of control over extremists is assumed to reduce the expected costs of opposing the conflict effort, thereby influencing both the rate of collapse of this effort and the difficulty of terminating the conflict (as noted in Section 7 below).

4. SEGREGATION, DIRECT INVOLVEMENT, MOBILITY, GAINERS, AND LOSERS

The degree of spatial separation of the conflicting parties is taken as an exogenous cause of the strength of G_1 goals, perhaps both positively and negatively, and also the closeness to home of the conflict activity and thus indirectly the percentage of the total membership actively or directly involved. The ability of the central authority to control information flow, and thus the degree to which costs can be kept secret or otherwise disguised, is also both directly and indirectly affected by the spatial separation of the conflicting parties. The degree of separation will, of course, also be relevant to the importance of the loss-of-power gradient discussed in Section 7.

The extent to which the conflict affords opportunities for upward mobility is taken as influenced by the power of extremist elements. Otherwise, mobility opportunities are here treated as primarily exogenous, though they perhaps could be explained in a more complex model as a function of the nature and extent of the conflict activity. The amount of upward mobility due to the conflict is presumed to have a negative impact on the extent to which conflict groups and other extremists are likely to be controlled. It also may be an important contributor to the extent to which those who are gaining from the conflict have more power than those who are net losers, thus indirectly impacting on the overall fatigue level, the expected costs of capitulation, and the rate of collapse of the conflict effort, as discussed below. The percentage of the total population directly involved in the conflict may or may not affect the rate of upward mobility produced by the conflict, and no arrow has been drawn to link this particular pair of variables.

5. RESOURCE DEPLETION, FATIGUE, AND CONSENSUS ON CONTINUATION

As noted, a number of factors will affect the resource depletion rate and level of fatigue. The actual (or perceived) depletion rate can be expected to affect the expected *future* depletion rate which, if greater than the expected replenishment rate (not included in the figure), will ordinarily increase the fatigue level. Both the fatigue level and this expected depletion rate can then be predicted to reduce the level of consensus on the desirability of continuing the conflict. Increases in the fatigue level are also expected to decrease the expected costs of capitulation relative to those of continuation, with such lowered expected capitulation costs further decreasing the level of consensus. This assumes that the predominant position still favors continuation and suggests that the above-named factors will operate to weaken such a position by increasing the level of *dissensus*. Expected capitulation costs are presumed to be positively affected by the degree to which the power of the conflict's beneficiaries exceeds that of the net losers. The greater the degree of trust in Y, the less the expected capitulation costs.

To the extent that there is a high degree of heterogeneity with respect to the relative costs and benefits to members, it is argued that this will increase the amount of resources needed to reduce or control internal cleavages, which will in turn increase the expected future resource depletion rate. Heterogeneity with respect to experienced costs and benefits will also tend to decrease consensus on the desirability of continuing, thereby also further increasing the resources needed to reduce internal cleavages. In general terms, most of the mechanisms modeled in this portion of the diagram link heterogeneity factors with resource depletion, fatigue, and *dissensus*—all of which operate to reduce the motivation to continue the conflict and to decrease the expected costs of capitulation relative to those anticipated if the conflict were to continue.

6. ROLE OF Y AND THIRD PARTIES

Variables located to the far right in the diagram refer more specifically to the other party Y and to possible roles to be played by third parties. There will, of course, be a similar set of variables affecting Y and its responses, as well as Y's trust in X and Y's willingness to negotiate. An additional factor affecting Y's level of trust will be X's ability to control the behaviors of its own extremists, with X's ability to disclaim such a responsibility tending to decrease Y's level of trust.

The clarity of the rules assumed to be operative once the conflict has ceased is expected to affect positively both X's and Y's willingness to negotiate. The power of neutral parties to enforce agreements and maintain the peace will tend to decrease X's vulnerability to Y, and of course Y's vulnerability to X as well. To the degree that regulatory procedures are precise and clear to both parties, this should help neutral parties enforce any agreements that have been made.

Finally, X's dependence on and vulnerability to Y will tend to increase X's sensitivity parameters in response to any changes in Y's behaviors, as well as X's ambivalence-to-indifference ratio. That is, high levels of dependence and vulnerability will tend to produce relatively more ambivalence (e.g., love-hate) than indifference. This ambivalence-to-indifference ratio, in turn, is expected to affect the rate at which a collapse may occur once fatigue levels have sufficiently reduced the expected costs of capitulation relative to those of continuation.

7. STALEMATES, RATE OF COLLAPSE, WILLINGNESS TO NEGOTIATE, AND TERMINATION

Toward the bottom right of the figure is a set of variables relating to the termination of a conflict. The steepness of the loss-of-power gradient is taken as an exogenous cause of the degree to which a stalemate situation becomes obvious and clear-cut, and thus is perceived by both parties. Perception of a stalemate, we have argued, is almost a necessary condition for *both* parties to be willing to negotiate, even though one of them may be willing to do so once the expected costs of capitulation have become small enough relative to those anticipated by continuation. The clarity of rules regulating the transition to peace will also positively affect the willingness of both parties to enter negotiations.

The ultimate dependent variable in the model—the difficulty of

terminating the conflict—is then taken as determined by both X's and
Y's willingness to negotiate, their ability to control their own extremists, lowered costs of actually opposing the conflict effort, and the
fatigue levels and rates of collapse of the conflict effort among both
parties.

Concluding Remarks

This completes our summary discussion of several very complex
models of the conflict process. Once more it is important to emphasize that any particular conflict will permit many kinds of simplifications, thus allowing one to delete a number of variables and causal
arrows from the models. Such deletions should be made on the basis
of theoretical considerations, however, and not merely for the sake of
convenience or the availability of empirical data. Variables that simply intervene between several others in a recursive portion of the
model can, indeed, be removed without our reaching misleading conclusions. Those that produce spurious relationships among included
variables, however, will result in correlated disturbance terms if deleted. Variables involved in complicated feedback loops can also be
deleted, provided that this is properly done (Blalock, 1982; Heise,
1975). If nonrecursive relationships are made recursive without
clearly stating the assumptions justifying this sort of simplification,
however, biases and misleading interpretations are likely to result.

The important point that we have tried to emphasize throughout is
that the genuine accumulation of knowledge requires us to avoid
premature ad hoc simplifications of complex social processes. As we
have seen, however, certain simplifications must inevitably be made.
Insofar as possible, such simplifications need to be brought out into
the open where they can be examined one by one. If, instead, they
are merely hidden from view, social scientists will have a much more
difficult time deciding precisely how and where they disagree. Our
attempts to communicate across disciplinary boundaries will also be
much less effective.

To those who may wish to extract policy recommendations appropriate to highly specific types of conflict situations, we may offer a
few additional suggestions. It will of course be crucial to appraise
each such situation in terms of the stage of the conflict process,

whether it is in an incipient state, one in which a Richardson-type conflict spiral is well underway, or one where the two parties are about to enter a stalemate stage. After making appropriate simplifications and other types of modifications that are deemed appropriate, the analyst may then wish to search among the exogenous factors or among those endogenous variables toward the beginning of the postulated causal sequence in order to locate factors that appear to be relatively easily manipulated by those who may wish to influence the conflict process. Perhaps these may be actions of third parties, rules that may be relatively easily modified, surveillance capabilities, or even grievance levels of the parties concerned. Perhaps mechanisms can be introduced to curtail the replenishment of both parties' resources or to increase their fatigue levels so as to dampen the escalation process. Mediative services may be introduced to help interpret each party's concerns and reactions to the other side, or to provide assurances that third-party interventions will be introduced in such a way that neither party will gain a permanent advantage over the other once overt hostilities have been curtailed.

To the extent that conflicts are caused by competition for scarce resources, then efforts to assure that such scarcities do not become pronounced will tend to work to reduce conflict levels. In the context of world politics, this implies an emphasis on the conservation of natural resources and the search for alternative sources of supply that are not easily controlled by parties that happen to be in the most advantageous positions. For example, solar energy might be more readily tapped in many parts of the world than would fossil fuels. An abundant food supply combined with efficient and relatively inexpensive means of transportation of widely different kinds would remove another major irritant among peoples of the world. Improved fertility control, if made uniformly and cheaply available, could also help reduce pressures of populations on restricted food supplies. The removal of marginal lands from agricultural production would at least slow down the infringement of deserts on more fertile regions of the world. Over the long term, it is critical to examine the nature and impact of exogenous factors such as these and to encourage worldwide cooperation so as to attempt to assure that critical scarcities do not increase the number of zero-sum game situations around the globe, thereby aggravating existing conflicts or further increasing the temptation to engage in instrumental aggression.

At the more micro level, many kinds of personal goals involve inherently scarce objectives. There are only a certain number of prestigious jobs, top political offices, or contest winners. Whenever invidious distinctions are not only encouraged but made into core elements of an ideological system—such as our own—conflicts are almost bound to be endemic, though perhaps reasonably well-regulated. If by definition there can only be a very few winners, the numerous losers may retreat gracefully, but they may very likely seek alternatives that make them "winners" in other respects. They may scapegoat members of a racial or ethnic minority or endorse chauvinistic foreign policy objectives that result in conflicts with others who are outside of the competitive arena that inevitably produced such a large number of losers.

To the degree that a belief system can downplay objectives that by their very nature force actors into zero-sum game situations or that encourage them to define them in these terms, this important source of conflicts can at least be reduced in both scope and magnitude. A belief system that places a premium on helping others and taking satisfaction in their improved lifestyles seems far less conducive to conflict than one that stresses extreme forms of individual competition or the out-and-out superiority of one set of behaviors or beliefs over another.

Obviously, the above account of conflict reduction or conflict controlling mechanisms is so sketchy as to be of little practical value in concrete conflict situations. What is being suggested, however, is that a careful search among exogenous factors or among those endogenous variables that are close to the beginnings of causal chain sequences may provide the analyst with a series of more specific suggestions as to how to gain a greater degree of control over these conflict processes. One must remain on guard against premature oversimplifications, however. If a factor has several indirect as well as direct effects on a given variable, one path may result in a change that is opposite in direction from that produced by other paths, so that the net change caused by a manipulated variable may be the very opposite of that which was intended.

As always, if social processes are indeed complex, so must be our models of these processes if we are to achieve our policy objectives. It has been a major theme of this work that theoretical simplifications need to be made with extreme caution. The same applies, of course, to any policy recommendations we wish to make concerning how these processes may be modified or controlled. Otherwise, we run the continued risk of making recommendations that, although they may seem on the face of it to make considerable sense, may do far more harm than good. Most certainly, power and conflict processes are sufficiently important that we can ill afford overly simplistic, though well-meaning, recommendations designed to modify their impacts.

References

Abelson, R. P. 1963. A "derivation" of Richardson's equations. *Journal of Conflict Resolution* 7: 13–15.

Allport, G. W. 1954. *The nature of prejudice*. Reading, MA: Addison-Wesley.

Arendt, H. 1951. *The origins of totalitarianism*. New York: Harcourt Brace.

Arendt, H. 1963. *On revolution*. New York: Viking.

Aristotle. 1893. *The politics of Aristotle*. Trans. by J. E. C. Welldon. New York: Macmillan.

Axelrod, R. 1970. *Conflict of interest*. Chicago: Markham.

Axelrod, R. 1980. Effective choice in the prisoner's dilemma. *Journal of Conflict Resolution* 24: 3–26.

Axelrod, R. 1981. The emergence of cooperation among egoists. *American Political Science Review* 75: 306–18.

Axelrod, R. 1984. *The evolution of cooperation*. New York: Basic Books.

Bacharach, S. B., and E. J. Lawler. 1980. *Power and politics in organizations*. San Francisco: Jossey-Bass.

Bacharach, S. B. and E. J. Lawler. 1981. *Bargaining: Power, tactics, and outcomes*. San Francisco: Jossey-Bass.

Barclay, S., and L. R. Beach. 1972. Combinatorial properties of personal probabilities. *Organizational Behavior and Human Performance* 8: 176–83.

Bar-Hillel, M. 1973. On the subjective probability of compound events. *Organizational Behavior and Human Performance* 9: 396–406.

Bendix, R. 1978. *Kings or people*. Berkeley: University of California Press.

Berk, R. A., and H. E. Aldrich. 1972. Patterns of vandalism during civil disorders as an indicator of selection of targets. *American Sociological Review* 37: 533–46.

Blalock, H. M. 1961. Theory, measurement, and replication in the social sciences. *American Journal of Sociology* 66: 342–47.

Blalock, H. M. 1964. *Causal inferences in nonexperimental research*. Chapel Hill: University of North Carolina Press.

Blalock, H. M. 1967. *Toward a theory of minority group relations*. New York: Wiley.

Blalock, H. M. 1982. *Conceptualization and measurement in the social sciences*. Beverly Hills, CA: Sage.

253

254POWERANDCONFLICT

Blalock. H. M. 1987. A power analysis of conflict processes. In *Advances in group processes, Vol. 4*, edited by E. J. Lawler and B. Markovsky, 1–40. Greenwich, CT: JAI.

Blalock. H. M., and P. H. Wilken. 1979 *Intergroup processes: a micro-macro perspective*. New York: Free Press.

Bonacich. E. 1973. A theory of middleman minorities. *American Sociological Review* 38: 583–94.

Bonacich. P. 1972. Norms and cohesion as adaptive responses to potential conflict: An experimental study. *Sociometry* 35: 357–75.

Boulding. K. E. 1962. *Conflict and defense: A general theory*. New York: Harper.

Brinton. C. 1938. *The anatomy of revolution*. Englewood Cliffs, NJ: Prentice-Hall.

Bueno de Mesquita. B. 1981. *The war trap*. New Haven: Yale University Press.

Caplow. T. 1956. A theory of coalitions in the triad. *American Sociological Review* 21: 489–93.

Caplow. T. 1968. *Two against one*. Englewood Cliffs, NJ: Prentice-Hall.

Cartwright. D. 1959. A field theoretical conception of power. Chap. 11 in *Studies in social power*, edited by D. Cartwright. Ann Arbor: University of Michigan Press.

Cook. K. S. and M. R. Gillmore. 1984. Power, dependence, and coalition formation. In *Advances in group processes: Theory and research, Vol. 1*, edited by E. J. Lawler. 27–58. Greenwich, CT: JAI.

Coombs. C. H., R. Dawes, and A. Tversky. 1970. *Mathematical psychology*. Englewood Cliffs, N. J.: Prentice-Hall.

Coombs, C. H., and D. C. Pruitt. 1960. Components of risk in decision-making: Probability and variance preferences. *Journal of Experimental Psychology* 60: 265–77.

Copeland. L. C. 1939. The Negro as a contrast conception. Chap. 6 in *Race relations and the race problem*, edited by E. T. Thompson. Durham, NC: Duke University Press.

Coser, L. 1956. *The functions of conflict*. New York: Free Press.

Cusak. T. R., and M. D. Ward. 1981. Military spending in the United States, Soviet Union, and the People's Republic of China. *Journal of Conflict Resolution* 25: 429–69.

Dahl, R. 1957. The concept of power. *Behavioral Science* 2: 201–15.

Dahrendorf. R. 1959. *Class and class conflict in industrial society*. Stanford: Stanford University Press.

Davies. J. C. 1962. Toward a theory of revolution. *American Sociological Review* 27: 5–19.

DeSwann. A. 1973. *Coalition theories and cabinet formation*. San Francisco: Jossey-Bass.

Dollard. J. 1937. *Caste and class in a southern town*. Garden City, NY: Doubleday Anchor.

Doyle, B. W. 1937. *The etiquette of race relations in the South*. Chicago: University of Chicago Press.

dwards, L. P. 1927. *The natural history of revolution.* Chicago: University of Chicago Press.

merson, R. M. 1962. Power-dependence relations. *American Sociological Review* 27: 31–41

merson, R. M. 1972. Exchange theory, part II: Exchange relations and network structures. In *Sociological theory in progress,* edited by J. Berger, M. Zelditch, and B. Anderson, 58–87. Boston: Houghton Mifflin.

anon, F. 1963. *The wretched of the earth.* New York: Grove.

reman, B., and W. A. Gamson. 1979. Utilitarian logic in the resource mobilization literature. In *The dynamics of social movements,* edited by M. N. Zald and J. D. McCarthy, 8–44. Cambridge, MA: Winthrop.

rench, J. R. P., and B. Raven. 1959. The bases of social power. Chap. 9 in *Studies in social power,* edited by D. Cartwright. Ann Arbor: University of Michigan Press.

riedan, B. 1963. *The feminine mystique.* New York: Norton.

romm, E. 1945. *Escape from freedom.* New York: Rinehart.

alenter, E. 1962. The direct measurement of utility and subjective probability. *American Journal of Psychology* 75: 208–20.

amson, W. A. 1961. A theory of coalition formation. *American Sociological Review* 26: 373–82.

amson, W. A. 1968. *Power and discontent.* Homewood, IL: Dorsey.

amson, W. A. 1975. *Strategy of social protest.* Homewood, IL: Boxwood.

iddens, A. 1987. *The nation-state and violence.* Berkeley: University of California Press.

illespie, J. V., D. A. Zinnes, G. S. Tahim, P. A. Schrodt, and R. M. Rubison. 1977. An optimal control model of arms races. *American Political Science Review* 71: 226–44.

illmore, M. R. 1987. Implications of generalized versus restricted exchange. Chap. 8 in *Social exchange theory,* edited by K. S. Cook. Beverly Hills, CA: Sage.

ist, N. P., and A. G. Dworkin, eds. 1972. *The blending of races: Marginality and identity in world perspective.* New York: Wiley.

ranovetter, M. 1978. Threshold models of collective behavior. *American Journal of Sociology* 83: 1420–43.

ruder, C. L. 1971. Relationship with opponents and partner in mixed-motive bargaining. *Journal of Conflict Resolution* 15: 403–16.

urr, T. R. 1970. *Why men rebel.* Princeton: Princeton University Press.

urr, T. R., and M. I. Lichbach. 1986. Forecasting internal conflict: A competitive evaluation of empirical theories. *Comparative Political Studies* 19: 3–38.

usfield, J. R. 1962. Mass society and extremist politics. *American Sociological Review* 27: 19–30.

all, T. D. 1989. *Social change in the Southwest, 1350—1880.* Lawrence: University Press of Kansas.

amblin, R. L. 1971. Ratio measurement for the social sciences. *Social Forces* 50: 191–206.

Hamblin, R. L., M. Hout, J. L. Miller, and B. L. Pitcher. 1977. Arms races: A test o two models. *American Sociological Review* 42: 338–54.

Hawley, A. H. 1963. Community power and urban renewal success. *American Journa of Sociology* 68: 422–31.

Hechter, M. 1987. *Principles of group solidarity.* Berkeley: University of Californi Press.

Heider, F. 1958. *The psychology of interpersonal relations.* New York: Wiley.

Heise, D. R. 1975. *Causal analysis.* New York: Wiley.

Hibbs, D. A. 1973. *Mass political violence.* New York: Wiley.

Himes, J. S. 1980. *Conflict and conflict management.* Athens: University of Georgi Press.

Hobsbawm, E. J. 1959. *Social bandits and primitive rebels.* Glencoe, IL: Free Press

Huntington, S. P. 1958. Arms races: Prerequisites and results. In *Public policy,* edite by C. J. Friedrich and S. E. Harries. Cambridge, MA: Harvard University Press

Isaac, L., E. Mutran, and S. Stryker. 1980. Political protest orientations among blac and white adults. *American Sociological Review* 45: 191–213.

Jaynes, G. D., and R. M. Williams, Jr., eds. 1989. *A common destiny: Blacks an american society.* Washington: National Research Council.

Jenkins, C. C., and C. Perrow. 1977. Insurgency of the powerless: Farm worker movements (1946–1972). *American Sociological Review* 42: 249–67.

Jones, E. E., and K. E. Davis. 1965. From acts to dispositions: The attribution proces in person perception. In *Advances in experimental social psychology, Vol. 2,* 219 66. New York: Academic Press.

Jones, E. E., and R. E. Nisbett. 1971. *The actor and the observer: Divergent percep tions of the causes of behavior.* Morristown, NJ: General Learning Press.

Kelley, H. H. 1971. *Attribution in social interaction.* Morristown, NJ: General Learn ing Press.

Kelley, H. H., and A. J. Stahelski. 1970. The social interaction basis of cooperator and competitors' beliefs about others. *Journal of Personality and Social Psychol ogy* 16: 66–91.

Kelley, H. H., and J. W. Thibaut. 1978. *Interpersonal relations: A theory of interdepen dence.* New York: Wiley.

Killian, L. M. 1984. Organization, rationality and spontaneity in the civil rights move ment. *American Sociological Review* 49: 770–83.

Klandermans, B. 1984. Social-psychological expansions of resource mobilizatio theory. *American Sociological Review* 49: 583–600.

Komorita, S. S., and J. Chertkoff. 1973. A bargaining theory of coalition formatio *Psychological Review* 80: 149–62.

Kornhauser, W. 1959. *The politics of mass society.* Glencoe, IL: Free Press.

Le Bon, G. 1896. *The crowd: A study of the popular mind.* New York: Macmillar

Lee, W. 1971. *Decision theory and human behavior.* New York: Wiley.

Leiserson, M. 1970. Power and ideology in coalition behavior: An experimental stud

In *The study of coalition behavior,* edited by S. Groennings, E. W. Kelley, and M. Leiserson, New York: Holt, Rinehart and Winston.

Lichbach, M. I., and T. R. Gurr. 1981. The conflict process: A formal model. *Journal of Conflict Resolution* 25: 3–30.

Lieberson, S., and A. R. Silverman. 1965. The precipitants and underlying conditions of race riots. *American Sociological Review* 30: 887–98.

McAdam, D. 1982. *Political process and the development of black insurgency.* Chicago: University of Chicago Press.

McCarthy, J. D., and M. N. Zald. 1977. Resource mobilization and social movements: A partial theory. *American Journal of Sociology* 82: 1212–39.

Mannheim, K. 1940. *Ideology and utopia.* New York: Harcourt, Brace.

March, J. G. 1966. The power of power. Chap. 3 in *Varieties of political theories,* edited by D. Easton. Englewood Cliffs, NJ: Prentice-Hall.

March, J. G., and H. A. Simon. 1958. *Organizations.* New York: Wiley.

Mason, P. 1970. *Patterns of dominance.* London: Oxford University Press.

Merton, R. K. 1949. *Social theory and social structure.* Glencoe, IL: Free Press.

Molm, L. D. 1987. Power-Dependence theory: Power processes and negative outcomes. In *Advances in group processes, Vol. 4,* edited by E. J. Lawler and B. Markovsky, 171–98. Greenwich, CT: JAI.

Moore, B. 1966. *Social origins of dictatorship and democracy.* Boston: Beacon.

Morgan, M. P. 1977. *Deterrence: A conceptual analysis.* Beverly Hills, CA: Sage.

Morgan, W. R., and T. N. Clark. 1973. The causes of racial disorders: A grievance-level explanation. *American Sociological Review* 38: 611–24.

Morgenthau, H. J. 1948. *Politics among nations: The struggle for power and peace.* New York: Knopf.

Murnighan, J. K. 1978. Models of coalition behavior: Game theoretic, social psychological, and political perspectives. *Psychological Bulletin* 85: 1130–53.

Myrdal, G. 1944. *An American dilemma.* New York: Harper.

Nagel, J. H. 1975. *The descriptive analysis of power.* New Haven: Yale University Press.

Nieburg, H. L. 1969. *Political violence: The behavioral process.* New York: St Martin's.

Nisbet, R. 1953. *The quest for community.* New York: Oxford University Press.

Oberschall, A. 1973. *Social conflict and social movements.* Englewood Cliffs, NJ: Prentice-Hall.

Ofsche, L., and R. Ofsche. 1970. *Utility and choice in social interaction.* Englewood Cliffs, N.J.: Prentice-Hall.

Oliver, P. 1984. Rewards and punishments as selective incentives: An apex game. *Journal of Conflict Resolution* 28: 123–48.

Olson, M. 1965. *The logic of collective action.* Cambridge, MA: Harvard University Press.

Ostrom, C. W. 1978. A reactive linkage model of the U.S. expenditure policymaking process. *American Political Science Review* 72: 941–57.

Paige, J. M. 1971. Political orientation and riot participation. *American Sociological Review* 36: 810–19.

Perrow, C. 1979. The sixties observed. In *The dynamics of social movements*, edited by N. M. Zald and J. D. McCarthy, 192–211. Cambridge, MA: Winthrop.

Pettee, G. S. 1938. *The process of revolution*. New York: Harper.

Pilisuk, M. 1984. Experimenting with the arms race. *Journal of Conflict Resolution* 28: 296–315.

Portes, A. 1971. Political primitivism, differential socialization, and lower-class leftist radicalism. *American Sociological Review* 36: 820–35.

Rattinger, H. 1975. Armaments, detente, and bureaucracy. *Journal of Conflict Resolution* 19: 571–95.

Richardson, L. F. 1960. *Arms and insecurity*. Pittsburgh: Boxwood.

Salert, B., and J. Sprague. 1980. *The dynamics of riots*. Ann Arbor: Inter-University Consortium for Political and Social Research.

Schelling, T. C. 1956. An essay on bargaining. *American Economic Review* 46: 281–306.

Schelling, T. C. 1966. *Arms and influence*. New Haven: Yale University Press.

Schermerhorn, R. A. 1970. *Comparative ethnic relations: A framework for theory and research*. New York: Random House.

Schopler, J., and D.B. Layton. 1974. Attributions of interpersonal power. In *Perspectives on social power*, edited by J.T. Tedeschi. Chicago: Aldine-Atherton.

Shorter, E., and C. Tilly. 1974. *Strikes in France, 1830—1968*. Cambridge: Cambridge University Press.

Simmel, G. 1955. *Conflict and the web of group affiliations*. Glencoe, IL: Free Press.

Simon, H. A. 1957. *Models of man*. New York: Wiley.

Singer, J. D. 1958. Threat perception and the armament-tension dilemma. *Journal of Conflict Resolution* 2: 90–105.

Skocpol, T. 1979. *States and social revolutions*. Cambridge: Cambridge University Press.

Snyder, D. 1975. Institutional setting and industrial conflict: Comparative analyses of France, Italy and the United States. *American Sociological Review* 40: 259–78.

Snyder, D., and C. Tilly. 1972. Hardship and collective violence in France, 1830 to 1960. *American Sociological Review* 37: 520–32.

Spilerman, S. 1970. The causes of racial disturbances: A comparison of alternative explanations. *American Sociological Review* 35: 627–49.

Spilerman, S. 1976. Structural characteristics of cities and the severity of racial disorders. *American Sociological Review* 41: 771–92.

Spruill, C. R. 1983. *Power paradigms in the social sciences*. Lanham, MD: University Press of America.

Stark, R. 1972. *Police riots*. Belmont, CA: Wadsworth.

Tedeschi, J. T., B. R. Schlenker, and T. V. Bonoma. 1973. *Conflict, power, and games*. Chicago: Aldine-Atherton.

Thibaut, J. W., and H. H. Kelley. 1959. *Social psychology of groups*. New York: Wiley.

Tilly, C. 1978. *From mobilization to revolution*. Reading, MA: Addison-Wesley.

Tilly, C., L. Tilly, and R. Tilly. 1975. *The rebellious century: 1830—1930*. Cambridge, MA: Harvard University Press.

Turner, R. H. 1969. The public perception of protest. *American Sociological Review* 34: 815–31.

Tversky, A. 1967. Utility theory and additivity analysis of risky choices. *Journal of Experimental Psychology* 75: 27–36.

Useem, B. 1980. Solidarity model, breakdown model, and the Boston anti-busing movement. *American Sociological Review* 45: 357–69.

Vann Woodward, C. 1965. *The strange career of Jim Crow*. New York: Oxford University Press.

Wagner, R. H. 1983. The theory of games and the problem of international cooperation. *American Political Science Review* 77: 330–46.

Wallace, M. D. 1979. Arms races and escalation: Some new evidence. *Journal of Conflict Resolution*. 23: 3–16.

Weitzman, L. J. 1985. *The divorce revolution: The unexpected social and economic consequences for women and children*. New York: Free Press.

Wyer, R. S., and L. Goldberg. 1970. A probabilistic analysis of the relationships among beliefs and attitudes. *Psychological Review* 77: 100–20.

Yamagishi, T. 1986. The structural goal expectation theory of cooperation in social dilemmas. In *Advances in group processes, Vol. 3*, edited by E. J. Lawler, 57–81. Greenwich, CT: JAI.

Young, O. R. 1967. *The intermediaries: Third parties in international crises*. Princeton: Princeton University Press.

Zald, M. N., and R. Ash. 1966. Social movement organizations: Growth, decay, and change. *Social Forces* 44: 327–41.

Zald, M. N., and J. D. McCarthy, eds. 1979. *The dynamics of social movements* Cambridge, MA: Winthrop.

Index

About the Author

Hubert M. Blalock, Jr. is Professor Emeritus at the University of Washington, having previously taught at the University of Michigan, Yale, and the University of North Carolina. He is past president of the American Sociological Association, a fellow in the American Academy of Arts and Sciences and the American Statistical Association, and a member of the National Academy of Sciences. His interests include applied statistics, conceptualization and measurement, race and ethnic relations, and sociological theory. His two most recent books, both published by Sage, are *Conceptualization and Measurement in the Social Sciences* and *Basic Dilemmas in the Social Sciences*.

NOTES

NOTES

NOTES

NOTES